blackwell great minds

edited by Steven Nadler

The Blackwell Great Minds series gives readers a strong sense of the fundamental views of the great western thinkers and captures the relevance of these figures to the way we think and live today.

locke

Samuel C. Rickless

WILEY Blackwell

This edition first published 2014
© 2014 Samuel C. Rickless

Registered Office
John Wiley & Sons Ltd, The Atrium, Southern Gate, Chichester, West Sussex, PO19 8SQ, UK

Editorial Offices
350 Main Street, Malden, MA 02148-5020, USA
9600 Garsington Road, Oxford, OX4 2DQ, UK
The Atrium, Southern Gate, Chichester, West Sussex, PO19 8SQ, UK

For details of our global editorial offices, for customer services, and for information about how to apply for permission to reuse the copyright material in this book please see our website at www.wiley.com/wiley-blackwell.

The right of Samuel C. Rickless to be identified as the author of this work has been asserted in accordance with the UK Copyright, Designs and Patents Act 1988.

All rights reserved. No part of this publication may be reproduced, stored in a retrieval system, or transmitted, in any form or by any means, electronic, mechanical, photocopying, recording or otherwise, except as permitted by the UK Copyright, Designs and Patents Act 1988, without the prior permission of the publisher.

Wiley also publishes its books in a variety of electronic formats. Some content that appears in print may not be available in electronic books.

Designations used by companies to distinguish their products are often claimed as trademarks. All brand names and product names used in this book are trade names, service marks, trademarks or registered trademarks of their respective owners. The publisher is not associated with any product or vendor mentioned in this book.

Limit of Liability/Disclaimer of Warranty: While the publisher and author have used their best efforts in preparing this book, they make no representations or warranties with respect to the accuracy or completeness of the contents of this book and specifically disclaim any implied warranties of merchantability or fitness for a particular purpose. It is sold on the understanding that the publisher is not engaged in rendering professional services and neither the publisher nor the author shall be liable for damages arising herefrom. If professional advice or other expert assistance is required, the services of a competent professional should be sought.

Library of Congress Cataloging-in-Publication Data applied for

Hardback ISBN: 978-1-4051-8935-4
Paperback ISBN: 978-1-4051-8936-1

A catalogue record for this book is available from the British Library.

Cover image: Engraving of John Locke. © Bettmann/Corbis.
Cover design by Cyan Design.

Set in 9/12 pt TrumpMediaevalLTStd- Roman by Toppan Best-set Premedia Limited
Printed in Malaysia by Ho Printing (M) Sdn Bhd

1   2014

To my mother,
Regina Sarfaty Rickless

contents

preface

Writing a book on the most important themes of John Locke's entire philosophical output is a singular challenge. One of the reasons he was such a great philosopher is that he was remarkably knowledgeable and instinctively curious, with a penchant for clarity and systematicity. His work covers topics in the philosophy of mind, metaphysics, philosophy of language, epistemology, moral philosophy, and political philosophy. I have done my very best to provide a concise, clear, and, I hope, relatively accessible conspectus of Locke's contributions in these areas. I would have liked to have been able to discuss more of Locke's theological views, as well as the details of his investigations into natural philosophy (science). But I had to leave these matters to one side for reasons of space. Readers who are interested in these topics will learn a great deal from the work of Victor Nuovo (on the first) and Peter Anstey (on the second), among others.

I have many people to thank for helping me to bring this book to fruition. First and foremost, I am grateful to Steven Nadler and the editorial staff at Wiley Blackwell for granting me the commission, and I thank Gideon Yaffe for encouraging me to take it. Although I had spent some years thinking about various aspects of Locke's philosophy, I had certainly not thought through his views on all the matters covered in the pages to follow. As I wrote, I tried out chapters (or parts thereof) on two audiences, for whose patience and constructive comments I am very grateful: the Roger Woolhouse Memorial Conference at the University of York in June–July 2012, and the History of Philosophy Roundtable at UCSD – with special thanks to Donald Baxter, Martha Bolton, Justin Broackes, Lisa Downing, Paul Lodge, Antonia LoLordo, Peter Millican, Lex Newman, Pauline Phemister, Gonzalo Rodriguez-Pereyra, Timothy Stanton, and Tom Stoneham. For their supremely clear-eyed and helpful contributions on a variety of matters Lockean, whether in conversation or on paper or both, I would also like to thank Peter Anstey, Margaret Atherton, Vere Chappell, Michael Jacovides, Nick Jolley, Jessica Gordon-Roth, Ruth Mattern, Ed McCann, David Owen, John Simmons, Galen Strawson, Matthew Stuart, Udo Thiel, Bill Uzgalis, Jeremy Waldron, Ken Winkler, Roger Woolhouse, and Gideon Yaffe: it really does take a village. For supporting my research with the help of a grant that enabled me to purchase most of Locke's correspondence, I would like to thank the UCSD Dean of Arts and Humanities, Seth Lerer, from whom I also learned a great deal about Locke's philosophy of education and his appreciation for, and translation of, Aesop's fables.

For their moral support and willingness to help me parcel out my research and teaching time in the most efficient way possible, I am very grateful to my colleagues David Brink and Don Rutherford, both of whom sacrificed a great deal as (consecutive) department chairs in order to make the UCSD philosophy department the vibrant and stimulating intellectual community that it is. The community of historians of philosophy at UCSD, including my colleagues David and Don, Eric Watkins, Clinton Tolley, Michael Hardimon, and Monte Johnson, and my doctoral student, Nate Rockwood, made excellent suggestions and provided useful objections that contributed to improvements in the book. More than anything, I thank my lucky stars for the fact that my wife and colleague, Dana Kay Nelkin, and our two wonderful children, Sophie and Alice, make it possible for me to live and work in an environment pervaded by intellectual honesty, boundless curiosity, and untrammeled love.

My first ever publication (in 1997) was on Locke's distinction between primary and secondary qualities. When I received the offprints, I immediately sent one to my mother. When I next visited her, she had found a special stand for it and had given it a prominent place in her study. Every day of my life she has been proud of me and given me unconditional love and support. So this book is dedicated to you, Mom: wife, mother, and opera singer extraordinaire. Thanks for everything, but especially for the banana cream pie.

abbreviations

AT	*Oeuvres de Descartes*, revised edition, edited by Charles Adam and Paul Tannery. Paris: Vrin/CNRS, 1964–1976.
CSM 1, CSM 2	*The Philosophical Writings of Descartes*, vols. 1 and 2, translated by John Cottingham, Robert Stoothoff, and Dugald Murdoch. Cambridge: Cambridge University Press, 1985, 1984.
CSM 3	*The Philosophical Writings of Descartes*, vol. 3, translated by John Cottingham, Robert Stoothoff, Dugald Murdoch, and Anthony Kenny. Cambridge: Cambridge University Press, 1991.
Draft A, Draft B	*Drafts for the Essay Concerning Human Understanding and OtherPhilosophical Writings*, edited by Peter H. Nidditch and G.A.J. Rogers. Oxford: Clarendon Press, 1990.
E	*An Essay Concerning Human Understanding*, edited by Peter H. Nidditch. Oxford: Clarendon Press, 1975.
ELN	*Essays on the Law of Nature and Associated Writings*, edited by W. von Leyden. Oxford: Clarendon Press, 1954.
T1, T2	*Two Treatises of Government*, edited by Peter Laslett. Cambridge: Cambridge University Press, 1960. Cited by section number only.
W	*The Works of John Locke*. A New Edition, corrected, 10 vols. London: printed for Thomas Tegg, 1823.

locke's life

If you ask what sort of a man he was, the answer is that he was contented with his modest lot. Bred a scholar, he used his studies to devote himself to truth alone.

Locke's description of himself, translated by Roger Woolhouse from the original Latin on his tombstone

John Locke was an accidental philosopher. For most of his intellectual life, he was attracted to the kinds of activities engaged in by the research scientists of his day: collecting data, formulating explanatory hypotheses on the basis of observation, and testing hypotheses by controlled experiments. But because of a broad and insatiable intellectual curiosity and a devotion to truth wherever it lay, as well as a deep antipathy to absolute power and its abuses, Locke found himself drawn into a number of important philosophical and political controversies that, as he saw it, required clear definition of terms, precise reasoning, and a firm grasp of the extent and limits of human understanding. His impatience with what he saw as the fruitless and endless disputation of his more Scholastically minded contemporaries, combined with his own investigations into the mental abilities of human beings and his liberal views on the inclusive nature of Christianity and the importance of toleration, led him to defend a number of controversial philosophical and theological doctrines that more than ruffled the feathers of prominent Anglican (Church of England) clergymen. His claim that the legitimacy of government is grounded in the consent of the people was anathema to supporters of the divine right of kings and of the importance of absolute rule as a bulwark against chaos and civil war. He was mostly lucky in that he was able to devote much of his life to the pursuits that gave him the greatest satisfaction: observing, cataloguing, discovering, reading, writing, and sharing ideas with like-minded friends. And he lived long enough and worked sufficiently tirelessly to leave us with a priceless intellectual legacy, one that rivals, in both quality and influence, the output of the rest of the Western world's greatest philosophers.

Locke, First Edition. Samuel C. Rickless.
© 2014 Samuel C. Rickless. Published 2014 by John Wiley & Sons, Ltd.

John Locke was born in Wrington, Somerset, in 1632, and spent the first 14 years of his life in the village of Belluton, 6 miles south of the thriving market town of Bristol. His mother, Agnes Keene, and father, John, 10 years her junior, lived in a house given to them by Locke's grandfather, who had made his fortune in the cloth trade. In later years, Locke would describe his mother as very pious and affectionate, but little else is known about her. He also had kind things to say about his father, approving of the strict discipline with which he was raised before adolescence and the gradual loosening of this discipline thereafter, allowing for the possibility of true friendship between parent and son in adulthood. Of Locke's two brothers, one died in infancy, and the other, Thomas, five years younger than John, died in 1663, most likely of tuberculosis.

Locke's parents were probably Puritans, Calvinists who leaned towards Presbyterianism. As Protestant dissenters, they opposed Anglican orthodoxy and demands for uniformity, as well as Catholicism. No doubt this dual hostility had a significant impact on Locke, much of whose later theological output (perhaps unsurprisingly) reflected the basic attitudes of his parents. Locke's father was a lawyer, charged in part with collecting local taxes to support the increasingly unpopular administration of King Charles I, who believed in his divine right to absolute rule. In 1642, when Locke was 10 years old, a two-year standoff between Parliament and Charles I led to civil war. Locke's father, at some cost to himself, joined a Parliamentary regiment organized by a local MP, Alexander Popham. The regiment was defeated, and John Sr returned home in 1643. But thanks to Popham's power to nominate boys for entrance into selective private schools, Locke's father was able to secure a place for him at Westminster School in 1646.

At Westminster, Locke's curriculum consisted of a steady diet of Latin, Greek, Hebrew, and Arabic, with some geography, arithmetic, and geometry (taught in Latin). Locke later described the school atmosphere as very severe, awash with the kind of corporal punishment he never ceased to detest. In 1649, Charles I was beheaded, and his son, Charles II, was defeated by Oliver Cromwell in 1651 and fled to the continent. In 1650, Locke earned a special scholarship that enabled him to board at Westminster and compete, successfully in 1652, for a place at Christchurch College, Oxford.

Locke's program of study at Christchurch was an extension of the Westminster curriculum, with the addition of lectures and tutorials on Aristotelian Scholastic logic, metaphysics, and moral philosophy, and a method of learning grounded in disputation, akin to what we now think of as formal debate. Locke developed a lifelong antipathy to Aristotelian doctrines (particularly to the procrustean conventions of syllogistic logic and the obscure terms and useless questions of Scholastic metaphysics) and to the method of disputation, which he thought inconducive to knowledge or discovery.

Locke's mother died in 1654, when he was 22, and the next year he was graduated with a BA from Oxford. He thought briefly of studying law, but returned to Christchurch to seek an MA, which included a slightly more extensive program of Scholastic study, including "natural philosophy" (i.e., science). By the time he earned his MA in 1658, Locke had a reputation as a very learned and ingenious scholar. In 1659, perhaps thinking of finding a spouse, Locke began spending time (and exchanging letters) with Elinor Parry, then 18, whose brother was a student at Jesus College. Neither Locke nor Elinor was willing to commit to anything more than friendship, and the correspondence shows evidence of ups and downs in the relationship, though over the next few years Elinor's interest in the possibility of more serious attachment grew.

After Cromwell's death in 1658, there was a brief battle for succession. Cromwell's son, Richard, was defeated in 1659 and Charles II was restored to the throne. Though unclear beforehand which way to lean, Locke embraced the Restoration as a form of "quiet and settlement."[1] Despite Charles II's liberal attitude to dissenters, a Parliamentary bill for religious (Anglican) uniformity was passed in 1661, the year of Locke's father's death. Worried about the consequences of a crackdown on dissenters, Locke wrote two (unpublished) *Tracts on Government* (in 1660 and 1662) supporting toleration of freedom of conscience, but trusting the king to enforce uniformity of religious *practices* as a way of preventing religious war. At the time, Locke was enjoying life as a student, making friends with the experimental chemist Robert Boyle (1627–1691), relishing his study of medicine, and gaining appreciation for the intelligibility (even if not the truth) of the physics of René Descartes (1596–1650).

Between 1661 and 1667 Locke was elected to various posts at Oxford: Lecturer in Greek, Lecturer in Rhetoric, Censor in Moral Philosophy, and Tutor. He attended medical lectures, investigating the function of respiration and looking to explain the various colors of blood, and conducted experiments with barometers, thermoscopes, and hygrometers in order to better understand the weather (and its potential relationship with disease). In 1663–1664, he composed *Essays on the Law of Nature* (in Latin), explaining that natural law, imposed by God to govern the wills of human beings for their own betterment, is not innate, but can be known by human beings on the basis of reason and sense-experience. In 1665, Charles II moved briefly to Oxford to avoid the plague that was about to sweep through London. On the basis of a recommendation, Locke was offered the chance to serve as part of a mission to Germany to prevail on the Elector of Brandenburg to remain neutral in case England fell to war with Holland. Locke's letters at the time reveal openness of mind and curiosity, and a willingness to learn about the manners and mores of foreigners (including Catholics).

In 1666, a friend asked Locke to bring some spring water for Anthony Ashley Cooper (1621–1683), later the 1st Earl of Shaftesbury, who was Chancellor of the Exchequer and a powerful man in Charles II's government. Ashley suffered from pain and jaundice, and found some relief in spring water. Locke was unable to secure the water and apologized to Ashley in person. A generous man, Ashley accepted the apology and invited Locke to stay for dinner. Thus started a friendship that lasted until Ashley's death and completely changed Locke's life.

Locke was thinking of pursuing an MD at Oxford, but, growing increasingly impatient with the demands of academic life, decided against it. He received an offer from Elinor Parry's brother to become an Anglican clergyman and (possibly) take up a position in Dublin, Ireland. Not wanting to take orders and unwilling to give up further study for a life in the church, Locke declined the offer. Though Elinor continued for a time to hope that Locke would join her in Dublin, she eventually realized that Locke was not going to give up his life in England for a life with her, and married a Richard Hawkshaw in 1670.

By 1667, Locke had joined Ashley's family at Exeter House in London, and was serving as a tutor to Ashley's son, and advising the household on medical matters. In his medical capacity, he met and interacted with Ashley's physician, Thomas Sydenham (1624–1689), from whom he learned that the best way to study any disease is by observation of its development and the effects of treating it in various ways. Locke came to see that the leading medical theories of his day, derived from Galen (130–200) and Paracelsus (1493–1541), had not been sufficiently well tested.

During the time that Locke held various academic posts at Oxford, Charles II was trying to resist repeated Parliamentary efforts to crush religious dissenters, efforts that both Ashley and Locke supported. In 1667, Locke wrote (without publishing) an *Essay Concerning Toleration*, in which he went back on his earlier claim that the king could regulate practices of religious *worship*. The next year, Ashley developed a tumor that was successfully cauterized and drained for six weeks under Locke's direction. As a result, Ashley credited Locke with having saved his life. Locke's confidence in treating Ashley reflected what he had acquired in the way of experience and testimony from numerous physicians. And it was this blend of curiosity and confidence that led him to join the Royal Society of London for Improving Natural Knowledge (founded in 1660) in 1668.

In 1669, Locke helped Ashley, who had become one of the eight Lords Proprietors of the American colony of Carolina, to draft the *Fundamental Constitutions of Carolina*, and served as secretary to the Lords Proprietors for the next six years. He continued work on diseases and cures therefor, but by 1670 had decided against becoming a practicing physician. Part of the reason for this was that Locke was developing what he himself took to be a "consumptive disposition,"[2] probably caused by asthma or chronic bronchitis, no doubt inflamed by air pollution in London caused by the burning of sea coal. Ashley's grandson, the future 3rd Earl of Shaftesbury (1671–1713), later to become a well-known philosopher in his own right, was born in 1671, and Locke was given responsibility for his education.

At Exeter House, Locke had been involved in discussions with friends about the principles of morality and revealed religion, and realized that these questions could not be answered without a grasp of the proper compass of the human understanding. Locke recognized that many disputes are really the product of misunderstanding prompted by the failure to clarify the meanings of words. Encouraged by friends to set down some thoughts about how such disputes might best be avoided, in 1671 Locke produced two early drafts (Draft A and Draft B) of what eventually became, after 18 years of on-and-off work during his leisure hours, *An Essay Concerning Human Understanding*. In these drafts, Locke defended the idea that the mind is initially a blank slate, that all of the materials of knowledge derive from sensation and reflection, and that there is an important difference between knowledge, which is certain and indubitable, and belief or judgment, which is based on (greater or lesser degrees of) probability.

Locke experienced the results of political instability during the years 1672–1675. In 1672, Charles II declared war on Holland and, acting unilaterally, issued a Declaration of Indulgence protecting both Protestant nonconformists and Catholics. In the same year, Ashley became the 1st Earl of Shaftesbury and was appointed Lord Chancellor. Thanks to Shaftesbury's influence, Locke took on various paid appointments, including the position of Secretary and Treasurer of the Council of Trade and Plantations. But the conflict between Charles II and Parliament did not abate, with Charles abandoning his Declaration in the face of political opposition and Parliament passing the Test Act (requiring persons in civil or military positions to take an oath disavowing the Catholic doctrine of transubstantiation) in 1673. Charles replaced Shaftesbury as Lord Chancellor with Thomas Osborne. Fearful that Osborne's influence might lead to absolute and arbitrary government without Parliamentary check, Shaftesbury, probably with Locke's assistance, published an anonymous polemical pamphlet, *A Letter from a Person of Quality, to his Friend in the Country* (1675), that was condemned by the Lords and ordered to be burned.

For Locke, who was experiencing regular debilitating coughs, this was an opportune time to leave the country for a time. In the end, he spent three and a half years in France, traveling (in two separate trips) to many destinations, including Paris, Orléans, Bordeaux, Montpellier, and Lyon. Locke kept a journal, divided into four categories: philosophy, history of manners, political wisdom, and productions of art and nature. He used Latin to communicate and worked on his French. On his travels, he met several people who came to play an important role in his life, not the least of whom was Thomas Herbert (later Earl of Pembroke in 1683), who became the patron to whom the *Essay* is dedicated. He met the Dutch physicist Christiaan Huygens (1629–1695), the astronomer Giovanni Cassini (1625–1712), and the physician François Bernier (1625–1688), who had translated the work of the French Epicurean atomist and critic of Descartes, Pierre Gassendi (1592–1655). In 1678, he hired Sylvanus Brownower, who served him as amanuensis, secretary, and in other capacities. Locke thought of marriage, but realized that this would result in the loss of his Christchurch studentship, and would require earning a living as a physician. He came to the conclusion that marriage and death are "nearly the same thing."[3]

While Locke was in France, Charles brought Shaftesbury back into the government because of his increasing popularity, in part to insulate himself against worries that his brother and heir to the throne, James, who had converted to Catholicism, would replace him and turn the country Catholic. With Shaftesbury now in a stronger position, Locke returned to England in 1679. But fearful that Shaftesbury's power and connections might make it difficult for James to succeed him, Charles dismissed Shaftesbury later that year. For two years, Charles fought with Parliament over the question of whether James should be excluded as heir to the throne or should be allowed to take the throne with limitations on his power. In 1681, Shaftesbury was arrested and charged with high treason, accused of encouraging false testimony of a "Popish Plot" to replace Charles with James. Eventually released on bail, fears that he would engage in armed rebellion because of Charles's repeated refusals to call Parliament into session led Shaftesbury to go into hiding and escape to Holland, where he died a few months later in January 1683.

During this time, Locke wrote one of the works responsible for his lasting fame, and met a person who was to become one of his closest friends, and perhaps more than that. The work was *Two Treatises of Government* (W5: 207–485), the first a detailed refutation of Robert Filmer's posthumously published *Patriarcha: or the Natural Power of Kings* (1680), which defended the divine right of kings, passed down through primogeniture from Adam's paternal right over his children and his right of dominion over the Earth granted him by God, the second a positive account of the source of governmental legitimacy in any political society formed by voluntary compact in a state of nature. The person was Damaris Cudworth (1659–1708), daughter of the Cambridge Platonist philosopher, Ralph Cudworth (1617–1688), to whom Locke was introduced in 1681 and of whom he said that there was "something more in her than is common to the rest of her sex," and later described as "a remarkably gifted woman and one of my familiar friends."[4]

In 1683, the Rye House plot to assassinate Charles and James was discovered, and warrants were issued for the conspirators. Locke began hiding and destroying papers, worried perhaps that he might be associated with the plot. A list of "damnable doctrines"[5] was drawn up at Oxford, at least some of which he knew he had included in the *Two Treatises*. Perhaps worried about being detained on charges of treason or defamation and thence dying in detention as a result of complications deriving from ill-health, Locke fled precipitously to Holland in August. He was to remain in Holland and the United Provinces, sometimes hiding under various assumed names, for five years.

Living with the help of monetary transfers from English friends, Locke spent most of his time abroad in Amsterdam and Utrecht. He joined a semi-formal group of physicians, including Philip van Limborch (1633–1712), a Remonstrant theologian, read the occasionalist Nicolas Malebranche's *Search After Truth* (1674–1675) and worked on the *Essay* because he had a great deal of time to himself. His asthma did not trouble him as much, given that the

Dutch burned peat, rather than coal. In 1684, he began drafting directions for the upbringing of a friend's son, emphasizing the importance of good habits, inculcated by praise and by example, rather than through corporal punishment, the spurring of curiosity, and the restraint of desire by means of reason. Because of his association with what were perceived as defamatory pamphlets and suspicious English expatriates living in Holland, Locke was formally expelled from Christchurch, even while he wrote to Pembroke to deny the allegations.

In 1685, Charles died and was succeeded by his brother, James II. Two failed invasions of England to depose James, led by the Duke of Monmouth and his supporters, led to the duke's execution. There is some evidence that Locke lent financial support to the invasion, even as he thought it rash. That same year, Damaris Cudworth married Sir Francis Masham, a widower 13 years her senior with several children, and went to live at Oates, near the village of High Laver in Essex, roughly 25 miles northeast of central London. There, as she reported to Locke in pining letters, life was dull and solitary. At the time, Locke was working on Draft C of the *Essay*, developing both the negative anti-innatist views of what would become Book I, as well as the positive theory of ideas contained in what would become Book II, and on an *Epistola de Tolerantia* (Letter on Toleration), refining views previously included in the *Tracts on Government* and the *Essay Concerning Toleration*. This was an apt time for Locke to be writing on the subject, given that the Catholic King Louis XIV had just revoked the Edict of Nantes (1598), which had previously provided Protestants with a measure of protection against persecution.

In the same year, Locke's first official publication, a *Method of Indexing a Commonplace Book* (W3: 331–349), appeared in a new periodical edited by a friend. It testifies to the obsessive compulsive side of his personality, given to the precise and efficient recording of multiple observations. Still writing to his friend about how to raise children properly, Locke recommended Aesop's Fables, Descartes's *Principles of Philosophy* (for their intelligibility), the learning of Latin as a living language, as well as disciplines built on observation, experiment, and reason: astronomy, geography, history, and geometry.

In 1686, Locke expanded what would become Books III and IV of the *Essay*, with significant discussion of the distinction between real and nominal essence and the distinction between knowledge and belief. Late in 1687, Locke approved the publication of a French abridgement of the *Essay* in the same journal that had published his indexing method. The initial reaction, judging by his friends' reports, was favorable. Damaris Masham, who understood the sophisticated pro-innatist views of her father's circle very well, challenged Locke in correspondence on the issue. Still voraciously interested in all matters scientific, Locke met with the microbiologist Anton van Leeuwenhoek (1632–1723), in Delft, and read (with some difficulty, given the undeveloped state of his geometrical knowledge) the newly published masterwork, *Philosophiae Naturalis Principia Mathematica* (1687), authored by Isaac Newton (1642–1727).

The controversy over the potential catholicization of England came to a head in 1687–1688. In April 1687, James issued a Declaration of Indulgence without Parliament's approval, eliminating a host of laws burdening both Protestant and Catholic dissenters, including the Test Act of 1673, which allowed him to bring Catholics into his government. In June 1688, James's wife gave birth to a son, assuring the real possibility of a Catholic succession. Seven important personages, including the Bishop of London, invited William of Orange, then Holland's Protestant ruler, to invade England and dethrone James. William accepted the invitation and came ashore with 15,000 soldiers in November. After numerous defections of Protestants from his army, James fled to France in December. William summoned a Convention Parliament in January 1689 to help decide who should become England's monarch. With James now no longer in power, and with a friendly Dutch Protestant in executive control, Locke accepted an invitation from one of his patrons, Lord Charles Mordaunt, to return to London in February 1689. At this point, Locke did not have a home, had lost his studentship at Oxford, did not have a job, and depended on rental income from his lands in Somerset and an annuity purchased before he left for Holland. But he had powerful and wealthy patrons, numerous well-placed friends, a reputation as a highly intelligent and fair-minded person, just-completed books to publish, and optimism about the future despite increased pulmonary congestion.

In April 1689, the *Epistola de Tolerantia* was published (anonymously, and in Latin) in Holland, in the same month that William and his wife, Mary, who was nearer to the succession than he, were crowned as joint sovereigns. With encouragement from William and Mary, Parliament passed the Act of Toleration, which protected Protestant (but not Catholic) non-conformists, and (in December) the Bill of Rights, which, among other things, restricted the royal prerogative by making it unlawful for English monarchs to suspend laws passed by Parliament or interfere with elections. In May, Locke was appointed to the Commission of Appeals for Excise, a salaried position, where his job was to adjudicate disputes over excise taxes. His petition to be restored to his studentship at Christchurch was approved, but he declined the invitation to return when he realized that doing so would deprive another student of his studentship. A sad letter from a newly widowed Elinor Parry, who now found herself in financial trouble with four children, led Locke to lend her some money. The *Two Treatises of Government* were published (anonymously) in August and an English translation of the *Epistola* (composed by an acquaintance) appeared in November as a *Letter Concerning Toleration* (W6: 3–58). The *Two Treatises* were (rightly) read as providing theoretical support for the legitimacy of James's removal from, and William and Mary's ascension to, the throne. In December, bearing the date "1690," *An Essay Concerning Human Understanding* was finally published (under his own name). Locke recognized that the work, having been written in fits and starts over a period of almost 20 years, was too long and repetitive, but described himself as "too lazie, or too busie to make it shorter" (*Essay*, The Epistle to the Reader: 8).

In 1690, Locke stayed with the Mordaunts on the outskirts of London to avoid the pollution that exacerbated the inflammation of his lungs, and worked on a reply to a recently published attack on his *Epistola* by Jonas Proast (1640–1710), chaplain of All Souls College, Oxford. *A Second Letter Concerning Toleration* (in English, W6: 61–137) was published in May, under the pseudonym "Philanthropus" (lover of humanity). Locke visited Oates for the first time in June, and clearly enjoyed his visit, because he moved himself along with all of his possessions (including a library of 2000 volumes that would eventually grow to almost 4000 at the time of his death), which had been scattered amongst friends during his time in Holland, to Oates in 1691. Locke paid for room and board for himself and his servant, Sylvanus, and undertook to shape the education of Francis and Damaris's five-year-old son, "little Frank." The Mashams clearly treated Locke as a valued member of the family: Locke ran errands, gardened with Damaris, and helped the household deal with various ailments.

Locke's interest in economics, which had developed from the time of his attachment to the Shaftesbury household, led to the (anonymous) publication of *Some Considerations of the Consequences of the Lowering of Interest, and Raising the Value of Money* (W5: 1–116) in 1691. The controversy concerned whether it was better or worse for the economy for the rate of interest on commercial loans to be lowered from 6% to 4% and for silver and gold coins, which were being "clipped" for the precious metals of which they were made, to be devalued. (Locke opposed both the lowering of interest rates and the devaluation of the currency.) That same year, Robert Boyle died, and Locke found himself editing Boyle's unfinished *General History of the Air* for publication. He also started making obsessively regular weather observations at Oates, and initiated what turned into a 12-year project of translating Aesop's Fables from Latin into English.

Faced with continued public criticism of his work on toleration, Locke could not resist penning an extraordinarily lengthy response to Proast's reply to his *Second Letter*, and *A Third Letter for Toleration* (W6: 141–546) was published in 1692. That same year, Locke came across a just-published book, *Dioptrica Nova*, by the Irishman William Molyneux (1656–1698), a Fellow of the Royal Society who had some complimentary things to say about the *Essay*. Locke wrote to thank Molyneux, and this initiated an intellectually fruitful long-distance friendship (eventually leading Molyneux to travel to Oates to spend five weeks with Locke just before his sudden and unanticipated death upon his return to Dublin in 1698) that did much to shape subsequent editions of the *Essay*. In the course of their correspondence, Molyneux asked Locke to say more about two important matters: (i) the "principium individuationis," or principle that establishes the identity of objects over time, and (ii) liberty and necessity (passing on questions and objections from William King, the Bishop of Derry), the worry here being that Locke was making "all sins to proceed from our understandings,"[6] rather than from our wills. Molyneux also sent Locke a hypothetical case that came to be known as "Molyneux's

Problem": whether a man born blind, and now adult, and taught by his touch to distinguish between a cube and a sphere, so as to tell which is which, could, if made to see, distinguish between them purely by sight (Locke's answer was "no"; see E II.ix.8: 146).

Collecting his thoughts (penned over the course of nine years) about the best way of educating children, Locke published *Some Thoughts Concerning Education* (W9: 1–205) anonymously in 1693. In response to Molyneux's questions, Locke drafted a lengthy extension to the *Essay*'s chapter "Of Power" (E II.xxi) on the will and freedom of action, an additional chapter (E II.xxvii), "Of Identity and Diversity," to propose his own principle of individuation and its application to personal identity, and a paragraph discussing Molyneux's Problem (E II.ix.8), among other (numerous, smaller) changes.

The second edition of the *Essay* was published in May 1694. Later that same year, Locke started thinking very seriously about Christianity, and in particular about what *makes* someone a Christian. His reason for focusing on this was that the fewer the theological doctrines adherence to which rendered someone a Christian, the less conflict among Christians would be generated by the existence of a variety of Christian practices and modes of worship. In the end, Locke came to the view, published anonymously in *The Reasonableness of Christianity, as delivered in the Scriptures* (1695, W7: 1–158), that the definition of a Christian is someone who believes that Jesus is the Messiah. A third edition of the *Essay*, involving minor alterations to the second edition, was published in 1695, and Locke was appointed Commissioner of Greenwich Hospital, to oversee the care of sailors in need of medical attention.

The *Reasonableness* included no mention (or serious discussion) of central Christian doctrines: the Trinity (three divine persons, God, the Son, and the Holy Spirit, in one substance), the Incarnation (the unity of human nature and divine nature in one person, Jesus), original sin, and bodily resurrection. This led several Anglican clergymen, notably a certain rather acerbic John Edwards (1637–1716), to worry that the author of the *Reasonableness* was a Socinian (generally speaking, one who denies these doctrines) and, indeed, because of this, a near-atheist. Locke became embroiled with Edwards in an increasingly acrimonious exchange of public letters (first in a *Vindication of the Reasonableness of Christianity, etc. from Mr. Edwards' Reflections* (1695, W7: 159–180), then in a *Second Vindication of the Reasonableness of Christianity* (1697, W7: 181–424)), defending himself, sometimes with sarcasm and invective, against the malicious accusation that he was engaged in a Socinian plot.

In December 1695, Locke was appointed Commissioner for Trade, another salaried position, this one devoted to the investigation of potential improvements to trade and manufacturing, the reduction of unemployment, and the administration of colonial plantations. This position took up a great deal of Locke's time (at least three long meetings per week, sometimes more), at a time when his health was worsening in part because the meetings were in London. In 1696, Locke became aware of remarks that the mathematician and philosopher Gottfried Wilhelm Leibniz (1646–1716) had made about the *Essay*.

As he told friends, Locke did not think much of Leibniz's criticisms (particularly the criticisms of Locke's views on innatism), which explains why Locke's exchanges of papers with Leibniz never led to any serious philosophical correspondence between them.

By 1697, Locke had given up any serious study of "physic," and was concentrating on his public service, possible alterations to the *Essay*, and defenses against published attacks on his work. In *A Discourse in Vindication of the Doctrine of the Trinity* (1697), Edward Stillingfleet (1635–1699), Bishop of Worcester, added a few criticisms of the *Essay* connecting Locke to skepticism about the external world, to Socinianism, and to unitarian doctrines recently defended by the free-thinker and satirist John Toland (1670–1722), in *Christianity Not Mysterious* (1696). Eager to defend himself against these charges and to distinguish between his views and Toland's, Locke published *A Letter to the Right Reverend Edward Lord Bishop of Worcester Concerning some Passages . . . in a late Discourse of his Lordship's in Vindication of the Trinity* (W4: 1–96) in 1697. In part because of his declining health and the many matters that engaged his attention, Locke offered to resign from the Board of Trade, but in the end was prevailed on to stay for what ended up being another three years. Stillingfleet, like Edwards, was not done. This led to further public letters, *Mr. Locke's Reply to the Bishop of Worcester's Answer to his Letter, etc.* (1697, W4: 97–189), which included an appendix replying to the criticisms of Thomas Burnet (1635–1715) about the voluntaristic aspects of Locke's moral philosophy, and *Mr. Locke's Reply to the Bishop of Worcester's Answer to his Second Letter* (1698, W4: 191–498), which was "too long" even by Locke's own standards.[7] In these years, Locke also drafted an unfinished chapter that he meant to include in the *Essay*, "Of the Conduct of the Understanding" (W3: 205–289), in which he catalogued the different ways in which the understanding might be misused, an essay on poverty, in which he defended public support for disabled adults but houses of correction and vocational schools for the able but idle poor and their children, and a short summary of current scientific theory, *Elements of Natural Philosophy* (W3: 301–330), for his 12-year-old tutee, "little Frank" Masham.

In 1700, Locke added two new chapters, "Of the Association of Ideas" (E II.xxxiii) and "Of Enthusiasm" (E IV.xix), as well as a significant number of smaller changes, to the fourth edition of the *Essay*. Citing ill-health, including what was now poor circulation in his legs, Locke resigned from the Board of Trade (though not from the Board of Appeals for Excise, which met infrequently). After an illness in 1702, he was left with deafness in his left ear. He spent much of his time corresponding with friends, including important letters on free will with van Limborch and a complimentary letter of thanks (followed by gifts of books and money) to Catharine Trotter (1679–1749), a convert to Catholicism who had written novels and plays, but also, at the age of 23, *A Defence of Mr. Lock's An Essay Concerning Human Understanding* (1702). Locke was asked for, and wrote, numerous letters of recommendation, was constantly asked for medical advice, and continued his weather observations.

He began a close study of St Paul's Epistles, which eventually led to the post-humous publication of *A Paraphrase and Notes on the Epistles of St. Paul* (1705–1707). He met, and was very much taken by, the young and dynamic Anthony Collins (1676–1729), who would eventually make a name for himself as a free-thinker. And he oversaw the publication of his translation of Aesop's Fables.

In 1704, Locke was told that some Oxford colleges were discussing the possibility of banning his books, because students were relying on the *Essay* instead of spending their time studying Scholastic logic and metaphysics (perhaps the ultimate compliment, though Locke did not take it well). Unable to stop himself, despite his bronchial condition, he penned *A Fourth Letter for Toleration* (W6: 547–574), which remained unfinished at his death. He died peacefully at Oates, surrounded by friends, letting them know that "this life is a scene of vanity that . . . affords no solid satisfaction but in the conscious-ness of doing well and in the hopes of another life."[8] His estate was valued at a little over £12,000, a significant sum, but he was buried in a plain wooden coffin (at All Saints' Church in High Laver) because the money for additional adornments would be better spent "covering . . . four honest poor labouring men of the neighborhood . . . with a coat and pair of breeches of cloth, a hat, a pair of shoes and stockings."[9]

notes

1 Roger Woolhouse, *Locke: A Biography*. Cambridge: Cambridge University Press, 2007, 45.
2 Woolhouse 2007, 96.
3 Woolhouse 2007, 149.
4 Woolhouse 2007, 175, 299.
5 Woolhouse 2007, 193.
6 Woolhouse 2007, 320.
7 Woolhouse 2007, 403.
8 Woolhouse 2007, 452.
9 Woolhouse 2007, 460.

further reading

Cranston, Maurice, *John Locke: A Biography*. London: Longman, 1957. Reprinted by Oxford University Press, 1985.
Marshall, John, *John Locke: Resistance, Revolution, and Responsibility*. Cambridge: Cambridge University Press, 1994.
Woolhouse, Roger, *Locke: A Biography*. Cambridge: Cambridge University Press, 2007.

the nature and role of ideas

I n his masterwork, *An Essay Concerning Human Understanding*, Locke introduces and defends what has since come to be known as the "way of ideas." It is difficult to overstate the influence and staying power of this mode of philosophical investigation. For years after Locke penned the *Essay*, philosophers were busy defending or attacking one or other aspect of his theory of ideas, in relation to philosophical subjects as diverse as ethics and epistemology. It is therefore of the utmost importance to understand how Locke conceives of ideas, for these entities lie at the heart of his philosophical system.

As we will see, ideas are the building blocks of Locke's theories of (i) perception, (ii) scientific classification, (iii) linguistic meaning, (iv) knowledge, and (v) judgment: (i) ideas are objects of perception; (ii) we classify substances (e.g., gold or water) into categories based on whether their qualities or properties match up with the ideas we associate with the relevant names ("gold" and "water"); (iii) the meaning of a linguistic term for a particular speaker is no more than the idea that the speaker associates with that term; (iv) knowledge is *perception* of agreement or disagreement between two ideas; and (v) judgment is *presumption* of the same sort of agreement or disagreement. There will be more on all these theories in the chapters that follow. But in order to understand them, we need to understand how Locke thinks of ideas. What, for Locke, is an idea?

It is commonly supposed that Locke holds that an idea is the object of perception or thought. The term "idea," Locke tells us, "serves best to stand for whatsoever is the Object of the Understanding when a Man thinks, [or] whatever it is, which the Mind can be employ'd about in thinking" (E I.i.8: 47; also Draft B, 3: 103).[1] It seems, then, that, for Locke, everything that I perceive or think of is an idea. And ideas, Locke goes on to say, are "Perceptions in our Minds" (E II.viii.7: 134). In this, ideas are to be distinguished from the properties or qualities of bodies that are external to the mind. As Locke puts the point in the title to a famous passage to which we shall return in

Locke, First Edition. Samuel C. Rickless.
© 2014 Samuel C. Rickless. Published 2014 by John Wiley & Sons, Ltd.

Chapter 6: "Ideas *in the Mind, Qualities in Bodies*" (E II.viii.7–8: 134, section heading).

It might be objected to this view that, although it seems true to say that when Macbeth hallucinates a dagger the object perceived or thought of is an idea in Macbeth's mind, it seems false to say that when Hamlet sees Yorick's skull, what he is perceiving is something in his own mind. The skull and its various qualities are outside, not inside, Hamlet's mind; hence they cannot be ideas, as Locke understands the term.

This would be an excellent criticism, were it not for the fact that Locke actually speaks loosely in saying that everything a human being perceives is an idea. When he is being careful, Locke says this: "Whatsoever the Mind perceives in it self, or is the immediate object of Perception, Thought, or Understanding, that I call *Idea*" (E II.viii.8: 134; also E IV.i.1: 525; W4: 130, 134, 145, 233, 362). The emphasis here should be on the word "immediate." Locke's considered view is that ideas are all *immediate* objects of perception. It does not follow from this that all objects of perception are ideas, for the view leaves open the possibility that (some) objects of *mediate* perception are not ideas.

But this raises the question of what differentiates immediate from mediate perception. Locke does not say much, if anything, about the nature of this distinction. But it is reasonable to suppose that mediate perception involves something that mediates between perceiver and perceived, in the following sense. An object O is mediately perceived by M when M perceives O by perceiving something numerically distinct from O that is in some way related to O; an object O is *immediately* perceived by M when M perceives O but not mediately. It is in a perfectly ordinary sense that I perceive my face mediately when I look at it in a mirror: I perceive my face by perceiving something else – namely an image of my face – in the mirror, an image that is related to my face by way of representing it. Locke's view seems to be that ideas are objects of perception that are not perceived this way: when I perceive an idea, I do not perceive it by perceiving something else to which it is related (e.g., by the relation of representation). I do not perceive ideas by perceiving images or representations of them: I perceive them, as it were, directly.

This view leaves open the possibility that tables and chairs, apples and pears, colors and shapes, and so on, are perceived without being ideas in our minds. And indeed, this is Locke's own view. The world that we experience is full of objects and properties external to our minds that are only mediately perceived, namely by perceiving ideas that conform to, or represent, them. Ideas themselves are only *immediate* objects of perception.[2]

Pointing out that when Locke speaks precisely he means to describe ideas as *immediate* objects of perception does not, however, tell us what ideas actually *are*. What sorts of things are immediate objects of perception? Are they substances or modes, mind-dependent or mind-independent, material or immaterial? The short answer here is that Locke takes ideas to be mind-dependent modes, while remaining agnostic about whether they are material or immaterial.

To understand this view, it helps to have a brief overview of Lockean ontology. According to Locke, everything that exists is either a substance, a mode, or a relation (E II.xii.3: 164; W8: 220). Locke writes that "[t]he *Ideas of Substances* are such combinations of simple *Ideas*, as are taken to represent distinct particular things subsisting by themselves" (E II.xii.6: 165), and thus treats substances as particular things that subsist by themselves. (In this, Locke joins all of his philosophical predecessors, most notably the Aristotelian Scholastics and the followers of Descartes.) Substances, then, are particular things (e.g., human beings, sheep, gold, and water) that can exist on their own – that is, things that do not depend for their existence on the existence of anything else. Modes, by contrast, "contain not in them the supposition of subsisting by themselves, but are considered as Dependences on, or Affections of Substances" (E II.xii.4: 165); that is, a mode is something that *does* depend for its existence on the existence of something else, namely a substance. Among modes, Locke counts, for example, distances and motions, gratitude, murder, and beauty. Relations are connections between modes (e.g., being longer than), between substances (e.g., being a sibling of), or between modes and substances (e.g., inhering in, being caused by).

Within this ontological framework, Locke's ideas are clearly mind-dependent modes, rather than substances or relations. For ideas are private and depend for their existence on the minds that perceive them.[3] On Locke's view (as on Descartes's or Aristotle's), there is no such thing as a free-floating idea, an idea whose existence is completely independent of the existence of anything else. Were there no perceiving minds in the world, there would be no ideas. By contrast, minds could exist even if there were no ideas to speak of.[4]

As for whether ideas are material or immaterial, Locke tells us that he is not in any position to provide an answer to this question. In Draft B of the *Essay*, Locke writes:

> I shall not at present medle with the physicall consideration of the minde or trouble my self to examin . . . by what motions of our spirits, or what alteration of our bodys we come to have any Ideas in our understanding & whether those Ideas be material or immateriall. These are speculations which however pleasant & profound I shall decline not only as lying out of my way in the designe I am now upon, but also out of my reach. (Draft B, 2: 102; see also E I.i.2: 43)

As we will see, Locke's agnosticism here is in keeping with the fundamental tenets of his epistemology. On Locke's view, knowledge consists in the perception of agreement or disagreement between two ideas (E IV.ii.15: 538). If, as Locke thinks, there is no agreement or disagreement to be perceived between the idea of an idea and the idea of materiality or immateriality, then it is impossible for us to know whether ideas are material or not. Indeed, the very nature or essence of ideas eludes the human understanding. We simply do not know what ideas are in themselves. To ask after the nature of ideas, then, is to ask a question that the human mind is unable to answer. Rather than push for an answer, we should "sit down in a quiet Ignorance" of an issue that is "beyond the reach of our Capacities" (E I.i.4: 45).[5]

Do we receive any more illumination from the fact that Locke tells us that he has used the term "idea" "to express whatever is meant by *Phantasm, Notion, Species*" (E I.i.8: 47)? Not much. Phantasms, notions, and species are theoretical posits that belong to the Aristotelian Scholastic theory of perception and knowledge to which Locke was exposed as an undergraduate at Oxford. A *phantasm* is (roughly) a sensible mental image that represents and resembles the external object that produces it by operating on the relevant sense organ. On the Scholastic picture, a red ball produces a phantasm of red (a mental image of red) that resembles the redness of the ball. It does this by emitting a *sensible species* of red that is propagated through the relevant medium (e.g., air, or water) towards the eye. The sensible species in this case is just the color red *as it exists in the relevant medium*, while the phantasm is the color red *as it exists in the organ of sight*. Once the phantasm is produced, the mind (*qua* intellect) is able to abstract it by considering it apart from other mental images (e.g., the phantasm corresponding to the ball's roundness), and the process of abstraction produces an *intelligible species* or *notion* (i.e., something like an abstract, general concept) of red, which is merely the color red *as it exists in the intellect*.

Although Locke does not have much patience for the terminology of Aristotelian Scholasticism (calling it "learned gibberish" – E III.x.9: 495), he does think that his term "idea" encompasses the Scholastics' phantasms, notions, and (intelligible) species, *supposing that there were any such things*. Locke himself thinks that the same immediate object of thought performs the role played by a Scholastic phantasm and performs the role played by the corresponding Scholastic species or notion. As we will see below, Locke's ideas of sense (e.g., the idea of this particular shade of red, which a Scholastic would categorize as a phantasm) are numerically identical to abstract ideas that result from their partial consideration (e.g., the general idea of red that represents all red things, which a Scholastic would categorize as an intelligible species or notion). But for Locke's theoretical (and particularly his epistemological) purposes, whether the immediate objects of thought belong to the same or different ontological categories does not much matter. This explains Locke's theoretical ecumenicalism when it comes to the Scholastic doctrines concerning the immediate objects of perception or thought, but it does not tell us what Locke thinks ideas are in themselves. And, given Locke's agnosticism on the subject, this should not surprise us.

Lockean ideas, then, are modes of mental substance. As such, they are numerically distinct from the mind-independent objects that produce them in our minds. To perceive the shape of a crossword puzzle, then, is not to perceive the puzzle in a certain way (as it were, squarely); it is to perceive something akin to a square image that is (more than likely) produced in one's mind by the motion of corpuscles (called "animal spirits") in one's optic nerve, motion itself caused by the rays of light that are reflected by the puzzle towards one's retina. In the *Essay*, Locke writes:

> The next thing to be consider'd, is how *Bodies* produce *Ideas* in us, and that is manifestly *by impulse*, the only way which we can conceive Bodies operate in.[6] If then external Objects be not united to our Minds, when they produce *Ideas* in it; and yet we perceive . . . *Qualities* in such of them as singly fall under our Senses, 'tis evident, that some motion must be thence continued by our Nerves, or animal Spirits, by some parts of our Bodies, to the Brains or the seat of Sensation, there to *produce in our Minds the particular* Ideas *we have of them.* (E II.viii.11–12: 135–136)

Philosophers who hold that mind-independent objects and properties (e.g., a chair and its shape and color) are immediately perceivable are called "direct realists." In this sense of the term, Locke is opposed to direct realism. His main reason for this is that causes (including the mind-independent causes of our ideas) are numerically distinct from their effects. Locke holds, rather, that (at least some of) the immediate objects of perception (i.e., ideas) *represent* or conform to their mind-independent causes, and therefore ranks among those philosophers who have come to be known as "representative realists."[7]

Among those who hold that Locke is a representative realist, there is a lively debate on the issue of whether Locke holds that all ideas are mental images. Call the position that all ideas are mental images, "imagism." As is usual in contested matters of interpretation, it is difficult to know whether Locke is an imagist. But it is probably most reasonable to think that Locke is simply agnostic on the question of imagism.

Perhaps the best evidence that Locke is an imagist comes from consistent and repeated references to "Ideas or Images of things" (Draft A, 1: 1; Draft B, 18: 128), "images or Ideas" (Draft A, 5: 15; Draft B, 21: 133; E II.i.25: 118; also E II.i.15: 112), and "the Idea or image as it is in the understanding" (Draft B, 58: 161). Here Locke appears to be using the word "or" epexegetically, as a synonym for "in other words," and thereby revealing his true view, which is that ideas are images that represent the things in the external world that produce them in our minds. This view is also reflected in passages in which Locke explicitly likens ideas to pictures. For example, in his chapter on memory, he writes that over time ideas "do quite wear out," that "there seems to be a constant decay of all our *Ideas*," that "the Print wears out . . . and the Imagery moulders away," that "[t]he *Pictures drawn in our Minds, are laid in fading Colours*," and that "we oftentimes find . . . the flames of a Fever, in a few days, calcine all those Images to dust and confusion" (E II.x.5: 151–152; also Draft B, 28: 138). And in a later chapter on maxims, he writes that "a Child having framed the *Idea* of a *Man*, it is probable, that his *Idea* is just like that Picture, which the Painter makes of the visible Appearances joyned together" (E IV.vii.16: 606–607; Draft A, 27: 48).

Even more tellingly, perhaps, Locke explicitly ascribes shape properties to ideas, an ascription that would make no sense unless Locke thought that the relevant ideas were imagistic representations. This is clearest in his discussion of our ideas of geometrical figures. Locke writes:

> The Mathematician considers the Truth and Properties belonging to a Rectangle, or Circle, only as they are in *Idea* in his own Mind . . . But yet the knowledge he has of any Truths of Properties belonging to a Circle, or any other mathematical Figure, are nevertheless true and certain, even of real Things existing . . . Is it true of the *Idea* of a *Triangle*, that its three Angles are equal to two right ones? It is true also of a *Triangle*, where-ever it really exists . . . [The mathematician] is sure what he knows concerning those Figures, when they have barely *an Ideal Existence* in his Mind, will hold true of them also, when they have a real existence in Matter; his consideration being barely of those Figures, which are the same, where-ever, or however they exist. (E IV.iv.6: 565; see also Draft B, 44: 152)

Here Locke suggests that triangles exist in two ways, in the mind and in reality, and that their properties are the same no matter *how* they exist. But a triangle that exists in the mind is just an idea of a triangle. So Locke must be thinking that the idea of a triangle literally has three sides, and that the three angles of that idea add up to two right angles, just as the three angles of a material triangle pictured by that idea add up to two right angles. And Locke must therefore be assuming that our ideas of shapes are images in just the way that drawings or paintings of shapes are images.[8]

On the other hand, there are passages (to which we shall return) that suggest that Locke explicitly rules out the view that all ideas are images. Locke distinguishes between two kinds of ideas: ideas of primary qualities (e.g., motion and shape), and ideas of secondary qualities (e.g., color and taste). In an important passage, Locke writes:

> [T]he *Ideas of primary Qualities* of Bodies, *are Resemblances* of them, and their Patterns do really exist in the Bodies themselves; but the *Ideas, produced* in us *by* these *Secondary Qualities, have no resemblance* of them at all. There is nothing like our *Ideas*, existing in the Bodies themselves. (E II.viii.15: 137)

And later, Locke repeats the point:

> Not that [our ideas] are all of them the Images, or Representations of what does exist, the contrary whereof, in all but the primary Qualities of Bodies, hath been already shewed. (E II.xxx.2: 372)

In these passages, Locke appears to be saying that ideas of *secondary* qualities (unlike ideas of *primary* qualities) *cannot* be images, for they do not *resemble* the qualities in objects that produce them in our minds. And this seems to follow from the general truth that all images resemble what they represent.

In addition to these reasons, it is difficult to understand *how* certain kinds of ideas could possibly be images. As we will see, Locke believes that we have ideas of various mental operations, such as *"Perception, Thinking, Doubting, Believing, Reasoning, Knowing,* [and] *Willing"* (E II.i.4: 105). And although Locke likens the mode in which we receive such ideas to sensation (E II.i.4: 105), it is difficult to imagine the sorts of mental images that Locke would have associated with these various operations. What could Locke possibly count as a mental image of perceiving, or doubting, or willing? Could he possibly have thought that thinking of thinking involves a mental image of thinking? If images resemble their objects, in what respects would an image of believing resemble believing itself? It seems difficult to fathom how Locke could have assimilated the process that results in ideas of our own mental operations to any process that results in the production of an image.

Perhaps the most reasonable position to hold on this issue is the following. Locke surely holds that *some* ideas are images (or, at least, image-like). Too much of his terminology suggests this, as well as passages in which Locke likens at least some ideas (ideas of triangles, ideas of human beings) to images. As to whether *all* ideas are images, Locke is probably agnostic, for the same reasons that drive him to agnosticism about whether ideas are material or immaterial. Indeed, Locke *should* be agnostic, because it is too much for him to suppose that one can *know* whether all ideas are images, such knowledge requiring the possession of something we do not have, namely perception that the idea of an idea agrees with the idea of an image. As for Locke's seemingly definite claim that ideas of secondary qualities do *not* resemble (and hence, could not be images of) secondary qualities themselves, we will see below that it is best understood as making a more restricted statement, to the effect that ideas of secondary qualities do not resemble any *real* properties of objects. And as long as secondary qualities are not *real* properties of objects (as we will see, Locke holds that they aren't), Locke's claim does not automatically rule out the possibility that ideas of secondary qualities resemble secondary qualities themselves.

If at least some ideas are images, it is possible to settle another long-standing debate in Locke scholarship regarding the nature of ideas. For many scholars, especially those who are allergic to the existence of private sense-data (some of them for reasons articulated by Wittgenstein), it would be uncharitable in the extreme to attribute to Locke a view that commits him to the existence of mental objects or entities (e.g., mental images) that mediate between our minds and the external world. These scholars are typically drawn to numerous passages in the *Essay* in which Locke refers to ideas as "perceptions" (e.g., E II.i.3: 105; E II.i.5: 106; E II.viii.7–8: 134; E II.xxxii.1: 384; E II.xxxii.14: 388). In these passages, they take Locke to be using the word "perceptions" to refer to mental acts of perceiving. This is all consistent with Locke's thesis that ideas are modes, mental acts in fact being more mode-like than any objects that might count as the contents or objects of such acts.

But Locke's claim that at least some ideas are images is not consistent with the claim that ideas are mental acts. For Locke, an idea of a triangle has three sides, and in this way resembles triangles drawn on paper or in the sand. Truths that we discover about our idea of the triangle transfer directly to real, external-world triangles. On this picture, it makes no sense to think of the idea of a triangle as a mental event, such as a mental act of perceiving a triangle. Such acts of perceiving do not have three sides and do not have internal angles that add up to 180 degrees. Much as we might be tempted to avoid foisting a sense-datum conception of ideas to Locke, it is really beyond dispute that at least some of Locke's ideas are mental objects, objects that are spatially isomorphic to the real objects to which they conform. And Locke's use of the term "perception" to refer to ideas is consistent with this picture. The reason is that the word "perception" is ambiguous, as between "object perceived" and "act of perceiving." In some cases, it is evident that Locke uses "perception" to refer to the latter. This happens, for example, when Locke tells us that "whatever impressions are made on the outward parts [of the body], if they are not taken notice of within, there is no Perception" (E II.ix.3: 143). But when Locke uses "perception" as a synonym for "idea," he means to refer to the former.

There is an important lesson in all this, a lesson that every reader of a 300-year-old text should take to heart, namely that there is a serious risk of imposing one's own standards of charity on the long-buried author of such a text. It may be that, by our own lights, it is wrong (indeed, philosophically foolish) to suppose that there are, or even could be, such entities in the world as private mental objects. But from the fact that some of us, as the result of complex and subtle philosophical argumentation, have concluded that a particular philosophical thesis is obviously wrongheaded or sophomoric, it does not follow that the author whose work we are interpreting would have been a fool to accept it. There is (or at least, can be) such a thing as progress in philosophy, and it does not detract from the greatness of a philosopher such as Locke that he is best read as holding a view that some of us believe to be false (or even crazy). In applying the principle of charity, Locke's views must be judged against the intellectual background in which he was working. And here it is quite plain that none of Locke's contemporaries, whether an opponent of his or a fellow traveler, would have balked at the thought that ideas are private mental objects.

It is important to note, however, that the thesis that ideas are mental *objects* does not entail that ideas are mental *substances*. As Locke makes clear in his criticisms of Malebranche's doctrine of "seeing all things in God" (according to which ideas perceived by human minds are substances, or at least quasi-substantial, in not being dependent for their existence on the human minds that perceive them), ideas are not (human-)mind-independent. As such, they must be modes, not substances, modes of human minds, not of God's mind (W9: 219–220).

notes

1 Here Locke is using "the Understanding" and "the Mind" interchangeably. His use of language suggests that he thinks of the mind (or understanding) as an agent, namely whatever in a human being is actually doing the thinking. But this is loose talk on Locke's part. What does the thinking is the human being, not something distinct from the human being.

2 It does not follow from this that every idea represents something, let alone that it represents something distinct from itself. Indeed, Locke leaves open the possibility that some ideas, such as pains and pleasures, do not represent anything: they are merely sensations, possessing nothing in the way of intentionality.

3 Locke writes that "one Man's Mind could not pass into another Man's Body, to perceive, what Appearances [i.e., ideas] were produced by those Organs" (E II. xxxii.15: 389).

4 Locke emphasizes (in opposition to Descartes) that, for all we know, it is possible for a mind to exist without having ideas. This likely happens, according to Locke, during sleep (E II.i.9–19: 108–116).

5 In Draft B of the *Essay*, Locke writes that he does not know "how the Ideas of our mindes are framed, of what materials they are made, whence they have their light & how they come to make their appearance" (Draft B, 105: 229).

6 In the early editions of the *Essay*, Locke wrote confidently that "bodies operate by impulse, and nothing else." But, as Locke explained in a letter to Stillingfleet, he softened this passage in later editions because he had been "convinced by the judicious Mr. Newton's incomparable book [i.e., *Principia*] that . . . the gravitation of matter towards matter . . . is not only a demonstration that God can, if he pleases, put into bodies powers and ways of operation above what can be derived from our idea of body, or can be explained by what we know of matter, but also an unquestionable and every where visible instance, that he has done so" (W4: 467–468). Still, even if we were to discover that external bodies do not produce ideas in our minds *by impulse*, Locke would still hold that bodies and their properties are numerically distinct from the ideas they produce in our minds.

7 Idealists agree with direct realists that sensible objects (e.g., chairs) and their qualities are immediately perceived, but part with direct realists in holding that these objects and qualities are mind-dependent. Representative realists agree with direct realists that sensible objects and their qualities are mind-independent, but part with direct realists in holding that these objects and qualities are mediately perceived.

8 Locke is here echoing the language, if not necessarily all of the theoretical commitments, of Descartes, for whom "the idea of the sun is the sun itself existing in the intellect – not of course formally existing, as it does in the heavens, but objectively existing, i.e. in the way in which objects normally are in the intellect" (AT 7: 102; CSM 2: 75).

further reading

Ayers, Michael, *Locke: Epistemology and Ontology*, 2 vols. London: Routledge, 1991, vol. 1, pp. 13–77.

Chappell, Vere, "Locke's Theory of Ideas," in *The Cambridge Companion to Locke*, edited by Vere Chappell. Cambridge: Cambridge University Press, 1994, pp. 26–55.

Yolton, John W., *Perceptual Acquaintance from Descartes to Reid*. Minneapolis: University of Minnesota Press, 1984.

the negative project: against innatism

Early on in the *Essay*, Locke explains that his "first Enquiry . . . shall be, how [ideas] come into the Mind" (E I.i.8: 48). This is not a question about the nature or role of ideas, but about their genesis. Locke assumes that "there are such Ideas in Men's Minds," for "every one is conscious of them in himself, and Men's Words and Actions will satisfy him, that they are in others" (E I.i.8: 48). His charge is to explain how the mind becomes furnished with them.

At first blush, it is not obvious why Locke is interested in this question. In very short order, Locke throws himself into the details of arguments on both sides, all without clearly explaining why his reader should care about the result of his investigation. But one need not look far for the reason Locke begins with a genetic question. Locke tells us that the very purpose of the *Essay* is "to enquire into the Original,[1] Certainty, and Extent of humane[2] Knowledge; together, with the Grounds and Degrees of Belief, Opinion, and Assent" (E I.i.2: 43). So Locke is primarily interested in what, if anything, we can know or be certain of, and what, if anything, we can no more than believe or assent to (on probable grounds). For a number of Locke's opponents, many of the propositions we know are innate – that is, "stamped upon the Mind of Man, which the Soul receives in its first Being; and brings into the World with it" (E I.ii.1: 48). As it happens, Locke agrees with his opponents that the innateness of a (true) proposition is sufficient for knowledge of it (E I.ii.5: 50). So if there were innate truths, we would be able to account for at least a good part of our knowledge. It is for this reason that Locke begins his epistemic investigation in Book I of the *Essay* with an enquiry into the origin of ideas, specifically focused on the question whether any ideas are innate.

Locke presents his anti-innatist arguments as if they were independent of the views he defends in the rest of the *Essay*. This procedure has the potential

Locke, First Edition. Samuel C. Rickless.
© 2014 Samuel C. Rickless. Published 2014 by John Wiley & Sons, Ltd.

to mislead the unwary reader. As we will see, some of his arguments are free-standing and others are *ad hominem*, displaying internal inconsistencies in the views of his innatist opponents. But, on occasion, Locke finds himself relying on assumptions that are not discussed at greater length until many pages on.

One important assumption is the claim that (mental)[3] propositions – that is, the bearers of truth-value and the objects of judgment and knowledge that are expressed by sentences or uses thereof – are constituted by ideas that are bound together by the mental act of joining (affirming) or separating (denying) (E IV.v.2: 574). On this view, for example, the proposition I express when I say that a particular line is divisible is the result of my joining my idea of that line with my idea of divisibility (in such a way as to affirm the latter of the former) (E IV.v.6: 576). Call this the Constitution Assumption. Locke takes this assumption on board without arguing for it, almost certainly because he takes it to be definitive of what propositions are and because his Scholastic and Aristotelian opponents also embrace it.

Another important assumption is that the innateness of a complex whole requires the innateness of each of its parts. Call this the Whole-Part Assumption. Locke considers this thesis self-evident, as indeed it appears to be. For it seems inconceivable that something should be stamped on a person's mind as soon as the mind comes into existence without all of its parts being stamped on the very same mind at the very same time. To suppose otherwise would be to suppose, absurdly, that a whole could be in a mind at a time without its parts being in the very same mind at the very same time.

From the Whole-Part Assumption and the Constitution Assumption, Locke logically derives a powerful tool with which to criticize innatists. This tool is the thesis that "no Proposition can be innate, unless the *Ideas*, about which it is [i.e., of which it is constituted], be innate" (E I.ii.18: 58). Call this the Proposition Assumption. If Locke can show that a particular idea is not innate, it will follow directly from the Proposition Assumption that *any* proposition that has the idea as a part is also not innate.

The innatism that Locke attacks consists of two separate theses. The first is that "there are in the Understanding certain *innate Principles*" (E I.ii.1: 48), principles "both *Speculative* and *Practical*" (E I.ii.2: 49). Principles are propositions (unlike commands, questions, or exclamations) that can be either true or false (E I.iii.12: 73–74). A principle is practical when it is a moral rule that "excites and directs the Actions of all Men" (E I.iii.12: 73). Examples of practical principles discussed by Locke include the propositions *"That one should do as he would be done unto"* (E I.iii.4: 68), "that Men should keep their Compacts" (E I.iii.5: 68), and that *"it is the Duty of Parents to preserve their Children"* (E I.iii.12: 74). Any principle that is not practical is speculative, concerned with what can be known or understood independently of its relation to human actions. Examples of speculative principles discussed by Locke include the propositions that *"whatsoever is, is"* and that *"it is impossible for the same thing to be, and not to be"* (E I.ii.5: 51). Locke focuses on these propositions because, as he reasons, these "of all others I think have the most allow'd Title to innate" (E I.ii.4: 49).

The second thesis is that there are innate *ideas*. The two theses (i.e., that there are innate principles and that there are innate ideas) are related, but not equivalent. The Proposition Assumption shows that there can be no innate principles unless there are innate ideas. But, logically, it might be possible for there to be innate ideas without there being innate principles. Locke focuses on whether there are innate speculative principles in E I.ii, on whether there are innate practical principles in E I.iii, and on whether there are innate ideas in E I.iv.1–20.

It is commonly thought that Locke's arguments against innatism are directed at straw men and flawed to boot. This explains why Book I of the *Essay* garners a fraction of the scholarly attention devoted to the rest of Locke's work. But the standard criticisms of Book I are flawed themselves. Locke's investigation into the innateness question is masterful and fascinating, and there is a great deal to be learned from it.

Let us begin with the straw man issue. A philosopher commits the straw man fallacy when no one actually holds the thesis, or makes the argument, to which his or her criticisms are directed. Now the most prominent innatists of Locke's day were Descartes and his followers. Descartes tells us that there are three kinds of ideas. Adventitious ideas ("such as the idea we commonly have of the sun") are produced by brain images received from the operation of sensible bodies on our senses; constructed ideas (e.g., the idea of a siren or hippogriff, or astronomers' ideas of the sun) are made up of other ideas; and innate ideas (e.g., "the idea of God, mind, body, triangle, and in general all those which represent true, immutable and eternal essences") derive from our own natures (AT 7: 37–38; CSM 2: 26; AT 3: 383; CSM 3: 183).

Descartes's innatism, however, is of a very particular sort. Descartes writes: "When we say that an idea is innate in us, we do not mean that it is always there before us. This would mean that no idea was innate. We simply mean that we have within ourselves the faculty of summoning up the idea" (AT 7: 189; CSM 2: 132). Further, Descartes likens this "summoning" faculty to the tendency to contract diseases that fetuses possess in the womb (AT 8B: 358; CSM 1: 304). According to this analogy, just as some fetuses are predisposed to contract gout or kidney stones, our minds are predisposed to frame (or become conscious of) certain kinds of ideas (e.g., the idea of God) when the appropriate triggering conditions are met. For Descartes, then, we have innate ideas inasmuch as we have the ability to become conscious of certain kinds of mental contents under certain conditions. Let us call this position "Dispositional Innatism."

As we will see, many of Locke's anti-innatist arguments take for granted that innate ideas would, by their very nature, be conscious if they existed. Locke writes that it seems to him "near a Contradiction, to say, that there are Truths imprinted on the Soul, which it perceives or understands not; imprinting, if it signify any thing, being nothing else, but the making certain Truths to be perceived" (E I.ii.5: 49; see also E I.ii.26: 63). Even if these arguments are sound, however, they cannot establish the falsity of Dispositional Innatism. The reason is that Dispositional Innatists do not accept that it is necessary for innate ideas to be conscious. So it might seem that Locke is committing the straw man fallacy when, as it is contended, he draws absurd conclusions from the supposition that we have innate ideas, where innateness is understood non-dispositionally.

Let us call the view that innate ideas are actually, and not merely potentially, conscious mental contents "Occurrent Innatism."[4] It is also commonly thought that even if there were Occurrent Innatists among his opponents, the arguments for innatism Locke criticizes would be straw men. For Locke not only attacks innatism itself; he also attacks one particular kind of argument for innatism that he finds "commonly taken for granted" by innatists (E I.ii.2: 49). According to this argument, which is "drawn from *Universal Consent*" (E I.ii.3: 49), there are truths "universally agreed upon by all Mankind," whence it is taken to follow that these truths "must needs be the constant Impressions, which the Souls of Men receive in their first Beings" (E I.ii.2: 49). But, so critics of Locke contend, no major opponent of Locke's offered this sort of argument for innatism. So the pages that Locke devotes to attacking the argument from universal consent simply miss their mark.

However, Locke did not commit either of the blunders that are commonly attributed to him. For, first, Locke attacks both Occurrent and Dispositional Innatism, focusing on the former because there are reasons for thinking that it is closer to the hearts of innatists (whatever else they may say) than the latter. And, second, there were prominent philosophers, well known in Locke's day but less well known now, who advanced the very versions of the argument from universal consent that Locke so ably criticizes.

Let us begin by examining Locke's reasons for thinking that most of his opponents are, or should be, Occurrent Innatists. Locke's focus here is on why nature should have endowed us with innate principles if it did. The vast majority of innatists insisted that innate principles do not simply appear in our minds by chance: they are imprinted on our minds by *God*. Descartes himself argues that the idea of God has the kind of content (or, as he puts it, objective reality) that could only be produced by an entity that has as much (formal) reality as there is objective reality in the idea itself. Given that the idea of God has infinite (indeed, the greatest possible amount and quality of) objective reality, it follows that God himself must be the cause of the idea of God that each of us possesses (AT 7: 40–45; CSM 2: 28–31). But it is a given that God (and hence nature, which is his product) always acts purposefully, for a good reason. Innatists reasoned, then, that God inscribes speculative and practical truths in our minds so that they might serve as "the Foundation, and Guide of all [our] acquired Knowledge" (E I.ii.25: 62; also E I.ii.21: 59). Certainly, Descartes's entire scientific edifice is built on the supposition of God's existence, for it is from God's perfection (and consequent immutability and constancy) that Descartes derives the laws of motion that are foundational for the rest of his physics (AT 8A: 61ff; CSM 1: 240 ff.).

Suppose, then, that God has imprinted certain principles on our minds to serve as sure epistemic guides in both science and ethics. Locke points out, not unreasonably, that there would be no point to God's having done this if the minds on which the principles were imprinted were ignorant, because unconscious, of them. He writes:

> Can it be imagin'd, with any appearance of Reason, That [children who are capable of thought] perceive the Impressions from things without; and be at the same time ignorant of those Characters, which Nature it self has taken care to stamp within? . . . This would be, to make Nature take Pains to no Purpose; Or, at least, to write very ill; since its Characters could not be read by those Eyes, which saw other things very well: and those are very ill supposed the clearest parts of Truth, and the Foundations of all our Knowledge, which are not first known, and without which, the undoubted Knowledge of several other things may be had. (E I.ii.25: 62)[5]

Locke's main point here is that it would be pointless for God to inscribe innate truths on our minds if we were to be (and, quite possibly, remain) unconscious of them until such time as consciousness of them were (contingently) triggered. Moreover, God would have no reason for endowing the mind with truths of which many would be known only *after* adventitious truths were known, if his aim were to have the innate truths serve as a foundation for acquired knowledge. Locke therefore reasons that, by their own lights, it would be better (because more in line with their independent theological commitments) for innatists to embrace Occurrent over Dispositional Innatism.[6]

But Locke then makes short work of Occurrent Innatism. As he argues, if speculative principles such as the principle of non-contradiction ("'tis impossible for the same thing to be, and not to be") and ideas such as the idea of God were occurrently innate, then all minds would be conscious of them, and hence would assent to the former (given their self-evidence) and recognize the existence of the latter. But a little empirical observation shows that "all *Children*, and *Ideots*, have not the least Apprehension or Thought of" the principle of non-contradiction (E I.ii.5: 49) and "bating, perhaps, some faint *Ideas*, of Hunger, and Thirst, and Warmth, and some Pains, which they may *have* felt in the Womb, there is *not* the least appearance of any settled *Ideas* at all in [new born children]" (E I.iv.2: 85). As to the question whether the idea of God himself is (occurrently) innate, Locke cites the travel journals of explorers as evidence that navigation has "discovered, in these latter Ages, whole Nations, at the Bay of *Soldania*, in *Brasil*, in *Boranday*, and the *Caribee* Islands, *etc.* amongst whom there was to be found no Notion of a God, no Religion" (E I.iv.8: 87–88).

In the realm of the practical, Locke provides additional reasons for thinking that moral rules are not (occurrently) innate. First, he claims, "moral

Principles require Reasoning and Discourse, and some Exercise of the Mind, to discover the certainty of their Truth" (E I.iii.1: 66). Even moral rules we take as axiomatic (e.g., the Golden Rule, "*That one should do as he would be done unto*") are not self-evident: we can "without any absurdity ask a Reason why" such a rule is true. But, argues Locke, the fact that moral rules are not self-evident entails that they are not innate. As he puts it, innate principles "neither want nor receive any Proof" (E I.iii.4: 68).[7]

Second, Locke claims that explorers have discovered whole societies whose members confidently and serenely transgress moral rules of the utmost importance, committing robbery, rape, infanticide, parricide, cannibalism, murders in duels, all "without remorse of Conscience" (E I.iii.9: 72). But if these moral rules were innate, it seems that it would be impossible for human beings to publicly "*transgress* [them], *with Confidence, and Serenity*" (E I.iii.9: 70). The reason for this is simple. All human beings are strongly motivated by self-interest. But any innate moral rule would be such that all humans knew it to be a law, indeed a law promulgated by God, who "would certainly punish the breach of [it] to a degree to make it a very ill Bargain to the Transgressor." So, although human beings are occasionally self-deceived (and may, for example, "give way to a present Appetite" despite knowing that they cannot "escape the Knowledge or Power of the Law-maker"), it is impossible to conceive that an *entire society* should "wantonly, and without scruple, . . . offend against a Law, which they carry about them in indelible Characters, and that stares them in the Face, whilst they are breaking it" (E I.iii.13: 74–75).[8]

Third, Locke claims that if men found practical propositions "stamped on their Minds, they would easily be able to distinguish them from other Truths, that they afterwards learned, and deduced from them; and there would be nothing more easy, than to know what, and how many there were." Unfortunately, claims Locke, "no body, that I know, has ventured yet to give a Catalogue of" innate moral rules, and this strongly suggests that it is not in fact as easy as innatists pretend it is to distinguish between non-innate and putatively innate practical principles (E I.iii.14: 76).[9]

Along with these considerations against Occurrent Innatism, Locke appeals to two additional assumptions to show that the speculative and practical principles commonly thought to be innate could not, in fact, be stamped on the mind at its inception. The first assumption is the Proposition Assumption, to the effect that no proposition is innate unless the ideas of which it is composed are innate. The second assumption, to which Locke assumes that any Occurrent Innatist would be committed, is that innate ideas "*should appear fairest and clearest*" and "must needs exert themselves with most Force and Vigour" in those (e.g., "*Children, Ideots, Savages,* and *Illiterate* People") who are "of all others the least corrupted by Custom, or borrowed Opinions" (E I.ii.27: 63). Call this the "Clarity Assumption." The reason Locke gives for the Clarity Assumption is that education casts our thoughts "into new Moulds" and "super-induc[es] foreign and studied Doctrines," thereby "confound[ing]" our ideas; so that in *uneducated* (and hence, uncorrupted) human beings, "native Beams of Light (were there any such) should . . . shine out in their full Lustre, and leave us in no . . . doubt of their being there" (E I.ii.27: 64).

Locke uses these assumptions to show that the ideas of impossibility, identity, God, worship, whole, part, and substance are not innate, and hence that no proposition of which any of these ideas is a constituent could be (occurrently) innate. Children, says Locke, do not possess the idea of impossibility or the idea of identity (E I.iv.3: 85–86), nor do they possess the idea of God (E I.iv.13: 92) or the idea of worship (E I.iv.7: 87). And yet, by the Clarity Assumption, we should expect children, above all, to be aware of these ideas. So, by the Proposition Assumption, it follows that the principle of non-contradiction (which contains the idea of impossibility), the principle of identity (which contains the idea of identity), and the principle that God is to be worshipped (which contains both the idea of God and the idea of worship) cannot be innate.

Concerning the ideas of whole and of part, Locke argues that each is relative to the ideas of extension and number. (Locke is assuming here that nothing can be a part unless it is part of a whole, and – more controversially – that nothing can be a whole unless it is both one and extended.) But the ideas of extension and number, says Locke, are adventitious. So if, as Locke avers, no idea that is relative to an adventitious idea can itself be innate, it follows that neither the idea of whole nor the idea of part can be innate. And from this it follows by the Proposition Assumption that the proposition that the whole is bigger than a part (a principle commonly thought innate, which contains both the idea of whole and the idea of part) is not innate. As for the idea of substance, Locke claims that it is no more than "an uncertain supposition of we know not what," that it is therefore unclear, and hence, by the Clarity Assumption, cannot be innate. Locke does not himself mention any principle containing the idea of substance one might think to be innate, but one plausible candidate is the Scholastic axiom that all accidents must inhere in a substance. And according to the Proposition Assumption, it would then follow from the fact that the idea of substance is not innate that this axiom is not innate either.

In the face of this sort of criticism, an innatist might retreat to a form of Dispositional Innatism. Indeed, most of Locke's innatist opponents, in addition to Descartes, were Dispositionalists. Among them were Lord Edward Herbert, Edward Stillingfleet, and the Cambridge Platonists, Benjamin Whichcote, Henry More, and Ralph Cudworth. But Locke could not see any way of distinguishing Dispositional Innatism from any reasonable version of anti-innatism. Most opponents of innatism, as Locke points out, are happy to accept that human beings are born with all sorts of *abilities*, such as the ability to perceive ideas and the ability to recognize the truth of self-evident propositions when perceived. What anti-innatists insist on is the fact that the ideas and principles we have the inborn ability to recognize and accept are not *themselves* stamped on the mind in its very first being. Dispositional Innatism being the view that human beings possess innate ideas and principles only inasmuch as they have the ability to become conscious of them under certain kinds of conditions, it follows directly that there is no significant theoretical gap between reasonable anti-innatism and Dispositional Innatism:

> [N]o Body, I think, ever denied, that the Mind was capable of knowing several Truths. The Capacity, they say, is innate, the Knowledge acquired. But then to what end such contest for certain innate Maxims? If Truths can be imprinted on the Understanding without being perceived, I can see no difference there can be, between any Truths the Mind is capable of knowing in respect of their Original: They must all be innate, or all adventitious: In vain shall a Man go about to distinguish them. (E I.ii.5: 50)[10]

Locke, then, provides reasons for dismissing Occurrent Innatism as false and reasons for assimilating Dispositional Innatism to his own version of anti-innatism. But he spends only a relatively small portion of Book I attacking these positions directly. The vast majority of his anti-innatist efforts consist of a methodical and merciless dismantling of every version of the argument from universal consent put forward by his intellectual opponents. It is to these arguments that we now turn.

The basic structure of the argument from universal consent (AUC) is simple:

1. There are speculative and practical principles to which every human assents.
2. Any principle to which every human assents is innate.

So, 3. There are innate speculative and practical principles.

The argument itself may be found in *De Veritate* (1624), in which Lord Herbert claims that "universal consent [is] the final test of truth . . . [and] the beginning and end of theology and philosophy."[11] And in his *Origines Sacrae* (1662), Stillingfleet writes approvingly of the Epicurean argument that "since the *belief* of a *Deity*, neither *rise* from *custom* nor was *enacted* by *Law*, yet it is unanimously *assented* to by all *mankind*; it necessarily *follows* that there must be a *Deity*, because the *Idea* of it is so *natural* to us."[12] So when Locke attacks this argument, he is not targeting a straw man.

Locke has two objections to AUC. The first is that premise (1) is false: simple observation reveals that "there are [no principles] to which all Mankind give an Universal Assent" (E I.ii.4: 49). The evidence in the case is the same as the evidence used to show that there are no principles of which every human is conscious. In order to assent to a principle, one must be conscious of it. So if there were a principle to which every human assents, then there would be a principle of which all humans (including the congenitally stupid and the neonates) are conscious. But there are no such principles. Locke recognizes, of course, that it is far more difficult to prove a negative than it is to prove a positive. To prove that there is a principle of a certain sort, all one needs to do is find *one*. But to prove that there is *no* principle of a certain sort, one needs to rule out *all* possible candidates. This appears to be a tall order. Locke therefore simplifies matters by focusing on paradigm cases, such as the principle of identity and the principle of non-contradiction. He writes that "if *these first Principles* of Knowledge and Science, *are* found *not* to be *innate, no other speculative Maxims can* (I suppose) *with better Right pretend to be so*" (E I.ii.28: 65). And, yet, as he points out, "these Propositions are so far from having an universal Assent, that there are a great Part of Mankind, to whom they are not so much as known" (E I.ii.4: 49). Similarly, Locke points out that none of the *practical* principles one might think innate is universally accepted. Laws of nature (e.g., the principle that one ought to keep one's promises) are not generally accepted (though many pay lip service to them), and although it is sometimes suggested that even villains adhere to these laws, the truth is that villains "practise them as Rules of convenience" rather than as moral imperatives (E I.iii.2: 66).

Locke's second objection to AUC is that premise (2) is false. It is, in fact, one of the recurring themes of Book I (and, in a way, one of the recurring themes of the entire *Essay*) that from the fact that a proposition garners universal assent it does not follow that the proposition is innate. For the innateness of a proposition is not the only, or perhaps even the best, explanation for the fact (if there were such a fact) that everyone assents to it (E I.ii.3: 49; E I.ii.28: 65). Everyone's assenting to a particular proposition might simply be the result of their recognizing its self-evidence. How this might happen if innatism were false is the burden of Book IV, in which Locke argues that recognizing the truth of (and hence assenting to) a self-evident proposition requires no more than perception of (immediate) agreement or disagreement between its ideational components (see E IV.vii, and Chapter 10 below). This is one of the ways in which Book I is not self-standing.

Locke's initial objections to AUC can be answered by making small changes to it, as he himself recognizes. For example, it might be granted to Locke that the first premise is false (i.e., that there are no principles to which every human assents), and yet it might also be maintained despite this that there are principles to which all humans assent *"when they come to the use of Reason"* (E I.ii.6: 51). And it might then be urged, not merely that universal assent is sufficient for innateness, but that universal assent *upon the use of reason* is sufficient for innateness. Acceptance of these premises results in a slight tweaking of the argument from universal consent. Call this the "argument from universal consent upon the use of reason," or "AUC-Reason":

1. There are speculative and practical principles to which all humans assent *when they come to the use of reason.*
2. Any principle to which all humans assent *when they come to the use of reason* is innate.

So, 3. There are innate speculative and practical principles.

Something similar to AUC-Reason may be found in *Origines Sacrae*, where Stillingfleet argues that "there is a *faculty* in the *Soul*, whereby upon the free use of *reason*, it can *form* within its self a settled *notion* of [God]."[13] Stillingfleet's point here concerns the innateness of *ideas* rather than the innateness of *principles*. But the basic line of reasoning is the same. The point is to weaken premise (1) of AUC to make it easier to accept, while strengthening premise (2) without detracting from its truth. So, again, when Locke attacks AUC-Reason, he is not attacking a straw man.

Locke's first reaction to AUC-Reason is to remove an ambiguity he finds in the phrase "when they come to the use of reason." The phrase, he says, could be taken in one of two senses:

(a) when "the Use and Exercise of Men's Reasons . . . makes [the relevant principle] known to them" (E I.ii.7: 51);

(b) "as soon as Men come to the use of Reason."

On the one hand, if the phrase is taken in sense (a), then premise (2) becomes (2a):

(2a) Any principle to which all humans assent when the use of reason makes it known to them is innate.

Locke then objects that this premise leads to the absurd consequence that all mathematical *theorems* (i.e., all mathematical propositions proved by means of reason from mathematical axioms) would turn out to be innate. (This is because every mathematical theorem is such that all humans assent to it when the use of reason makes it known to them.) The consequence here is absurd presumably because the number of theorems is (potentially) infinite and our minds finite.[14]

On the other hand, if the phrase is taken in sense (b), then premise (1) becomes (1b):

(1b) There are speculative and practical principles to which all humans assent as soon as they come to the use of reason.

Locke then objects that empirical observation reveals that (1b) is false, at least in the case of general propositions such as the principle of non-contradiction and the principle of identity. As he puts the point: "How many instances of the use of Reason may we observe in Children, a long time before they have any Knowledge of this Maxim, *That it is impossible for the same thing to be, and not to be*? and a great part of illiterate People, and Savages, pass many Years, even of their rational Age, without ever thinking on this, and the like general Propositions" (E I.ii.12: 53). Moreover, if the phrase is taken in sense (b), then premise (2) becomes (2b):

(2b) Any principle to which all humans assent as soon they come to the use of reason is innate.

Locke then objects that (2b) leads to absurdity. He begins by noting that the province of reason is distinct from the set of propositions that are commonly thought innate. Reason considers *all* propositions, not just a small set of self-evident maxims. In this way, the faculty of reason is similar to the faculty of speech. But then, reasons Locke, if assent to a proposition P as soon as the faculty of *reason* begins to exert itself were sufficient for P's innateness, then, by the same token, assent to P as soon as the faculty of *speech* begins to exert itself would also be sufficient for P's innateness. And this is absurd. Locke makes the point by means of a rhetorical question: "[B]y what kind of Logick will it appear, that any Notion is Originally by Nature imprinted in the Mind in its first Constitution, because it comes first to be observed, and assented to, when a Faculty of the Mind, which has quite a distinct Province, begins to exert it self?" (E I.ii.14: 54).

Given that AUC-Reason is unsound (by reason of its reliance on at least one false premise) no matter which way the phrase "when they come to the use of reason" is disambiguated, Locke concludes that AUC-Reason fails as a way of avoiding his original criticism of AUC. But Locke recognizes that innatists who wish to defend an argument along the lines of AUC have one more trick up their sleeves. It might be suggested that, even though it is false that there are principles to which every human assents, it is true that there are (speculative and practical) principles to which every human assents *as soon as proposed and the terms they are proposed in understood* (E I.ii.17: 56). Furthermore, it might be urged not that any proposition to which all humans assent is innate, but rather that any proposition to which all humans assent *as soon as proposed and the terms it is proposed in understood* is innate. This tweaking of AUC results in what we might call "AUC-Proposal":

1. There are speculative and practical principles to which all humans assent *as soon as proposed and the terms they are proposed in understood*.
2. Any principle to which all humans assent *as soon as proposed and the terms they are proposed in understood* is innate.

So, 3. There are innate speculative and practical principles.

The Cambridge Platonists, Benjamin Whichcote and Henry More, clearly advanced one or another version of AUC-Proposal, a fact of which Locke could not possibly have been unaware. Whichcote claims in one of his *Discourses* that "things of natural knowledge, or of first inscription in the heart of man by God, these are known to be true as soon as ever they are proposed."[15] And in his *Antidote Against Atheisme*, More writes that there are "severall complex Notions [e.g., that the whole is bigger than the part, that if you take equal from equal the remainders are equal, and that every number is either even or odd] which are true to the soul at the very first proposal," truths to which the soul "will certainly and fully assent," and which "must therefore be concluded not fortuitous or arbitrarious, but Natural to the Soul."[16] So, yet again, when Locke criticizes AUC-Proposal, he does not have a straw man in his sights.

In response, Locke argues that (2) leads to absurd results, and must therefore be rejected. The basic problem is that there are simply *too many* propositions to which all humans assent as soon as proposed and the terms they are proposed in understood. Locke writes: "If it be said, that [assent, given to a proposition upon first hearing] is a mark of innate, [those who put forward AUC-Proposal] must then allow all such Propositions to be innate, which are generally assented to as soon as heard, whereby they will find themselves plentifully stored with innate Principles" (E I.ii.18: 57). In particular, a whole host of propositions in mathematics (e.g., "*That One and Two are equal to Three, That Two and Two are equal to Four*") and science (e.g., "*That two Bodies cannot be in the same place*") would turn out to be innate if (2) were true. Worse, according to the criterion of innateness represented by (2), there will be "as many innate Propositions, as Men have distinct *Ideas* . . ., [s]ince every Proposition, wherein one different *Idea* is denied of another [e.g., "*That White is not Black*," "*That a Square is not a Circle*," and "*That Yellowness is not Sweetness*"], will as certainly find Assent at first hearing and understanding the Terms, as this general one, *It is impossible for the same to be, and not to be*" (E I.ii.18: 57). The existence of an absurdity here, as in the earlier argument against premise (2a) of AUC-Reason, depends on the assumption that the number of innate principles, if there are any, must be finite.

Locke also uses the Proposition Assumption to argue that premise (2) of AUC-Proposal must be false. He notes, to begin, that propositions such as "that white is not black" are clearly assented to as soon as proposed and the terms they are proposed in understood. If (2) were true, it would then follow that these propositions are innate. But according to the Proposition Assumption, no proposition can be innate unless all the ideas of which it is composed are also innate. Given that the proposition that white is not black is innate, it follows directly from the Proposition Assumption that the ideas of white and black are innate. But this result is absurd. If any ideas are adventitious, the ideas of white and black are. Even if there were innate ideas, it strains credulity to think that ideas of *colors* are to be ranked among them. It follows that premise (2) of AUC-Proposal cannot be true.

How successful are Locke's criticisms of innatism and of the various versions of the argument from universal consent in support of innatism? Part of the answer, I think, is that Locke's reasons for rejecting the various versions of AUC are unassailable. If innatism is true, it is not because AUC establishes its truth. But Locke's direct argument for the falsity of innatism is less obviously persuasive. The main point here is that although Locke's criticism of innatism works against *Occurrent* Innatism, it is not as clear that it succeeds against *Dispositional* Innatism. The problem, as it turns out, is also exacerbated by changes Locke made in the second edition of the *Essay* to explicate his theory of memory.

Locke's basic reason for rejecting Occurrent Innatism is that there is plenty of empirical evidence to suggest that many human beings, including most notably those in whom one would expect occurrently innate ideas to shine forth most brightly, are not so much as conscious of the speculative and practical principles (and the ideas of which these principles are composed) most commonly thought to be innate. This seems right. Children in particular need to *learn* the principles of non-contradiction and identity, as well as the Golden Rule. But these facts are logically compatible with Dispositional Innatism, according to which innate ideas and principles are in the mind only in the sense that we are capable of thinking of them under the right sorts of conditions. For the fact that children and others *are* not conscious of the principle of non-contradiction or the Golden Rule does not mean that they are not *disposed* to think of them in the right circumstances. Similar remarks apply to the additional considerations Locke uses to establish that practical principles are not innate. If moral rules are only dispositionally and not occurrently innate (and hence, not conscious), then there is nothing to prevent human beings from transgressing them with confidence and serenity, and there is no reason to suppose that human beings would be able to distinguish innate from non-innate principles.

This problem is exacerbated by changes Locke made to his theory of memory in the second and subsequent editions of the *Essay*. Locke's official theory of memory is in some ways unusual, and is forced on him by his view that ideas cannot exist without being perceived. Although Locke describes memory as "as it were the Store-house of our *Ideas*," he does not want his readers to take the "storehouse" metaphor seriously. The reason is that ideas are "nothing, but actual Perceptions in the Mind, which cease to be any thing, when there is no perception of them." To say that ideas are "stored" in memory, then, is to say that "the Mind has a Power . . . to revive Perceptions, which it has once had, with this additional Perception annexed to them, that it has had them before." Ideas that are stored in memory "are actually no where, but only there is an ability in the Mind, when it will, to revive them again; and as it were paint them anew on it self" (E II.x.2: 150).

Yet, in the second edition of the *Essay*, Locke adds remarks to the end of his discussion of innatism that suggest that he does not want to abandon the thought that "stored" ideas are in the mind in some sense. He writes: "If there be any innate *Ideas*, any *Ideas*, in the mind, which the mind does not actually think on; they must be lodg'd in the memory . . . Whatever *Idea* is in the mind, is either an actual perception, or else having been an actual perception, is so in the mind, that by the memory it can be made an actual perception again" (E I.iv.20: 96–97). This is not straightforwardly consistent with Locke's claim that ideas in the memory are, strictly speaking, "nowhere." Moreover, the thought that there could be ideas in the mind that are not *actually* perceived does not sit well with Locke's attempted confutation of innatism. For if there could be ideas in the mind that are not, but could become, present to consciousness with the awareness of having been previously perceived, why could there not be ideas in the mind that are not, but could become, present to consciousness *without* the awareness of having been previously perceived? And wouldn't such ideas have good title to count as dispositionally innate?[17]

Locke's best response to this criticism, I believe, is to renounce the second edition claim that ideas that are stored in memory are in the mind. If ideas in the memory are *not* in the mind, and the storehouse metaphor is completely forsworn, then there is no reason to think that there might be ideas that are in the mind without being present to consciousness. The problem, of course, is that Locke's official theory of memory doesn't persuade. If remembering consists in repeating an idea with the thought that one has had it before, and if it is possible to have an idea with that accompanying thought without one's having had the idea in mind previously, then it is possible to recall an idea that one has never perceived. But this consequence flies in the face of the fact that recalling something logically requires having had it in mind previously. False memories are not real memories; yet Locke's official theory of memory does not distinguish between them.

Locke's best response, at this point, is to acknowledge that there is no good argument against Dispositional Innatism. And this is as it should be, given that Locke himself assimilates Dispositional Innatism to his own brand of anti-innatism. In the *New Essays*, Leibniz tries gamely to distinguish between them, claiming that "the mind is not merely capable of knowing [innate truths], but also of finding them within itself."[18] But this merely begs the question against anti-innatism, given that the evidence that establishes that we are capable of knowing maxims such as the principle of non-contradiction does not itself establish that we are drawing the principles from the unconscious depths of the mind. And, as Locke will later argue, there is an alternative explanation of our ability to know these truths, an explanation that does not presuppose that the truths already exist in the mind, whether occurrently or latently.

notes

1 The word spelled "O-r-i-g-i-n-a-l" here is our noun, "origin." English spelling and punctuation had not yet become standardized in 1689, and there are many words in the Nidditch edition of the *Essay* that have not been modernized. Nouns (but not all nouns) are capitalized, and archaic spelling remains.
2 As we spell it, the relevant word is "human," not (our word) "humane."
3 Later Locke distinguishes explicitly between propositions and sentences, calling the former "mental propositions" and the latter "verbal propositions" (E IV.v.5: 575–576).
4 I have borrowed the terms "dispositional" and "occurrent" from Kim, who distinguishes between dispositional and occurrent nativism (Halla Kim, "Locke on Innatism," *Locke Studies* 3 (2003): 15–39).

5   See also E I.iii.13: 75, where Locke writes: "[I]f Men can be ignorant or doubtful of what is innate, innate Principles are insisted on, and urged to no purpose; Truth and Certainty (the things pretended) are not at all secured by them: But Men are in the same uncertain, floating estate with, as without them."

6   Of course this sort of argument only works against innatists who are also theists or who think, perhaps on adaptationist grounds, that every natural capacity has a function or purpose. Locke's argument is therefore more successful as an *ad hominem* than as an independent consideration in support of Occurrent Innatism.

7   This argument does not sit well with Locke's theory, articulated later in the *Essay*, that "*Morality is capable of Demonstration*" (E III.xi.16: 516). Locke writes: "I doubt not, but from self-evident Propositions, by necessary Consequences, as incontestable as those in Mathematicks, the measures of right and wrong might be made out, to any one that will apply himself with the same Indifferency and Attention to the one, as he does to the other of these Sciences" (E IV.iii.18: 549). But then there must be at least some self-evident propositions from which the rules of morality may be deduced. For more on Locke's ethics, see Chapter 11.

8   Notice that this argument is predicated on the assumption that moral rules are laws and that every law requires a law-maker with the power to reward (for compliance) and punish (for non-compliance): "But what Duty is, cannot be understood without a Law; nor a Law be known, or supposed with a Law-maker, or without Reward and Punishment" (E I.iii.12: 74). The conception of morality as natural law is fundamental to Locke's ethical system. For further details, see Chapter 11.

9   At E I.iii.15–19, Locke considers the catalogue of innate practical principles provided by Lord Edward Herbert in *De Veritate* (1624), arguing, *ad hominem*, that the moral principles that Herbert identifies as innate do not satisfy the marks of innateness that Herbert himself lays out.

10 In response to this line of criticism, the Dispositional Innatist might retreat to the more sophisticated claim that what our minds are stamped with in their first being is not the *disposition* to frame certain sorts of ideas and principles, but rather the *ground* of this disposition. This is the sort of position occupied by Gottfried Wilhelm Leibniz, who, in his extended comments on Locke's *Essay* (composed in 1704, and later published as the *New Essays on Human Understanding* (1765)), writes that innate ideas are in the mind in something like the way a statue of Hercules is present in a block of marble that has "veins in the block which [mark] out the shape of Hercules rather than other shapes" (Gottfried Wilhelm Leibniz, *New Essays on Human Understanding*, edited by Peter Remnant and Jonathan Bennett. Cambridge: Cambridge University Press, 1981, 52). The question is whether the theoretical difference between this sort of "Dispositional Ground" innatism and anti-innatism *makes* a difference. Nothing much seems to hang on whether one follows Locke or Leibniz here.

11 Edward Herbert, *De Veritate*, translated by Meyrick H. Carré. Bristol: University of Bristol, 1937, 117–118.

12 Edward Stillingfleet, *Origines Sacrae, or a Rational Account of the Grounds of Christian Faith, as to the Truth and Divine Authority of the Scriptures, and the matters therein contained*. London: printed by R.W. for Henry Mortlock, 1662, 365–366.

13   Stillingfleet 1662, 369.
14   Note that there is no absurdity here if AUC-Reason is designed to establish the truth of *Dispositional* Innatism. The reason is that there is no inconsistency in the claim that finite human minds are capable of knowing a potentially infinite number of mathematical theorems. However, as we have already seen, Locke sees no relevant theoretical difference between Dispositional Innatism and his own reasonable version of anti-innatism.
15   Benjamin Whichcote, "The Glorious Evidence and Power of Divine Truth" (1698), in *The Cambridge Platonists*, edited by E.T. Campagnac. Oxford: Clarendon Press, 1901, 4–5.
16   Henry More, *An Antidote Against Atheisme, or, an Appeale to the Natural Faculties of the Minde of Man, Whether There be not a God*. London, 1653, 17–18.
17   Leibniz raises this criticism in the *New Essays*. He writes: "Since an item of acquired knowledge can be hidden [in the soul] by the memory, . . . why could not nature also hide there an item of unacquired knowledge?" (Leibniz 1981, 78).
18   Leibniz 1981, 79.

further reading

De Rosa, Raffaella, "Locke's *Essay, Book I*: The Question-Begging Status of the Anti-Nativist Arguments," *Philosophy and Phenomenological Research* 69 (2004): 37–64.

Herbert, Edward, *De Veritate*, translated by Meyrick H. Carré. Bristol: University of Bristol, 1937.

Kim, Halla, "Locke on Innatism," *Locke Studies* 3 (2003): 15–39.

Leibniz, Gottfried Wilhelm, *New Essays on Human Understanding*, edited by Peter Remnant and Jonathan Bennett. Cambridge: Cambridge University Press, 1981.

More, Henry, *An Antidote Against Atheisme, or, an Appeale to the Natural Faculties of the Minde of Man, Whether There be not a God*. London, 1653.

Rickless, Samuel C., "Locke's Polemic Against Nativism," in *The Cambridge Companion to Locke's "Essay Concerning Human Understanding"*, edited by Lex Newman. Cambridge: Cambridge University Press, 2007, pp. 33–66.

Stillingfleet, Edward, *Origines Sacrae, or a Rational Account of the Grounds of Christian Faith, as to the Truth and Divine Authority of the Scriptures, and the matters therein contained*. London: printed by R.W. for Henry Mortlock, 1662.

Whichcote, Benjamin, "The Glorious Evidence and Power of Divine Truth" (1698), in *The Cambridge Platonists*, edited by E.T. Campagnac. Oxford: Clarendon Press, 1901, pp. 1–28.

the positive project: ideational empiricism

If, as Locke argues in Book I of the *Essay*, there are no innate ideas, then all the ideas with which human minds are furnished, without exception, must be acquired. The main point of Book II is to explain where our ideas come from and how it could be that not a single one of them is innate. If this project is successful, then Locke will have shown that the innateness hypothesis is, at the very least, theoretically gratuitous. This is why he writes that the anti-innatism of Book I "will be much more easily admitted, when I have shewn, whence the Understanding may get all the *Ideas* it has, and by what ways and degrees they may come into the Mind" (E II.i.1: 104).

Locke tells us that our ideas come from two experiential sources: sensation and reflection (about which, more below). Sensation (but not reflection) provides us with ideas of light and colors, sounds, odors, tastes, heat and cold, hardness, smoothness, solidity, space, extension, shape, motion and rest. Reflection (but not sensation) provides us with ideas of mental operations, such as perceiving, retaining, discerning, comparing, combining, abstracting, doubting, believing, reasoning, knowing, and willing. Both sensation and reflection provide us with ideas of pleasure and pain, existence, and unity.[1]

In saying that our ideas come from sensation and reflection, Locke does not mean that sensation or reflection is the immediate cause of every one of our ideas. His view is that there is an important distinction to be drawn between simple ideas and complex ideas, that all *simple* (but no *complex*) ideas derive directly from sensation or reflection, and that every *complex* idea (but no *simple* idea) is the result of mentally combining some simple ideas into a unity. Locke tells us that "all our Knowledge is founded in [*Experience*]" (E II.i.2: 104). But he means by this, not that every idea has experience for its *immediate* source, but rather that every idea has experience for its *ultimate* source.

Locke, First Edition. Samuel C. Rickless.
© 2014 Samuel C. Rickless. Published 2014 by John Wiley & Sons, Ltd.

The claim that all ideas derive from experience, at least ultimately, might be called the thesis of *ideational empiricism*. It should be carefully distinguished from a very different kind of empiricism with which it is often, and unfortunately, confused. In truth, Locke's own words conduce to the confusion. For in telling us that all *knowledge* is founded in experience, Locke *seems* to be saying that experience provides the sole justification or warrant for any true belief to count as an item of knowledge. That is, Locke *seems* to be advocating not merely *ideational* empiricism, but also what might be called *epistemic empiricism*. And in telling us, as he does early in Book II, that the method he will use to discover the ultimate sources of our ideas involves an "appeal to every one's own Observation and Experience" (E II.i.1: 104), Locke seems to be applying epistemic empiricism to his own philosophical investigations into the nature and contents of the mind.

However, as becomes clear in Book IV of the *Essay*, Locke is not an *epistemic* empiricist. This is a matter about which the text is unambiguous. Although Locke does think that *many* propositions can be justified only on the basis of experience, he does not think that this is true of *all*. As we have seen, Locke defines knowledge as the perception of agreement or disagreement between two ideas (E IV.i.2: 525). And in some cases, the fact that two ideas agree or disagree is something that the mind can easily perceive without the aid of empirical observation. This happens, for example, in the case of the ideas of white and black. Although these ideas themselves derive from experience (in accordance with ideational empiricism), our minds can immediately see, without reasoning or experiment, that the ideas disagree – that is, that white is not black (E IV.ii.1: 530–531). So it is too simple to claim that Locke is an empiricist. He is an ideational, but not an epistemic, empiricist.

In the rest of this chapter, I will discuss the distinction between simple and complex ideas, the thesis that all simple ideas derive from sensation or reflection, the question of how complex ideas are formed, the (vexed) question of which of our ideas should be taken to count as simple and which as complex, the proper way to understand Locke's doctrine of abstract ideas, and finally whether his ideational empiricism is subject to counterexample (particularly with respect to the potentially recalcitrant ideas of substratum and infinity).

4.1 Simple Ideas

One of the most crucial aspects of Locke's ideational empiricism is his distinction between simple and complex ideas. It is crucial because, without it, the empiricist thesis that all ideas derive from experience would be false, and obviously so. As was understood well before Locke's time, humans are capable of creating, out of the ideas they already have, new ideas that do not correspond to anything in inner or outer experience. Recall Descartes's claim that there are three kinds of ideas: adventitious, constructed, and innate. Examples of constructed ideas include the idea of a hippogriff (mare-griffin) or chimera (lioness-snake-goat). These ideas of mythical creatures do not themselves derive from experience. The distinction between simple and complex ideas is what enables Locke to get around this difficulty, for he can say that while all simple ideas derive immediately from experience, complex ideas derive from experience only in the sense that all their simple ideational components do.

The critical issue here, of course, is how Locke means to distinguish between simple and complex ideas. What is the criterion according to which ideas are slotted in one category or the other? This is something of a vexed question. When Locke first introduces the simple/complex distinction, he writes that each simple idea "contains in it nothing but *one uniform Appearance*" (E II.ii.1: 119). This suggests that he is working with a *phenomenal* criterion, according to which an idea is simple inasmuch as it is visually, aurally, tangibly, olfactorily, and gustatorily (in sum, phenomenally) undifferentiated. But this seems too narrow a criterion for Locke's purposes, because it does not make sense of Locke's claim that ideas of some of our mental operations are simple.

Locke claims that simple ideas derive from two separate sources: sensation and reflection. Ideas derived from sensation are produced in our minds (most likely) by the motion of small particles of matter impinging on our eyes, ears, skin, nose, and tongue (E II.viii.13: 136). Ideas derived from reflection are produced in our mind by inner contemplation (introspection) of our own mental activities. It makes no sense to suppose that the latter ideas are phenomenally undifferentiated, given that they have no phenomenal characteristics to begin with. There is nothing it is *like* to think, or believe, or will, or doubt, or know. By contrast, there is something it is *like* to see red, hear a symphony, touch glue, smell a rose, or taste a pineapple. So it is unlikely that Locke would have thought that what *makes* a simple idea simple is the fact that it presents a uniform appearance.

Luckily, Locke tells us more about simple and complex ideas, and the additional information he provides about them can help us identify the criterion he uses to distinguish between them. Locke writes that each simple idea is "in it self uncompounded, . . . and is not distinguishable into different *Ideas*" (E II.ii.1: 119). This suggests that Locke is relying on a *mereological* criterion – that is, a criterion related to the concepts of whole and part. But there are many mereological criteria. According to the simplest criterion (call it the "No Part" criterion), simple ideas, unlike complex ideas, *have no parts*. According to a slightly different criterion (call it the "No Idea-Part" criterion), simple ideas, unlike complex ideas, have no parts *that are also ideas*. And according to a third criterion (call it the "No Idea-Parts of One Kind") criterion, simple ideas, unlike complex ideas, have no parts that are ideas *of the same kind*. Which of these criteria, if any, does Locke favor?

The "No Part" criterion, clearly the simplest of the three, is suggested by Locke's description of simple ideas as "uncompounded" (E II.ii.1: 119) and "pure & unblended" (Draft B, 20: 131). But careful examination of the *Essay* reveals that this cannot be the criterion on which he relies. Locke tells us that the ideas of space (or extension) and duration are simple (E II.v: 127; E II.xiii.2: 167; E II.xv.9: 201), and that it is possible to combine these simple ideas to produce complex ideas (ideas of simple modes – for more on which, see Section 4.3 below), such as the idea of a foot or a yard (E II.xiii.4: 167) and the idea of an hour or a day (E II.xiv.1: 181). But he also claims that "none of the distinct *Ideas* we have of either [space or duration] is without all manner of *Composition*, it is the very nature of both of them to consist of Parts" (E II.xv.9: 201–202). It follows that Locke's criterion for distinguishing between simple and complex ideas cannot be that the former, unlike the latter, lack parts.[2]

Locke also tells us that a simple idea "is not distinguishable into different *Ideas*" (E II.ii.1: 119). This suggests the "No Idea-Part" criterion, according to which simple ideas, unlike complex ideas, have no parts *that are also ideas*. The vast majority of the passages in the *Essay* in which Locke discusses simple and complex ideas are consistent with this interpretation. The reason is simple. When Locke turns his attention from simple to complex ideas, he tells us that complex ideas are those that are "made up of several simple ones put together" (E II.xii.1: 164). So if every complex idea has *some* ideas as constituents, it is natural to suppose that every simple idea, by contrast, has *no* ideas as constituents.

Unfortunately, Locke finds himself in a bit of a bind when he tries to apply his criterion of simplicity to the ideas of space (or extension) and duration. For he notices that the parts of which the ideas of space and duration are composed are themselves ideas, indeed ideas of sensible points and moments, the least parts of extension and duration our minds can discern (E II.xv.9: 203). So if Locke wants to treat the ideas of space and duration as simple, he needs a criterion of simplicity other than the "No Idea-Parts" criterion, for he clearly holds that the ideas of space and duration have parts that are also ideas.

Locke struggles with this problem, one has to say, not quite successfully. His official solution consists of an endorsement of the "No Idea-Parts of One Kind" criterion. Locke writes that the parts of the ideas of space and duration "being all of the same kind, and without the mixture of any other *Idea*, hinder them [i.e., the ideas of space and duration] not from having a Place amongst simple *Ideas*" (E II.xv.9: 202). This solution is also endorsed in a footnote added to the fifth (posthumous) edition of the *Essay* (dictated by Locke to his friend Pierre Coste, who translated the *Essay* into French), where Locke writes (in the third person) that "that Composition which he designed to exclude in that Definition [of simplicity], was a Composition of different *Ideas* in the Mind, and not a Composition of the same kind in a Thing whose Essence consists in having Parts of the same kind" (E II.xv.9: 201). The thought here is that the ideas of space and duration count as simple because, although they have ideas as parts, the ideas of which they are composed are not of different kinds.

But in the very same footnote, Locke also acknowledges the possibility (again in the third person) that "if the *Idea* of Extension is so peculiar, that it cannot exactly agree with the Definition that he has given of those *Simple Ideas*, so that it differs in some manner from all others of that kind, he thinks

the positive project: ideational empiricism

'tis better to leave it there expos'd to this Difficulty, than to make a new Division in his Favour" (E II.xv.9: 201–202). Locke's point here is that although it may indeed be the case that the ideas of extension and duration do not count as simple in accordance with his official criterion of simplicity, it would be too much trouble to come up with a more subtle criterion according to which they would count as simple. He tells us that he has observed "intelligible Discourses spoiled by too much Subtilty in nice [i.e., excessively fine-grained] Divisions," and that it suffices "that his Meaning can be understood" (E II.xv.9: 202).

It is fair, I think, to read this protestation of humble simple-mindedness as overdone. Locke himself goes to some pains to construct a fairly elaborate system of classification of ideas. As we will see, he divides complex ideas into ideas of modes, substances, and relations, divides ideas of modes into two kinds (ideas of simple modes and ideas of mixed modes), divides ideas of substances into two kinds (ideas of single substances and ideas of collective substances), and divides ideas of relations into four kinds (proportional, natural, instituted, and moral). So it is disingenuous of him to suggest that the consistent accommodation of the ideas of extension and duration into his classificatory scheme would require subtlety in excess of what may reasonably be demanded.

The long and short of it is that Locke faces a choice here, one that he prefers not to make. On the one hand, he can endorse the "No Idea-Parts of One Kind" criterion of simplicity. On the other, he can give up the claim that the ideas of extension and duration are simple. Not wanting to commit to either, he simply avoids the issue. More charitably, perhaps, one might read him as claiming that it does not much matter for theoretical purposes whether the ideas of extension and duration come out as simple or complex. And about this, Locke is probably right.

4.2 Sensation and Reflection

Locke claims that the two sources of simple ideas are sensation and reflection. "*Our Senses,*" he tells us, "conversant about particular sensible Objects, do *convey into the Mind*, several distinct *Perceptions* of things, according to those various ways, wherein those Objects do affect them . . ., which when I say the senses convey into the mind, I mean, they from external Objects convey into the mind what produces there those *Perceptions*" (E II.i.3: 105). The ideas thus conveyed include ideas of sensible qualities (e.g., ideas of colors, sounds, tastes, smells, heat, hardness, shape, size, and motion), as well as the ideas of pleasure and pain, existence and unity.

Locke's description of how we come by our simple ideas of sensation is potentially somewhat misleading, a fact of which he is not completely unaware. At first blush, it may seem as if he is telling us that external objects transmit simple ideas to our sense-organs, organs that then transmit these ideas to our minds. But this is actually the picture of perception endorsed by Locke's Aristotelian opponents, according to whom the accidental forms of objects (e.g., color and shape) travel through a medium (e.g., air or water) in the guise of sensible species to our common sense via our sense-organs, there to be abstracted as intelligible species or notions by the intellect. Recognizing the potential for confusion, Locke makes clear that external objects do not transmit *ideas*, and that ideas are neither present in nor transmitted by sense-organs. Rather, Locke's view is that external objects affect our sense-organs in a way that results in these organs transmitting *something* that then results in the production of ideas in our minds. Locke is officially agnostic both about exactly *how* external objects affect our sense-organs, about exactly *what* effects our sense-organs produce in our bodies (particularly in our brains), and about how those effects then produce ideas in our minds. There are no ideational agreements in this area of investigation for us to perceive, and hence no knowledge is as yet available to us of the way ideas are produced in our minds through our senses. As he puts it:

> We are so far from knowing what figure, size, or motion of parts produce a yellow Colour, a sweet Taste, or a sharp Sound, that we can by no means conceive how any *size, figure, or motion* of any Particles, can possibly produce in us the *Idea* of any *Colour, Taste,* or *Sound* whatsoever; there is no conceivable *connexion* betwixt the one and the other. (E IV.iii.12–14: 545–546)

This does not prevent Locke from putting forward a version of corpuscularian mechanism as part of the most plausible account of the genesis of our ideas of sensation. Locke writes that *"Bodies* produce *Ideas* in us . . . by impulse,"* that "some singly imperceptible Bodies must come from [larger Bodies] to the Eyes [and other senses]," that "some motion must be thence continued by our Nerves, or animal Spirits, by some parts of our Bodies, to the Brains or the seat of Sensation, there to *produce* [*Ideas*] *in our Minds"* (E II.viii.12: 136). The explanation is *corpuscularian* inasmuch as it relies on the hypothesis that there are bodies (corpuscles) that are too small to be perceived by our senses (without the aid of a microscope), and it is *mechanistic* in that it invokes nothing but the shape, size, motion, and configuration of these "singly imperceptible" particles. As we will see, Locke is both attracted to, but understands the limitations of, corpuscularian mechanism, writing that it is "that which is thought to go farthest in an intelligible Explication of the Qualities of Bodies" (E IV.iii.16: 547), and yet that it has not been able to explain the cohesion of the solid parts of matter (E II.xxiii.23–27: 308–311), nor does it seem capable of explaining gravitational phenomena (W4: 467–468; W9: 169; W3: 303–305).

The second source of our simple ideas is reflection. Locke does not tell us much about this very important source, and the little he tells us is understandably problematic. Locke's view of the human mind is that it is many ways active. Our minds voluntarily think of ideas, combine them, separate them, and compare them. In Locke's parlance, thinking, combining, separating, comparing, and so on, are mental *operations* (E II.i.4: 105), where operations include both *actions* (E II.i.10: 108; E II.vi.2: 128; E II.xix.1: 226; E II.xxiii.5: 297; Draft A, 2: 7; Draft A, 27: 42; Draft B, 19: 129–130) and "some sort of Passions arising sometimes from them," such as pains and pleasures (E II.i.4: 106).[3] And when our minds are thus active, we are conscious of these activities (and their pleasurable and painful upshots), a form of awareness that Locke calls "reflection." So far, so good. But reflection, Locke tells us, "though it be not Sense, as having nothing to do with external Objects; yet it is very like it, and might properly enough be call'd internal Sense" (E II.i.4: 105; see also Draft B, 19: 129). The problem here, of course, is that if reflection is *unlike* sense only inasmuch as it has "nothing to do with external objects," then reflection must be *like* sense in any other way. And hence, because sensation requires organs of sense, it would appear that Locke is committed to reflection requiring one or more *organs* of reflection. Yet Locke does not (nor is it likely that he could, even if he wanted to) identify anything in our bodies that might serve as an organ of reflection.

Worse, Locke tells us that in the reception of simple ideas, whether from sensation or from reflection, "the *Understanding* is merely [i.e., wholly] *passive*" (E II.i.25: 118; E II.xii.1: 163; E II.xxii.2: 288; E II.xxx.3: 373).[4] To say that the mind is passive, in the relevant sense, is to say that the perception of simple ideas of sensation and reflection is non-voluntary. As Locke puts it:

> [W]hether or no, [the understanding] will have these Beginnings . . . of Knowledge, is not in its own Power. For the Objects of our Senses, do, many of them, obtrude their particular *Ideas* upon our minds, whether we will or no: And the Operations of our mind, will not let us be without, at least some obscure Notions of them . . . These *simple Ideas*, when offered to the mind, *the Understanding can* no more refuse to have, nor alter, when they are imprinted, nor blot them out, and make new ones in it self, than a mirror can refuse, alter, or obliterate the Images or *Ideas*, which, the Objects set before it, do therein produce. (E II.i.25: 118)

So Locke's picture is that the mind cannot help but be aware of its mental activities, activities that "obtrude" on it in much the way that sensible things "obtrude" on it. The mind acts, and thereby non-voluntarily produces in itself an idea of its activity that stems from its (voluntary?) awareness of that activity. It is not clear that the mind's actively causing passive changes of this sort in itself is ultimately coherent. But Locke does not see this as a problem, happy as he is to liken mental operations to "floating Visions" that "pass [in the mind] continually," making "deep Impressions" when the mind considers them "attentively" but leaving no "clear distinct lasting *Ideas*" otherwise (E II.i.7–8: 107).

Assuming, though, that Locke's picture of how the mind comes by its ideas of reflection is consistent, it might then be asked whether the mind's awareness of its mental operations is mediate or immediate. Are we aware of our own mental operations by being aware of ideas that represent them, or are we aware of our own mental operations, as it were, directly? The answer is that it cannot be the former. Were I aware of my doubting, say, by being aware of an idea that represents this mental operation, Locke's account of the genesis of my idea of my doubting would presuppose the very existence of that idea as a (partial) cause of its own production. This *would* be incoherent. So Locke's view *must* be that the mind's awareness of its own mental operations is not mediated by ideas that represent them.

However, if this is so, then it may seem that Locke must change his characterization of ideas as the immediate objects of perception. For, as he sees it, the mind's activities are not themselves ideas, and yet are immediately perceived. It follows that they too are immediate objects of perception, and hence that his official ecumenical account of ideas cannot stand. But perhaps there is a way out of this conundrum. The word "object" is ambiguous, as between "intentional object" and "thing." Ideas are *intentional objects*, for they are the contents of our mental operations, but they are also *things*, inasmuch as they are bearers of properties (e.g., clarity, distinctness, reality, adequacy, and their opposites – see E II.xxix–xxxi: 362–384) that mediate between our minds and the world of our experience. By contrast, although mental operations, like ideas, are intentional objects, they are not *things*, but temporally extended (albeit very quickly performed – E II.ix.10: 147) activities or processes. So when Locke says that ideas are immediate objects of perception, he may be read as saying that ideas are immediate intentional objects of perception that are also objects (i.e., things). In *this* sense, mental operations are *not* immediate objects of perception, and hence Locke's official characterization of ideas remains uncontroverted.

4.3 Complex Ideas

On Locke's version of ideational empiricism, simple ideas are derived from experience (sensation or reflection), while complex ideas are derived from simple ideas. In this way, *all* ideas derive *ultimately* from experience. As we have seen, Locke makes clear that our reception of simple ideas is passive. But he is equally emphatic that the derivation of complex ideas is active. Complex ideas are produced by mental acts of one particular kind, namely the process of combining (joining, composing) (E II.xi.6: 158; E II.xii.1–2: 164).

What sort of thing does the process of combination yield? There are three possibilities: complex ideas could be (i) aggregates, (ii) sets, or (iii) structured wholes. A physical aggregate is a concrete, unstructured bundle of physical objects, and, correspondingly, a mental aggregate would be a concrete, unstructured bundle of mental objects. A set (at least on conceptions of it that do not treat it as an aggregate) is an abstract (rather than a concrete), unstructured whole, whose identity is wholly determined by its elements: the set {A, B} is identical to the set {B, A}, and if X and Y are sets each of which has exactly A and B as its elements, then X is numerically identical to Y. Like both aggregates and sets, structured wholes cannot be composed of elements that are numerically distinct from their actual parts. But by contrast to both aggregates and sets, structured wholes are not bundles: it is essential to what they are that their parts be related to one another in determinate ways. A chess position at a determinate point in a particular chess game, for example, is a structured whole, determined not only by the board and the various chess pieces on it, but also by the relative positions of the pieces on the board. Are complex ideas aggregates, sets, or structured wholes, so conceived?

In keeping with the general agnostic tenor of his theory of ideas, Locke does not speak to this question directly. But he does offer us a clue, one that clearly suggests that he thinks of complex ideas as structured wholes. Late in Book II of the *Essay*, Locke turns to the various properties he takes ideas to have. Here Locke follows Descartes's nomenclature: some ideas are clear, others obscure; some ideas are distinct, others confused. Locke (at least roughly) shares Descartes's conception of clarity. For Descartes, an idea is clear when "it is present and accessible to the attentive mind – just as we say that we see something clearly when it is present to the eye's gaze and stimulates it with a sufficient degree of strength and accessibility" (AT 8A: 22; CSM 1: 207). For Locke, simple ideas are clear when "they are such as the Objects themselves, from whence they were taken, did or might, in a well-ordered Sensation or Perception, present them," and complex ideas are clear when and only when their simple ideational constituents are clear (E II.xxix.2: 363). But Locke explicitly distances himself from Descartes's conception of confusion. For Descartes, an idea is confused when it is not distinct – that is, when it is not "so sharply separated from all other perceptions that it contains within itself only what is clear" (AT 8A: 22; CSM 1: 208). For Locke, "[n]o *Idea* can be undistinguishable from another, from which it ought to be different, unless you would have it different from it self" (E II.xxix.5: 364). So, as Locke sees it, confusion is not an intrinsic property or feature of ideas; it is, rather, partly a function of *language*. As he conceives of it, an idea is confused when "it may as well be called by another Name, as that which it is expressed by, the difference which keeps the Things (to be ranked under those two different Names) distinct, and makes some of them belong rather to the one, and some of them to the other of those Names, being left out" (E II.xxix.6: 364).

Locke explains that there are three ways in which complex ideas can become confused. Sometimes, he says, a complex idea is made up of "*too small a number of simple Ideas*, and such only as are common to other Things." This happens, for example, when one associates the idea of a beast with spots with the name "leopard." Confusion arises, because the idea of a spotted beast applies as much to other animals (e.g., a lynx) as it does to a leopard (E II. xxix.7: 365). At other times, it is uncertain or undetermined which ideas a given speaker associates with a particular word, as when the speaker does not keep to "any one precise Combination of *Ideas*" that makes up the idea of idolatry. And this too can yield a confused complex idea (E II.xxix.9: 366). But Locke also finds a third cause of confusion. He writes:

> Another default, which makes our *Ideas* confused, is, when though the particulars that make up any *Idea*, are in number enough; yet they are so *jumbled together*, that it is not easily discernable, whether it more belongs to the Name that is given it, than to any other. (E II.xxix.8: 365)

Locke then provides the analogy of a picture of a man in which there is "no Symmetry nor Order," a picture that could as easily belong to the name "man" as to the name "baboon," though when placed in front of a cylindrical mirror, "the Eye presently sees, that it is a Man . . . and that it is sufficiently distinguishable from a Baboon" (E II.xxix.8: 366).

If *confused* complex ideas are, as Locke puts it, "mental Draughts" relevantly like pictures with no such symmetry or order (E II.xxix.8: 366), then Locke must be thinking of *distinct* complex ideas as "mental Draughts" that possess the very order and symmetry that confused complex ideas lack. What this means is that the simple ideas that constitute a (distinct) complex idea must be organized in a particular way that partly determines the very nature and identity of the complex idea itself. Complex ideas, then, must be structured wholes of simpler ideational parts, rather than aggregates or sets of simple ideas.

Let us see how the structured whole thesis might apply to particular cases. Locke tells us that the idea of a friend is made up of the following ideas: the idea of a man, the idea of love, the idea of readiness, the idea of doing, and the idea of good. But the (distinct) idea of a friend is not a mere set or aggregate (as Locke puts it, a "jumble") of these five ideas, for a friend is "a Man, who loves, and is ready to do good to another [Man]" (E II.xxviii.18: 360–361). It is readily apparent that the (distinct) complex idea of friendship is not a mere aggregate or set of ideational components when one notices that the same five ideas could be organized differently, so as to pick out "a man, who does good, and is ready to love another man." But, so organized, these simple ideas would not combine to compose the (distinct) complex idea of a friend, but rather a completely different complex idea. Similarly, Locke tells us that the idea of a father is made up of three ideas: the idea of a man, the idea of generation, and the idea of a child (Draft B, 153: 264). But it is absolutely essential to the idea of a father that it be understood to be "a man who generates a child," and not "a child who generates a man." So it is of the very essence of the (distinct) idea of a father that its three ideational components be arranged in a particular way. Unfortunately, Locke gives us no information about the *kind* of arrangement or organization of simple ideas that complex ideas presuppose. But we may reasonably suppose that the organization is functional, in that some ideas are functions that take ideas (or n-tuples of ideas) to other ideas.

Let us now turn to Locke's own categorization of complex ideas. Locke tells us that there are three kinds of complex ideas: ideas of substances, ideas of modes, and ideas of relations (E II.xii.3: 164).[5] Ideas of substances "are such combinations of simple *Ideas*, as are taken to represent distinct particular things subsisting by themselves." These ideas fall into two categories: ideas of single substances and ideas of collective substances. Ideas of single substances are ideas of substances "as they exist separately," while ideas of collective substances are ideas of "several [substances] put together" (E II.xii.6: 165). Included among ideas of single substances are the ideas of lead, man, sheep (E II.xii.6: 165), horse, sun, water, iron (E II.xxiii.6: 298), gold (E II. xxiii.10: 301), swan (E II.xxiii.14: 305), violet, apple (E II.xxiv.1: 317), immaterial spirit, and matter (E II.xxiii.15: 305). Included among ideas of collective substances are the ideas of an army of men, a flock of sheep (E II.xii.6: 165), a swarm [of bees], a fleet [of ships] (E II.xxiv.2: 318), and a constellation [of stars] (E II.xxiv.3: 318).

Ideas of modes, by contrast, are "such complex *Ideas*, which however compounded, contain not in them the supposition of subsisting by themselves, but are considered as Dependences on, or Affections of Substances" (E II.xii.4: 165). These ideas too fall into two categories: ideas of simple modes and ideas of mixed modes. Ideas of simple modes are "variations, or different combinations of the same simple *Idea*, without the mixture of any other," while ideas of mixed modes are "compounded of simple *Ideas* of several kinds" (E II.xii.5: 165). Among the former are to be found the ideas of number (e.g., a dozen, a gross, or a million – E II.xiii.1: 167), infinity (E II.xvii.1: 209), shape (E II.xiii.5: 168), place (E II.xiii.7: 169), time, eternity (E II.xiv.1: 181), kinds of motion (E II.xviii.2: 224), types of sound (E II.xviii.3: 224), shades of the same color (E II.xviii.4: 224), and various modes of thinking or perception – such as sensation, remembrance, recollection, contemplation, reverie, attention, intention, dreaming, ecstasy, reasoning, judging, knowing, and willing (E II.xix.1–2: 226–227). Among the latter is a whole host of ideas, including the ideas of gratitude, murder (E II.xii.4: 165), beauty, theft (E II.xii.5: 165), obligation, drunkenness, lie (E II.xxii.1: 288), hypocrisy (E II.xxii.2: 289), sacrilege (E II.xxii.3: 289), reprieve, appeal (E II.xxii.7: 291), triumph, apotheosis (E II.xxii.8: 291), wrestling, and fencing (E II.xxii.9: 292). As an example, Locke analyzes the idea of a lie, which, he tells us, includes the following simple ideas: "1. Articulate sounds. 2. Certain *Ideas* in the Mind of the Speaker. 3. Those words the signs of those *Ideas*. 4. Those signs put together by affirmation or negation, otherwise than the *Ideas* they stand for, are in the mind of the Speaker" (E II.xxii.9: 292).

Finally, there are ideas of relation, which, Locke tells us, somewhat unhelpfully, consist in "the consideration and comparing one *Idea* with another" (E II.xii.7: 166). Examples of such ideas include the ideas of husband, father, son, whiter, stronger, weaker, older, younger, bigger, less, cause, effect, like, and unlike (E II.xxv.1–7: 319–322).

Locke underlines the fact that the mental acts that produce our complex ideas of substances, modes, and relations are *voluntary* (E II.xii.2: 164, heading; E II.xxx.3: 373, heading and main text; E II.xxxii.12: 387). And yet, somewhat unfortunately, Locke's statements on this issue are not entirely consistent. Surprisingly, he claims that ideas of mixed modes are derived in one of three ways: (i) "By Experience and *Observation* of things themselves," as when "by seeing two Men wrestle, or fence, we get the *Idea* of wrestling or fencing," (ii) "By *Invention*, or voluntary putting together of several simple *Ideas* in our own Minds," or, the most usual way, (iii) "by *explaining the names* of Actions we never saw, or Notions we cannot see" (E II.xxii.9: 291–292). And Locke keeps to this account of the acquisition of ideas of mixed modes in that chapter, claiming only that "[t]he Mind often *exercises an active Power in the making*" of ideas of mixed modes (underlining added), that such ideas (including, for example, the idea of hypocrisy) "might be taken from Observation" (e.g., "observation of one, who made shew of good Qualities which he had not") (E II.xxii.2: 288–289), and that *an usual way of getting* [ideas of mixed modes] *is by the explication of those terms that stand for them*" (E II.xxii.3: 289). So Locke seems to be saying that at least *some* complex ideas are not produced by voluntary acts of mind. For some ideas of mixed modes (e.g., the modes of wrestling and fencing) are derived directly from observation (i.e., sensation), and others stem directly from the explication of word meanings.

What are we to make of the tension here? On balance, I think, it is best to understand Locke as having strayed in E II.xxii from his own considered view. In the first place, the third type of process that Locke thinks can lead to the formation of ideas of mixed modes (i.e., the explanation of terms) is not theoretically distinguishable from the second (i.e., the voluntary combination of ideas). Locke writes that "a Man may come to have the *Idea* of *Sacrilege*, or *Murther*, by enumerating to him the simple *Ideas* which these words stand for" (E II.xxii.3: 289). And although this is supposed to constitute an example of how the explanation of terms can produce an idea of a mixed mode, it is clear that the idea thereby introduced into the man's mind is the result of his putting the various enumerated ideas into a unity. Considered as scattered, the various ideas that constitute the idea of murder do not make up a single idea of any kind, and mere enumeration will not suffice on its own to give anyone a single representation of anything.

In the second place, Locke actually provides us with an *argument* for the claim that *all* complex ideas, including all ideas of mixed modes, must be produced voluntarily, and so actively rather than passively. Locke writes:

> Though the Mind be wholly passive, in respect of its simple *Ideas*: Yet, I think, we may say, it is not so, in respect of its complex *Ideas*: For those being Combinations of simple *Ideas*, put together, and united under one general Name; 'tis plain, that the Mind of Man uses some kind of Liberty, in forming those complex *Ideas*: How else comes it to pass, that one Man's *Idea* of Gold, or Justice, is different from anothers? But because he has put in, or left out of his, some simple *Idea*, which the other has not. (E II.xxx.3: 373)

The reasoning here is simple. Locke claims (and indeed, as we will see, makes much of the fact) that one person's idea of gold (a substance) or justice (a mixed mode) can differ greatly from another's.[6] Were these ideas derived passively from experience, they would not differ much from person to person, given how similar nuggets of gold (and individual instances of justice) are to each other. It follows, then, by generalization, that no ideas of substances or mixed modes are derived passively from experience.

Interestingly, this result applies no less to the very examples Locke uses at E II.xxii to suggest that ideas of mixed modes are sometimes passively received by the mind. Locke tells us that "by seeing two Men wrestle, or fence, we get the *Idea* of wrestling or fencing" (E II.xxii.9: 292). But this is not clear at all. If I come upon two people who are fencing, I may observe what they are doing and construct an idea of highly ineffective dueling with blunt swords, or an idea of a complex form of sword-based signaling, or an idea of a highly ritualized form of hole-poking. The very concepts of wrestling and fencing are paradigmatic constructs, for these forms of activity are not natural but invented. Indeed, it would be exceedingly difficult, if not impossible, for an alien anthropologist to discover the nature and rules of the relevant sports merely by watching two people wrestling or fencing. I conclude that it would have been better for Locke not to have introduced the complication he did in E II.xxii. It would have served his purposes better to have kept to his official line, according to which *all* complex ideas, without exception, are produced by the voluntary activity of mental combination.

We have seen that Locke occasionally strays from his official pronouncements. Unfortunately, matters are no different when it comes to the question whether all complex ideas are produced by a single sort of mental act, or whether some complex ideas are produced by one kind of mental act while others are produced by another. In various places, Locke tells us that complex ideas are produced by the mental act of composition or combination (E II.xi.6: 158; E II.xii.2–8: 164–166; E II.xxx.3: 373). He also tells us unambiguously that ideas of relation are complex (E II.xii.3: 164). However, he also distinguishes between the mental act of combination and the mental act of comparison, claiming that while the former is responsible for the production of complex ideas, the latter is responsible for the production of ideas of relations (E II.xi.4: 157; E II.xi.6: 158). These statements are not mutually consistent. If ideas of relation are produced by the mental act of comparing, and the mental act of comparing differs from the mental act of combining, and the mental act of combining is responsible for the production of all complex ideas, then ideas of relation are not complex ideas. And yet, for Locke, it seems that they are.

This problem is exacerbated by a passage added to the fourth and fifth editions of E II.xii.1. In the first three editions, Locke uses this section to contrast simple ideas, which are passively received, with complex ideas, which are "made up of several simple ones put together" (E II.xii.1: 164). This is so far consistent with his claim that all complex ideas are produced by combination and that ideas of relation are, by this definition, complex. But in the fourth edition, Locke adds the following passage:

The Acts of the Mind wherein it exerts its Power over its simple *Ideas* are chiefly these three, 1. Combining several simple *Ideas* into one compound one, and thus all Complex *Ideas* are made. 2. The 2*d*. is bringing two *Ideas*, whether simple or complex, together; and setting them by one another, so as to take a view of them at once, without uniting them into one; by which way it gets all its *Ideas* of Relations. 3. The 3*d*. is separating them from all other *Ideas* that accompany them in their real existence; this is called *Abstraction*: And thus all its General *Ideas* are made. This shews Man's Power and its way of Operation to be muchwhat the same in the Material and Intellectual World. For the Materials in both being such as he has no power over, either to make or destroy, all that Man can do is either [1] to unite them together, or [2] to set them by one another, or [3] wholly separate them. (E II.xii.1: 163–164)[7]

For reasons he does not clarify, Locke therefore draws attention to, and deepens the mystery surrounding, the inconsistency with respect to the classification of ideas of relation within his ideational system. Not only does he tell us, contrary to his initial classification of complex ideas (into ideas of substances, modes, and relations), *that* ideas of relation are *not* complex; he also tells us *why* they are not complex. Although both ideas of relation and complex ideas have ideas as *parts*, and are therefore composed of ideas, complex ideas possess a *unity* that ideas of relation lack: the mind combines the constituents of complex ideas "into one compound one," while the mind "sets" the constituents of ideas of relation "by one another . . ., without uniting them into one."

How, if at all, are we to make sense of all this? The answer is: with difficulty. For even as Locke adds a passage that unambiguously distinguishes between complex ideas and ideas of relations, he fails to remove other passages that unambiguously preserve the original claim that ideas of relation are complex. One of these passages is in the very same chapter Locke amends in the fourth edition. There he writes that "[t]he last sort of complex *Ideas*, is that we call *Relation*" (E II.xii.7: 166). In other passages, Locke writes that relative ideas are "compounded of others" (E II.xxiii.35: 315; Draft B, 94: 213), speaks of "the simple *Ideas* that make up any Relation I think on, or have a Name for" (E II.xxv.8: 322), and states that "all the *Ideas* we have of *Relation*, are made up, as the others are, only of simple *Ideas*" (E II.xxv.11: 323). Worse, Locke actually gives examples of ideas of relation that are "made up" of simple ideas. At one point, he discusses "the Word Friend, [which] being taken for a Man, who loves, and is ready to do good to another, has all those following *Ideas* to the making of it up," namely the idea of man, the idea of love, the idea of readiness, the idea of action, and the idea of good (E II.xxviii.18: 360–361). Moreover, when he turns to the analysis of language, Locke holds that "[t]he *Names of simple* Ideas *are not capable of any definitions*; the Names of all complex *Ideas* are" (E III.iv.4: 421). The reason for this is that "a definition is best made by enumerating those simple *Ideas* that are combined in the signification of the term Defined" (E III.iii.10: 413). So when Locke actually enumerates simple ideas (of man, of love, of readiness, of action, of good) in defining the term "friend," he is thereby indicating that the *idea* of friend must be complex, rather than simple.

The answer to this conundrum, I believe, is that although the bulk of Locke's theoretical commitments push towards his original view that ideas of relation are complex, his fixation on the fact that ideas of relation are produced by the mental operation of comparing (rather than by the mental operation of combining), together with a glimmer of hope that he might be able to make room for a third category of idea in between the simple and the complex, result in textual and doctrinal incoherence. As to the fixation, it seems to me that it can be readily accommodated within a system that treats ideas of relation as complex. All Locke needs to say is that ideas of relation are produced when the mental operation of comparing results in the combination of the ideas of "the two things which are compard one with an other & the occasion or ground of that comparison" (Draft A, 20: 35). In this way, ideas of relation can be distinguished from other complex ideas by pointing to the essential role of comparison in their aetiology, all without supposing that comparison is the *only* mental act responsible for their production.

And as to the glimmer of hope, I do not see how it can possibly lead to further enlightenment. Locke suggests that what distinguishes ideas of relation from complex ideas is that while the latter are unified, the former are not. Ideas of relation, he says, stem from setting some simple ideas by one another without uniting them (E II.xii.1: 163). But if simple ideas are not united into *one*, how can they come to constitute any (i.e., any *one*) idea? Locke insists, through all the editions of the *Essay*, that the idea of friend is one idea, the idea of brother another, that the idea of whiter is one idea, the idea of bigger another. Clearly Locke thinks of ideas of relations as individual units, units that can themselves contribute to the constitution of complex ideas. The thought that there could be a single, non-unified idea of friend or brother is not merely a pipe dream: it is a self-contradiction. I conclude that Locke *should* treat all ideas of relation as complex, and that the fourth edition addition to the *Essay* on this topic is misbegotten.

Locke's version of ideational empiricism therefore consists of the following theses. Simple ideas, which (except perhaps for the ideas of extension and duration) have no ideas as parts, are passively received by us through sensation (of external bodies) and reflection (on our own internal mental operations and their painful or pleasurable upshots). All other ideas, which are complex, are derived by voluntarily combining simple ideas into a unity of which the latter are parts. All complex ideas are either ideas of substances, ideas of modes, or ideas of relation. When the combination is taken to represent something that can exist independently of other things, the relevant complex idea is an idea of a substance (e.g., gold, or a human being) or an idea of a collective substance (e.g., an army). When the combination is taken to represent something that cannot exist independently of other things, the relevant complex idea is an idea of a mode. When the relevant idea is constituted by ideas of the same kind, it is an idea of a simple mode (e.g., twelve, or a yard). But when the relevant idea is constituted by ideas of different kinds, it is an idea of a mixed mode (e.g., gratitude or murder). Unlike ideas of substances and ideas of modes, ideas of relation (e.g., the idea of a friend or a sister) are produced in part by the mental operation of comparison, and are constituted by ideas of the compared items and an idea of the ground of the comparison. If Locke's classificatory scheme is accurate, then it provides an elaborate vindication of his anti-innatism.

However, there remain a few points of controversy regarding whether – and if so, how – certain specific ideas fit into this classificatory scheme. One idea that has garnered some attention is the idea of power. Once again, Locke seems to say contradictory things in the *Essay* about the proper classification of this idea. On the one hand, he includes the idea of power in his list of the "simple *Ideas*, which convey themselves into the Mind, by all the ways of Sensation and Reflection" (E II.vii.1: 128; see also E II.xxii.10: 293). He maintains this thesis elsewhere, writing that "*Power* also is another of those simple *Ideas*, which we receive from *Sensation and Reflection*" (E II.vii.8: 131), that "[o]ur *Idea . . .* of *Power . . .* may well have a place amongst other simple *Ideas*, and be considered as one of them," and that "many of the simple *Ideas* that make up our specifick *Ideas* of Substances, are Powers" (E III.xi.22: 519; see also E II.xxxi.8: 381). On the other hand, Locke also writes that "these Powers [to change the sensible qualities of other substances], considered in themselves, are truly complex *Ideas*" (E II.xxiii.7: 299).[8]

Can we make sense of this without dismissing or disregarding one set of texts to the advantage of the other? I think we can. It helps to begin with the reason why Locke thinks that the idea of power is complex. Every idea of power represents a power, and every power is either active (i.e., a power to make or cause change of a certain kind) or passive (i.e., a power to receive change of some sort) (E II.xxi.2: 234). For example, "Fire has a *power* to melt Gold" (active power) and "Gold has a *power* to be melted" (passive power) (E II.xxi.1: 233). Because every power is a power to make a change *in something else* or a power to receive a change *from something else*, it follows that powers are *relations*. This is a consequence Locke embraces, writing that "*Power includes in it some kind of relation*, (a relation to Action or Change)" (E II.xxi.3: 234), and, less cagily, that "*Powers* are Relations" (E II.xxi.19: 243). It follows directly that the *idea of* power is an *idea of* relation, and hence, given that all ideas of relation are complex (see above), that the idea of power is a complex idea. The complexity of the idea of power therefore derives from the very nature of what the idea represents. This consequence of Locke's theory of ideas is simply unavoidable.

How, then, are we to make sense of Locke's repeated claims that the idea of power is *simple*? The answer is that Locke's word "simple," as applied to ideas, is ambiguous. In one sense, the sense with which we are familiar and that we have been using thus far, the idea of power is not simple. But in *another* sense, the idea of power is clearly simple. The sense in which the idea of power is *not* simple is the sense in which simplicity is defined as the failure to possess constituents (or perhaps constituents of different kinds) that are also ideas. Call this kind of simplicity "absolute." By contrast with *absolute* simplicity, we can define a kind of simplicity that is *relative*. Locke writes:

> Our *Idea* therefore of *Power*, I think, may well have a place amongst other simple *Ideas*, and be considered as one of them, being one of those, that make a principal Ingredient in our complex *Ideas* of Substances. (E II.xxi.3: 234)

His point here is that the idea of power can be thought of as simple *inasmuch* as it is an ingredient (i.e., a constituent) of more complex ideas. Because substance-ideas are *more complex* (in having a greater number of constituents) than the idea of power that partly constitutes them, we can say that the idea of power is *simpler than* (i.e., simple relative to) the substance-ideas it partly constitutes, even if it is not itself *absolutely* simple. It is with *this* relative sense in mind, I think, that Locke tells us, as he does in so many places in the *Essay*, that the idea of power is simple.

Elsewhere, Locke underlines the fact that it is in a "looser sence" that ideas of powers count as simple. He writes that ideas of substances are composed in large part of ideas of powers, and that these powers are of two kinds. There are powers to produce ideas of certain kinds in our minds by *immediately* affecting our senses. Among these powers are heat (the power to produce in our minds the idea of heat) and color (the power to produce in our minds the idea of color). But there are also powers to produce ideas of certain kinds in our minds by *mediately* affecting our senses – that is, by affecting other objects that immediately affect our senses. Among these powers are the "Power in Fire, which it has to change the colour and consistency of Wood" (E II.xxiii.7: 299). This power is a power to produce the ideas of color and consistency in our minds, but only by producing changes in the wood that then itself directly produces those ideas. Locke calls the former sorts of powers "*Secondary Qualities, immediately perceivable*" and the latter sorts of powers "*Secondary Qualities, mediately perceivable*" (E II.viii.26: 143). He then writes:

> [A]ll those Powers, that we take Cognizance of [i.e., secondary qualities, immediately perceivable, and secondary qualities, mediately perceivable], terminating only in the alteration of some sensible Qualities, in those Subjects, on which they operate, and so making them exhibit to us new sensible *Ideas*, therefore it is, that I have reckoned those Powers amongst the simple *Ideas*, which make the complex ones of the sorts of *Substances*; though these Powers, considered in themselves, are truly complex *Ideas*. And in this looser sence, I crave leave to be understood, when I name any of these *Potentialities amongst the simple Ideas*, which we recollect in our Minds, when we think of particular Substances. (E II.xxiii.7: 299–300; see also Draft B, 61: 164)

It is reasonable to suppose that the looser sense of "simple" that Locke has in mind here is the concept of relative simplicity just outlined. Locke again mentions the fact that ideas of powers (i.e., ideas of secondary qualities, whether immediately or mediately perceivable) "make up" the more complex ideas of substances, and so may be counted as simple relative to the substance-ideas they partly constitute. But there is also a slight hint of a different conception of relative simplicity. For Locke, the ideas produced in our minds by objects that possess immediately and mediately perceivable secondary qualities are ideas of color, heat, sound, taste, odor, hardness, and their ilk. These ideas are all paradigmatically absolutely simple. So Locke could be read as hinting at a different criterion of relative simplicity according to which an idea counts as relatively simple if and only if it represents a power to produce (whether mediately or immediately) something absolutely simple.[9]

In any event, Locke clearly does not want to be understood as saying that the idea of power is *absolutely* simple when he says (as he does) that the idea of power is simple: he wants to be understood as saying that the idea of power is, in one or other of the two senses I have just described, *relatively* simple. And this clears up the textual conundrum produced by sentences in the *Essay* about the idea of power that appear to be mutually inconsistent.

4.4 Abstract Ideas

According to Locke, the mental faculty that enables the mind to produce ideas of modes and substances is the faculty of combination, while the mental faculties that enable the mind to produce ideas of relations are the faculties of comparison and combination. But Locke claims that there is another faculty conversant about ideas, a faculty that was widely derided by some of his philosophical successors (most notably, George Berkeley). This is the faculty of *abstraction*, responsible for the production of *abstract ideas*. There is a fair amount of scholarly disagreement about how this faculty functions and what sorts of ideas it is designed to produce in Locke's ideational system. This is important, not least because the products of the faculty of abstraction play an important role in Locke's theories of language and scientific classification. A proper understanding of these theories requires a proper understanding of Locke's doctrine of abstraction.

When Locke introduces us to the faculty of abstraction, he writes that what one does by means of this faculty is to consider particular ideas "as they are in the Mind such Appearances, separate from all other Existences, and the circumstances of real Existence, as Time, Place, or any other concomitant *Ideas*." One thereby frames "precise, naked Appearances in the Mind, without considering, how, whence, or with what others they came there." He illustrates these points by discussing abstraction of the idea of whiteness: "Thus the same Colour being observed to day in Chalk or Snow, which the Mind yesterday received from Milk, it considers that Appearance alone." Locke then claims that the ideas produced by the mental operation of abstraction, unlike unabstracted ideas, represent anything that conforms to them and thereby acquire universal (or general) signification, a kind of universality that is then passed on to the words that stand for them. Thus, having produced an abstract idea by considering what the ideas produced in us by chalk, snow, and milk all share, one can give it "the name *Whiteness*, [and] by that sound signif[y] the same quality wheresoever to be imagin'd or met with" (E II.xi.9: 159).

In a passage we have already discussed that was added to the fourth edition of the *Essay*, Locke writes that abstract ideas are produced by means that differ from the means that produce complex ideas and ideas of relation. He writes that there are three "Acts of the Mind wherein it exerts its Power over its simple *Ideas*," namely combination, comparison, and abstraction, the last of which produces abstract ideas by "separating [ideas] from all other *Ideas* that accompany them in their real existence" (E II.xii.1: 163).

Later, in passages meant to explicate his theory of general signification, Locke writes that "Words become general, by being made the signs of general *Ideas*: and *Ideas* become general, by separating from them the circumstances of Time, Place, and any other *Ideas*, that may determine them to this or that particular Existence" (E III.iii.6: 410–411). To illustrate this "way of abstraction," Locke explains how children come to have the general idea of humanity. At first, he writes, children are acquainted with particular human beings, and thereby frame particular ideas that represent these people, to which they give names such as "*Nurse*" and "*Mamma*." As their experience grows, youngsters become acquainted with "many other Things in the World, that in some common agreements of Shape, and several other Qualities, resemble their Father and Mother, and those Persons they have been used to," and then "frame an *Idea*, which they find those many Particulars do partake in; and to that they give, with others, the name *Man*." Locke then insists that, when they frame the abstract idea of human being, children "make nothing new, but only leave out of the complex *Idea* they had of *Peter* and *James*, *Mary* and *Jane*, that which is peculiar to each, and retain only what is common to them all" (E III.iii.7: 411). Indeed, he writes, ideas produced in this way are nothing else "but such abstract and partial *Ideas* of more complex ones" (E III.iii.9: 412).

It is perfectly natural to read this passage as saying that there is a single mental operation of abstraction which, when applied to different ideas in different circumstances, sometimes yields abstract ideas that are simple and at other times yields abstract ideas that are complex. Indeed, I believe that this is the best way to understand Locke's doctrine of abstraction. But there is an influential line of interpretation according to which Locke describes one kind of abstraction in Book II and a different kind of abstraction in Book III, two mental operations that are distinguished both by their products (simple ideas in the Book II case, complex ideas in the Book III case) and by the way in which they arrive at them. The thought is that, although both types of abstraction begin with a single complex idea (e.g., C), Book II abstraction works by picking out a single simple idea that is a component of C, focusing on it alone, and ignoring the rest of C's components, while Book III abstraction works by removing some of C's components and then focusing on the complex constituent of C that remains.[10]

But this sort of view, which would significantly complicate our reading of Locke's doctrine of abstraction, is not required by the text. When Locke comes to illustrate the Book II type of abstraction, he does not claim that the simple idea of whiteness is abstracted from a single complex idea, such as the idea of milk, by focusing on it and ignoring the other constituents of the idea of milk (e.g., the idea of liquidity and the idea of sweetness). What he says is that the idea of whiteness is abstracted from *three* complex ideas (the ideas of milk, chalk, and snow) by focusing on an idea that they all have in common. Although he does not tell us exactly *how* one focuses on this idea, it is reasonable to suppose that he means that one mentally separates it from (a) the ideas that together with it make up the idea of milk, (b) the ideas that together with it make up the idea of chalk, and (c) the ideas that together with it make up the idea of snow. This process is no different from the process that yields the abstract idea of human being in Book III. There Locke tells us that one begins with some number of complex ideas (e.g., the ideas of Peter, Mary, and Jane), and that the idea of human being is abstracted from them by focusing on an idea that they all have in common. This is done by mentally separating the idea of human being from (a) the ideas that together with it make up the idea of Peter, (b) the ideas that together with it make up the idea of Mary, and (c) the ideas that together with it make up the idea of Jane. In both cases, the process of abstraction yields a partial idea – that is to say, an idea that is part of another idea. It just happens to be the case that the same process of mental separation sometimes enables one to abstract a *simple* idea that is part of a complex idea and sometimes enables one to abstract a *complex* idea that is part of a (more) complex idea. There is no reason to suppose that it is somehow *essential* to the kind of abstraction described in Book II that it yield *simple* ideas, and similarly no reason to suppose that it is somehow *essential* to the kind of abstraction described in Book III that it yield *complex* ideas.

Indeed, we might go even further and say that it is not even essential to abstraction as Locke conceives of it that it begin with one or more *complex* ideas. Locke tells us that abstraction works by separating from a given idea whatever concomitant ideas determine it to some particular existence. This happens, of course, when an idea is mentally separated from the other constituents of a more complex idea of which it is a part. But it can also happen when an idea is mentally separated from other ideas that happen to "accompany" it in its "real existence." For example, I might see white in the Louvre on Sunday and then see the same color in the Accademia on Monday. Moreover, it might be that the idea of whiteness I perceived in the Louvre on Sunday is accompanied by the idea of the Louvre and the idea of Sunday, while the idea of whiteness I perceived in the Accademia on Monday is accompanied by the idea of the Accademia and the idea of Monday. It then seems possible for me to focus on both sets of ideas, leaving out what distinguishes them, and focusing on what they have in common (i.e., the idea of whiteness). If I do this, I engage in Lockean abstraction and frame an abstract idea of white, but I do not do so by focusing on an idea that is a component of one or more complex ideas. For I am assuming that I have created neither a complex idea of which the ideas of the Louvre, Sunday, and whiteness are constituents, nor a complex idea of which the ideas of the Accademia, Monday, and whiteness are constituents.[11]

Locke tells us that abstraction is the means by which the mind forms general ideas or universals (E II.xi.9: 159; E III.iii.6: 410–411). It has been argued that abstract ideas are intrinsically general – that is, general *in their own nature*.[12] But the worry here is that the very idea of intrinsic generality appears to conflict with a general principle of metaphysics that Locke states explicitly at the very beginning of his discussion of general terms: "All things that exist are only particulars" (E III.iii.6: 410; see also E III.iii.1: 409, E III.iii.11: 414, and W9: 241).[13] Is reconciliation of these two claims possible? It might be thought that the way out of this difficulty is to suppose that Locke means his nominalistic principle to apply only to the realm of *real* existence – that is, only to physical objects (and their qualities) and mental events (and their qualities). If ideas were thought of as *intentional* objects, rather than as *real* objects (e.g., mental events), then they would be exempted from the nominalistic principle and *could*, consistently with it, be deemed intrinsically universal.

But it is quite plain that Locke would not have endorsed this solution. For Locke underlines the fact that ideas fall under his nominalistic principle when he writes that "universality belongs not to things themselves, which are all of them particular in their Existence, even those Words, and *Ideas*, which in their signification, are general" (E III.iii.11: 414). If Locke, as seems clear, endorses the principle that all *ideas* are particular, then he cannot without inconsistency accept that abstract ideas are *intrinsically* general. For this would commit him to the self-contradictory view that some things are both intrinsically particular and intrinsically general. Instead, Locke claims that ideas are general *in their signification*. By this, Locke means that ideas function as signs that represent many other things, signs that are nothing but the "*Inventions and Creatures of the Understanding*" (E III.iii.11: 414). Thus, the abstract idea of whiteness is not something that exists in many different things or places at the same time (in the way that universals would exist if they did exist). Rather, the abstract idea of whiteness is a particular idea that has been made general by being treated (by the mind) as a representative of all things that conform to it – that is, as a representative of all white things.

It would be a mistake to leave discussion of Locke's doctrine of abstraction without considering a famous passage in which Locke appears to attribute strange, indeed mutually contradictory, properties to abstract ideas. It is a passage on which his anti-abstractionist opponents, particularly Berkeley, fastened as indicating the doctrine's intrinsic incoherence. Let us consider briefly whether the criticisms of this passage are well taken.

Locke says, more than once, that the mental separation involved in abstraction is a process that does not come to the mind easily. Early in Book I, he writes that "Children commonly get not those general *Ideas* . . . till having for a good while exercised their Reason about familiar and more particular *Ideas*, they are by their ordinary Discourse and Actions with others, acknowledged to be capable of rational Conversation" (E I.ii.14: 54). He repeats the point later, claiming that "abstract *Ideas* are not so obvious or easie to Children, or the yet unexercised Mind, as particular ones" (E IV.vii.9: 595). His explanation for this is what appears to land him in hot water:

> For example, Does it not require some pains and skill to form the *general Idea* of a *Triangle* (which is yet none of the most abstract, comprehensive, and difficult,) for it must be neither Oblique, nor Rectangle, neither Equilateral, Equicrural [i.e., isosceles], nor Scalenon; but all and none of these at once. In effect, it is something imperfect, that cannot exist; an *Idea* wherein some parts of several different and inconsistent *Ideas* are put together. (E IV.vii.9: 596)

Locke seems to be saying that the abstract idea of a triangle must have "all and none" of the properties in the set S = {oblique, rectangular, equilateral, isosceles, scalene} "at once," and that it is by reason of this fact that it is difficult to form the idea. Moreover, he seems to be saying that the very idea that he takes to be possible "cannot exist," and that the reason for this is that it contains parts of inconsistent ideas. The obvious inference here is that the fact that the idea cannot exist derives from the fact that it is internally inconsistent.

If Locke is indeed committed to these claims, then his critics are surely right to criticize him for it. But it is possible to read the relevant passage in a far more charitable vein. As Chappell rightly notes, "Locke does not state that the general idea of a triangle itself contains inconsistent parts, but that it contains parts of other ideas which are, taken as a whole, inconsistent with one another."[14] Moreover, as Chappell also notes, Locke's (somewhat loosely stated) "all or none" claim could be understood to mean that the abstract idea of a triangle represents *all* triangles and has *none* of the ideas in set S as constituents. And the claim that the abstract idea of a triangle "cannot exist" could mean no more than that, indeterminate idea that it is, it cannot exist *in reality*. (After all, everything that exists in reality is particular, and hence determinate.) But from this it does not follow that the idea cannot exist *in the mind* – that is, as the intentional content of some mental act.

One wonders, though, whether this interpretation may not be *excessively* charitable. The question that remains unanswered in the charitable interpretation is why Locke finds a connection between his various statements about the abstract idea of a triangle, on the one hand, and his statement about the relative difficulty of framing the idea, on the other. Why should it be more difficult to frame an idea that contains parts of other ideas which, when taken as a whole, are mutually inconsistent? The idea of whiteness is part of the following pair of mutually inconsistent complex ideas: the idea of a white square and the idea of a white circle. And yet this does not make it particularly difficult to frame the idea of whiteness. Indeed, this idea is one of the earliest that children perceive. Furthermore, why should it be particularly difficult to frame an idea that represents a host of things, some of which are equilateral, some of which are isosceles, some of which are scalene, at the same time that it contains none of the ideas in set S as constituents? After all, the idea of a triangle is an idea of a three-sided, closed plane figure, and it is the very fact that the idea does *not* include any of the ideas in set S that *enables* it to represent triangles of all sorts! Finally, why does Locke appear to conclude that the abstract idea of a triangle cannot exist in reality from the fact that it contains parts of mutually inconsistent ideas? And in what way does the fact that this abstract idea cannot exist in reality explain why it is more difficult to frame it? After all, it does not seem terribly difficult to frame the idea of a square circle (just combine the idea of a square with the idea of a circle!), even though it is plain that no square circle could possibly exist in reality.

Part of the answer must be that Locke thinks it a tall order for a child to focus on all and only those features of all the triangles she has experienced that apply to all triangles and only to triangles, just as it is difficult for her to focus on all and only those features of all the *human beings* she has met that apply to all humans and only to humans. If her experience of triangles has been limited, say, to equilateral and isosceles triangles, she may end up mentally focusing on a complex idea that does not apply to scalene triangles. Similarly, if her experience of human beings has been limited to those who are overweight and pale-skinned, she may end up mentally focusing on a complex idea that does not apply to thin or dark-skinned humans. Another part of the answer may be that, in saying that the abstract idea of a triangle (an idea that contains none of the ideas in set S) cannot exist in reality, Locke means no more than that every real triangle must have at least one of the properties represented by the ideas in set S. But these suggestions do not remove all trace of awkwardness, the remainder of which seems only attributable to infelicity of expression. Indeed, it is difficult to believe that Locke would not have rewritten the passage substantially, had he been made aware of the criticisms subsequently raised by his intellectual opponents.

4.5 Challenges to Ideational Empiricism: The Ideas of Infinity and Substratum

Locke claims that all (absolutely) simple ideas are derived from (inner or outer) experience, and that all other ideas result from the arbitrary act of combining simple ideas into complex organized wholes. The greatest challenge faced by this ideational empiricism results not from its opposition to the innateness hypothesis, but from its potential inability to account for the existence and nature of two ideas: the idea of infinity and the idea of substance. These ideas are of great importance inasmuch as both are constituents of the idea of God, thought of as a perfect, and hence infinite, substance. If Locke's theory cannot provide an intelligible account of the idea of God, then it will follow from his theory that theistic discourse is unintelligible. For Locke's contemporaries (and quite possibly for many of ours), this result would be sufficient in itself to doom Locke's version of ideational empiricism.

How successful, then, is Locke's account of the nature of the ideas of infinity and substance? Let us focus first on the idea of infinity, before moving on to discuss the idea of substance.

Locke's view is that the idea of infinity is (absolutely) complex, not (absolutely) simple. Within his classificatory scheme, it is an idea of a simple mode of quantity that is produced by enlarging the (absolutely) simple idea of space, duration, or number (E II.xvii.1: 209). As Locke sees it, the mental operation of enlarging is a form of mental combination (or composition) that consists in "a putting several *Ideas* together, though of the same kind" (E II.xi.6: 158). When one enlarges the idea of space (or extension) by repeating the idea of a particular length (e.g., one foot), one obtains the idea of immensity, or infinite space (E II.xvii.3: 210–211; E II.xvii.5: 212); when one enlarges the idea of duration by repeating the idea of a particular duration (e.g., one hour), one obtains the idea of eternity (E II.xvii.5: 212); and when one simply enlarges the idea of number by repeating the idea of a particular number (e.g., one), one obtains the idea of infinity *per se*, or infinite number (E II.xvii.9: 215).

Locke's claim that we are able to enlarge by repeating ideas of the same kind seems incontrovertible. It is in this way that one obtains the idea of ten, or one yard, or one year. But these, of course, are only ideas of finite quantities. What Locke must account for is the existence and nature of an idea of a non-finite quantity. It is here that his ideational empiricism faces what may be its sternest test, and arguably leads him into unfortunate incoherence.

Locke writes that our idea of infinity "lies only in a Power still of adding any Combination of Unites to any former Number, and that as long, and as much as one will" (E II.xvii.13: 216). If Locke means by this that there is no end in principle to the number of times one can add any combination of units to any former number, then he is surely right. But Locke shifts easily from this statement to the claim that the idea of infinity "[is] got from the Power, we observe in our selves, of repeating without end our own *Ideas*" (E II.xvii.6: 212). That is, Locke moves all too easily to the claim that what one can do is endlessly add any combination of units to any former number. This, of course, is absurd in itself.

The shift, in essence, is from (1) to (2):

(1) Without end it is possible [to add one unit to another].
(2) It is possible [to add one unit to another without end].

The move is fallacious, involving illicit importation of the negation of an existential quantifier ("without end") into the scope of a modal operator ("it is possible that"). But it is also understandable, given that it is only in the late nineteenth and early twentieth centuries that logicians were able to diagnose this kind of error and thereby provide philosophers with the tools to avoid it. As we will see, this is not the only time that Locke succumbs to the fallacy of illicit importation, for an even more egregious version of the error dooms his proof of God's existence (see Chapter 10, Section 10.3).

Having committed a logical fallacy, but unaware of having done so, Locke struggles to find a coherent description of the idea of infinity. Understandably not wanting to describe the idea as endless in itself, Locke fixes on the unfortunate language of endless growth. He tells us that the idea of infinity is *"an endless growing Idea"* (E II.xvii.7: 213), that it is *"a growing and fugitive Idea, still in a boundless Progression, that can stop no where"* (E II.xvii.12: 216), and that it *"consists in a supposed endless Progression"* (E II.xvii.8: 214). It is no surprise, then, that Locke finds himself describing the relevant idea, incoherently, as "imperfect and incompleat" (E II.xvii.15: 218). The problem, of course, is that if the idea of infinity is itself endless or boundless, and hence incomplete, then it is not itself finite, but infinite. Locke thinks he can avoid this result by speaking of the idea of infinity as finite but in the process of increasing, as if it were a finite balloon in the process of being endlessly filled with air. But this is incoherent: no finite idea is capable of endless growth. It must therefore be conceded that Locke's own account of the construction of the idea of infinity from simple ideas fails.

Luckily for Locke, the fact that his own account of the idea of infinity fails does not entail that ideational empiricism itself is doomed. And there are hints that Locke sees the way out. The key is to argue that the idea of infinity is not positive, but negative; that it is no more than the result of combining the idea of finitude or boundedness with the idea of negation, in the same way that the idea of immortality is the result of combining the idea of mortality with the idea of negation. Locke glimpses this solution when he speaks of the idea of eternity as involving *"the Negation of a Beginning"* (E II.xvii.17: 220), and when he recognizes that the idea of infinity includes the *"plain Negative"* idea of *"so much greater, as cannot be comprehended"* (E II.xvii.15: 218). Unfortunately, according to Locke's official philosophy of language, "not" and its cognates "are not truly, by themselves, the names of any *Ideas*" (E III.vii.2: 472); they are all, rather, *"marks of some Action, or Intimation of the Mind"* (E III.vii.4: 472), namely denial (or the mental act of negation) (E III.vii.1: 471). So the result of combining the idea of finitude with the mental act of negation would be a kind of bizarre hybrid rather than a (absolutely) simple or (absolutely) complex idea. Locke therefore finds himself caught between equally unpalatable consequences: (i) preservation of his theory of negation and abandonment of any reasonable hope of accounting for the idea of infinity, and (ii) preservation of a reasonable account of the idea of infinity and abandonment of his theory of negation.

Let us now consider the idea of substance. Locke distinguishes between the idea of a particular substance (e.g., the idea of a particular man) or sort of substance (e.g., the idea of humanity) and what he calls "the idea of substance" (or substratum, or substance-in-general) (E II.xxiii.1–2: 295). At times, Locke also speaks of the idea of the substance of a substance (e.g., the "*Idea* of the *Substance* of a Spirit" (E II.xxiii.5: 298) or "the *Idea* of the Substance of Body" (E II.xxiii.16: 306)), by which he means to refer to the idea of the *substratum* of the relevant (sort of) substance. The idea of substratum, Locke then tells us, is "a Supposition of [one] knows not what support of such Qualities, which are capable of producing simple *Ideas* in us; which Qualities are commonly called Accidents" (E II.xxiii.2: 295). The idea of substratum is therefore the idea of "a support to Accidents" (W4: 19) and the idea of an accident appears to be the idea of a sensible quality that is supported by a substratum.

The idea of substratum plays a significant role in Locke's theory of complex ideas, especially his theory of the ideas of particular (sorts of) substances. As he sees it, every idea of a particular substance or sort of substance is composed of (i) the idea of substratum, and (ii) the ideas of the qualities that distinguish one (sort of) substance from another. He writes:

> The *Ideas* of *Substances* are such combinations of simple *Ideas*, as are taken to represent distinct particular things subsisting by themselves; in which the supposed, or confused *Idea* of Substance [i.e., substratum], such as it is, is always the first and chief. Thus if to Substance [i.e., the idea of substratum] be joined the simple *Idea* of a certain dull whitish colour, with certain degrees of Weight, Hardness, Ductility, and Fusibility, we have the *Idea* of *Lead*; and a combination of the *Ideas* of a certain sort of Figure, with the powers of Motion, Thought, and Reasoning, joined to Substance [i.e., the idea of substratum], make the ordinary *Idea* of *a Man*. (E II.xii.6: 165)

So Locke seems committed not only to the existence of the idea of substratum, but also to its role as a separate and *bona fide* constituent of the (complex) idea of any particular (sort of) substance.[15]

However, Locke also has some scathing things to say about the idea of substratum, some of them in terms that suggest contempt for those who suppose its existence. In one place he mentions "our not having any notion of the *Substance* of a Spirit" (E II.xxiii.5: 298), and in another he titles a section "*No* Idea *of abstract Substance*" and then writes in it that "we are as far from the *Idea* of the Substance of Body, as if we knew nothing at all" (E II.xxiii.16: 306). And in two sections dripping with sarcasm directed at purveyors of "the Doctrine of *Substance and Accidents*," Locke first likens them to "the poor Indian Philosopher . . . who imagined that the Earth also wanted [i.e., lacked] something to bear it up" and went to "the trouble to find an Elephant to support it, and a Tortoise to support his Elephant," and then claims that "an intelligent *American*, who enquired into the Nature of Things, would scarce take it for a satisfactory Account, if desiring to learn our Architecture, he should be told, That a Pillar was a thing supported by a *Basis*, and a *Basis* something that supported a Pillar" (E II.xiii.19–20: 175). Locke's point seems to be, first, that the supposition of a substratum to support accidents is no better than what he takes to be the obviously silly supposition that the Earth is supported by an elephant, and, second, that the same supposition, involving as it does a circular definition of one term by another and vice versa, is useless "in deciding Questions in Philosophy" (E II.xiii.20: 175).

Some scholars believe that these texts show that Locke either dismisses the existence of substratum and its corresponding idea or is simply of two minds on the issue. But this would be a mistake. Carefully read, the texts show that Locke is not skeptical of the *existence* of substratum or its corresponding idea; what he wants to emphasize is (i) how obscure and confused the idea of substratum is, and (ii) how its obscurity and confusedness render the idea philosophically useless. For example, Locke ends the section in which he discusses the "poor Indian philosopher" with these words: "So that of *Substance*, we have no *Idea* of what it is, but only a confused obscure one of what it does" (E II.xiii.19: 175). And in the section in which he discusses the "intelligent American," Locke makes fun, not of the idea of substratum itself, but of "the very great clearness there is in the Doctrine of *Substance and Accidents*" (E II.xiii.20: 175).

Moreover, the passages in which Locke appears to deny the existence of an idea of substratum involve infelicities of expression. For example, when Locke talks of our "not having any notion of the *Substance* of Spirit," what he says more fully is this:

> and therefore from our not having any notion of the *Substance* of Spirit, we can no more conclude its non-Existence, than we can, for the same reason, deny the Existence of Body; It being as rational to affirm, there is no Body, because we have no clear and distinct *Idea* of the *Substance* of Matter; as to say, there is no Spirit, because we have no clear and distinct *Idea* of the *Substance* of a Spirit. (E II.xxiii.5: 298)

It is quite plain here that Locke is not saying that we should avoid concluding the non-existence of spiritual substratum from the fact that there is no idea of such a substratum, but rather that we should avoid concluding the non-existence of spiritual substratum from the fact that there is no *clear and distinct* idea of such a substratum. Similarly, when Locke writes that there is "*No* Idea *of abstract Substance*" and that "we are as far from the *Idea* of the Substance of Body, as if we knew nothing at all," what he *means* is that there is no *clear and distinct* idea of abstract substratum (not that there is no idea of abstract substratum at all), and that we are as far from the *clear and distinct* idea of the substratum of body, as if we knew nothing at all about it (E II. xxiii.16: 306). As the overall context of these passages makes clear, Locke's point is that "we have as clear a perception, and notion of immaterial Substances, as we have of material . . . The one is as clear and distinct an *Idea*, as the other" (E II.xxiii.15: 305). In other words, the idea of material substratum is as clear and distinct as the idea of immaterial substratum because both ideas are equally obscure and confused.

So Locke is committed to the idea of substratum, as well as to the existence of the entity in the world that the idea represents. However, as Edward Stillingfleet notes in their acrimonious public correspondence on this issue, it appears to be difficult for Locke to explain how we come by the idea of substratum. For it seems plain that the idea of substratum does not itself derive from sensation or reflection: when we perceive sensible objects (e.g., tables and chairs), we do not see, hear, smell, touch, or taste the substrata that support their sensible qualities, and when we perceive our own mental operations (e.g., doubting and willing), we do not introspect the substratum in which these mental acts inhere. Does it not follow, then, that the idea of substratum must derive from some other source than sensation or reflection, a source such as one's own soul?

The answer is that it does not. As Locke makes plain in his first letter to Stillingfleet, the idea of substratum is not simple, but rather (absolutely) complex:

> I never said that the general idea of substance comes in by sensation and reflection; or, that it is a simple idea of sensation and reflection, though it be ultimately founded on them: for it is a complex idea, made up of the general idea of something, or being, with the relation of a support to accidents. (W4: 19)

The idea of substratum, then, is the result of combining two ideas: (i) the (absolutely simple) abstract idea of existence, and (ii) the (absolutely complex) relative idea of supporting qualities. Locke tells us that the idea of existence is a simple idea derived from sensation and reflection, "suggested to the Understanding, by every Object without, and every *Idea* within" (E II.vii.7: 131), and then abstracted from all other concomitant ideas. And the idea of a support to qualities is clearly an idea that represents a relation, and although Locke does not say so, it is reasonable to suppose that this idea too is abstracted from ideas of particular relations of support to accidents.

Locke's reply to Stillingfleet is therefore successful, as far as it goes. The problem is that it also raises another question. According to Locke's official aetiology of complex ideas, particular ideas of relation are formed by the operation of comparison and combination: a particular relative idea is formed by comparing two things and combining ideas of these things with the ground of the comparison. The relative idea of architectural support, for example, is derived by comparing, say, a beam of a house (relatum 1) with its roof (relatum 2), and then combining these ideas with the basis of the comparison (i.e., architectural function). This idea can then be abstracted by mentally separating it from its particular determinations and concomitant ideas. The problem is that the idea of a support to qualities cannot be derived by comparison in this way, for there is no idea of anything to compare with the ideas of various qualities we associate with particular substances. Perhaps Locke thinks of the process as one of comparing the idea of a quality with the general and indeterminate idea of existence (or something). But such comparison cannot yield anything, for it does not have a ground. Simply put, in comparing a general, indeterminate idea with anything else, there is no aspect of the idea for the mind to latch onto. In this way, the general, indeterminate idea of existence differs from the idea of a particular, determinate beam. The idea of a support to accidents, then, though a relative idea, cannot be formed by the mental operation of comparison. And this contradicts Locke's official account of the formation of relative ideas.

Is there a way out of this conundrum? Possibly. Locke tells us that our idea of a quality is an idea of something that (i) cannot exist or subsist of itself (W4: 21) and (ii) cannot be something in which something else exists or subsists (E II.xxiii.4: 297). From this, we conclude that the idea of a quality is an idea of something that requires a support – that is, something on which it depends for its existence. From the existence of any quality, then, we *infer* the existence of something that supports it, something that cannot itself be a quality, and we call the entity that supports the quality a "substratum." Arguably, then, it is not via the operation of *comparison*, but rather via the operation of *inference* or *reasoning* that we construct the (relative) idea of substratum. But if this is so, then Locke's official aetiology of relative ideas requires modification. For, on this account, relative ideas can be produced not only by combination preceded by *comparison*, but also by combination preceded by *reasoning*.

In the end, then, although it must be admitted that Locke himself struggles to explain how the ideas of infinity and substratum can be constructed from the (absolutely) simple ideas we receive from sensation and reflection, there is reason to hope that the resources of his theory of ideas and mental operations might be ample (perhaps if suitably modified) for us to provide at least the beginnings of a coherent and satisfactory explanation on his behalf. In the case of the idea of infinity, Locke would need to abandon his theory of negation as a mental act, and in the case of the idea of substratum, he would need to abandon his claim that relative ideas all have their source in the mental operation of comparison. Whether the theoretical benefits obtained by making these changes are worth the cost is a question for further investigation.

notes

1   Locke tells us that the idea of power is a simple idea derived from both sensation and reflection (E II.vii.1: 128). But, as I argue in Section 4.3 below, Locke does not think that the idea of power is simple (in the relevant sense).

2   At one point, Locke writes that the simple ideas of white and sweet (among others) are "capable of Parts or Degrees, and that ideas of proportional relations, such as the ideas of *"Whiter, Sweeter, Bigger, Equal, More*, etc." stem from "Equality and Excess of the same simple *Idea*" (E II.xxviii.1: 349). This might suggest that Locke does not even think of the ideas of white and sweet as lacking parts. But elsewhere Locke insists that ideas of sensible qualities

(e.g., the idea of white) "consist not of Parts," and that this explains why they (unlike the ideas of space and duration) "cannot be augmented to what proportion Men please, or be stretched beyond what they have received by their Senses" (E II.xvii.6: 213).

3 Locke later classifies passions as simple modes of pleasure and pain, and hence as complex ideas (E II.xx.3–14: 229–232). But here he treats them as simple ideas. There is a tension here, perhaps best resolved by supposing that the word "passion" is ambiguous, as between "the product of an activity" and "a simple mode of pleasure or pain." It may then be the former sense rather than the latter that is at issue when Locke writes (at E II.i.4: 106) that "Passions" rank among the simple ideas of reflection. It is also possible that Locke is using the word "simple" here in its relative, as opposed to absolute, sense (see Section 4.3 below).

4 It might seem that Locke actually *denies* that the perception of simple ideas that derive from sensation is *always* wholly passive. He writes that ideas of sensation "*are often* in grown People *alter'd by the Judgment*, without our taking notice of it." This happens, for example, when our perception of "a flat Circle variously shadow'd, with several degrees of Light and Brightness" is converted "by an habitual custom" into the perception of "a convex Figure, and an uniform Colour" (E II.ix.8: 145). But, in fact, there is no inconsistency here. Strictly understood, the idea of a convex figure of uniform color is *not* a simple idea derived from sensation, but is rather an idea (perhaps complex) derived from the separate mental operation of judging.

5 Unfortunately for the unwary reader, Locke confuses matters by often referring to *ideas of modes* as "modes" and by often referring to *ideas of relations* as "relations," while being rather careful to refer to *ideas of substances* as "ideas of substances." I am going to avoid this complication by clearly marking the distinction between ideas and what they represent. It will almost always be clear from the context whether Locke means to refer to modes/relations, or to the ideas in our minds that represent them.

6 See, for example, his discussion (at E III.vi.26: 453) of the various combinations of ideas to which different people assign the name "man" (including "rational animal" and "featherless biped with wide nails"), and his discussion (at E III. ix.17: 485) of the various definitions of gold.

7 For the present, I am going to ignore the part of this passage that concerns abstract ideas. Abstract ideas are discussed in Section 4.4 below.

8 Note that in saying this Locke means to say, not that *powers themselves* are complex ideas, but rather that *ideas that represent powers* are complex ideas. In the *Essay*, Locke often moves carelessly from talk of ideas to talk of what those ideas represent, and vice versa. He is actually aware of doing so, but for reasons that will be discussed below, does not think it important to remove the risk that he will be misread.

9 In an early draft of the *Essay*, Locke writes: "[T]hese powers [such as the active power in fire to melt gold and the passive power in gold to be melted] being conversant about the production, destruction or alteration of simple Ideas may I conceive be well enough recond under that head. as making up part of the complex Ideas of substances" (Draft A, 19: 35). Locke here again puts together two criteria of relative simplicity, the first concerning a relation to absolutely

simple ideas produced in our minds, the second concerning a relation to more complex ideas.

10   A view of this sort is defended by Vere Chappell, "Locke's Theory of Ideas," in *The Cambridge Companion to Locke*, edited by Vere Chappell. Cambridge: Cambridge University Press, 1994, 26–55.

11   Locke does write that simple sensory ideas (e.g., the idea of whiteness) "enter by the Senses simple and unmixed" (E II.ii.1: 119). But all Locke means by this is that simple sensory ideas do not enter the mind as parts of complex ideas that are passively received. This is perfectly consistent with Locke's view that simple ideas often enter the mind accompanied by – that is, at the same time as and mentally associated with – other simple ideas.

12   See Chappell 1994 for details.

13   This nominalism of Locke's puts him at odds with the Scholastic embrace of universals, and it is one of the many ways in which Locke's metaphysics differs from that of his Aristotelian teachers and predecessors.

14   Chappell 1994, 44.

15   There appears to have been some evolution in Locke's thoughts on this issue. In the early drafts of the *Essay*, Locke claims that ideas of particular (sorts of) substances are composed entirely of ideas of qualities. Not having any theoretical need for the concept of a substratum, Locke does not mention it in the drafts.

further reading

Bolton, Martha Brandt, "The Taxonomy of Ideas in Locke's *Essay*," in *The Cambridge Companion to Locke's "Essay Concerning Human Understanding"*, edited by Lex Newman. Cambridge: Cambridge University Press, 2007, pp. 67–100.

Chappell, Vere, "Locke's Theory of Ideas," in *The Cambridge Companion to Locke*, edited by Vere Chappell. Cambridge: Cambridge University Press, 1994, pp. 26–55.

Jacovides, Michael, "Locke's Construction of the Idea of Power," *Studies in History and Philosophy of Science* 34 (2003): 329–350.

Jolley, Nicholas, *Locke: His Philosophical Thought*. Oxford: Oxford University Press, 1999, chapter 3.

Mackie, J.L., *Problems from Locke*. Oxford: Clarendon Press, 1976, chapter 4.

Newman, Lex, "Locke on the Idea of Substratum," *Pacific Philosophical Quarterly* 81 (2000): 291–324.

substances

We have seen that in the first two books of the *Essay*, Locke argues against innate ideas and then attempts to establish that all ideas are ultimately derived from sensation (outer experience) or reflection (inner experience). In subsequent chapters, we will see that Locke uses the theory of ideas to provide a theory of linguistic meaning and communication, a theory of (scientific) classification, and, most importantly, a theory of knowledge and assent. The work therefore appears focused on the theory of ideas, and there is no doubt that this is its dominant theme. But it is a singular aspect of the *Essay* that Locke, despite his protestations of agnosticism concerning all sorts of metaphysical issues, addresses a significant number of metaphysical questions and attempts to provide systematic answers to them. Sometimes his forays into metaphysics are woven together with his theory of ideas, and sometimes they are, by and large, bracketed off as extended digressions. To many, the metaphysical passages are (among) the most philosophically engaging and fruitful parts of the work.

As we have seen, Locke's ontology is populated by substances, properties, and relations. In this chapter, I discuss Locke's philosophy of substance, paying particularly close attention to his theory of body and mind. In Chapter 6, I turn to Locke's theory of the properties of body (including the distinction between primary and secondary qualities) and, in Chapter 7, to his theory of the properties and operations of mind (including volitions and freedom). In Chapter 8, I discuss Locke's theory of relations, paying special attention to his theory of identity, including personal identity.

5.1 Body, Matter, Space, and Vacuum

Locke's philosophy of body is a good example of the way in which his theory of ideas is intertwined with his account of what those ideas represent. He begins his investigations into the nature of body by discussing our idea of body,

Locke, First Edition. Samuel C. Rickless.
© 2014 Samuel C. Rickless. Published 2014 by John Wiley & Sons, Ltd.

distinguishing it from our ideas of matter, space, and extension. He then considers the ontological implications of these investigations, finding, among other results, that there is every reason to suppose that a vacuum (a space devoid of body or matter) is not only possible but also actual. In the context of seventeenth-century science, this is an important claim, inasmuch as Locke is allying himself with the resurgent atomism of his day as against the new anti-atomist Cartesian research program.

The simple ideas that lie at the foundation of Locke's theory of body are the ideas of space and solidity, with occasional appeal to the ideas of shape and motion. Locke tells us that the idea of space (sometimes, "pure space" – E II.iv.3: 124) is simple and derived from both sight and touch (E II.v: 127). This is an already problematic claim, inasmuch as pure space "is capable neither of Resistance nor Motion" (E II.iv.3: 124). For if space is incapable of resistance, then it cannot resist the pressure of our bodies, and thus it would seem that it cannot be *felt*. And if space itself does not move, but it is rather bodies that move in space, then in what sense can space be *seen* if what we perceive by sight are *bodies* that are either at rest or in motion? Locke, for his part, does not so much as recognize the existence of a problem here, and passes over these embarrassing questions.

Locke holds that the idea of space is neither an idea of *a* (material or immaterial) substance nor an idea of relation. But he does consider the question whether the idea of space is the idea of substratum or an idea of a mode. Locke's answer to this question is consistent with his general proclivity towards agnosticism. He writes that he does not know whether (pure) space "be *Substance* [i.e., substratum] or *Accident*," but that he will only be ashamed of his ignorance on this score if someone is able to show him "a clear distinct *Idea of Substance*" (E II.xiii.17: 174). The point here, as we have seen, is that the idea of substratum is obscure and confused (E II.xiii.19: 175; E II.xxiii.2: 295–296), and from this Locke draws the (reasonable) conclusion that it can be difficult to know whether, and under what circumstances, something counts as a substratum. A substratum is something that supports properties without being in any need of support itself. Whether space is in need of support (by God, perhaps?) and whether space is something that itself supports properties are questions that we do not possess enough information to answer.

Locke is more forthcoming when he discusses the simple idea of solidity. He tells us that the idea is derived from the sense of touch, "from the resistance which we find in Body, to the entrance of any other Body into the Place it possesses, till it has left it" (E II.iv.1: 122–123). Locke is of two minds whether to identify the idea of solidity with the idea of impenetrability, saying on the one hand that "if any one think it better to call [solidity] *Impenetrability*, he has my Consent," but also that "*Impenetrability*, which is negative, . . . is, perhaps, more a consequence of *Solidity*, than *Solidity* itself" (E II.iv.1: 123). The positive aspect of the idea of solidity that is missing from the idea of impenetrability may be the idea of filling space, for Locke writes that solidity "is the *Idea* belongs to Body, whereby we conceive it *to fill space*" (E II.iv.2:

123). But if this is so, then the idea of solidity is at least partly relational, including as parts both the idea of space and the idea of filling, in which case it cannot be an absolutely simple idea. Although it is possible that Locke takes the idea of solidity to be only relatively simple, this is unlikely. For Locke writes that "[i]f any one asks me, *What this Solidity is*, I send him to his Senses to inform him: Let him put a Flint, or a Foot-ball between his Hands; and then endeavour to join them, and he will know" (E II.iv.6: 126–127). As usual, Locke does not worry much about these issues, presumably because it does not much matter to him how they should ultimately be resolved.[1]

With the help of the ideas of space and solidity (and the ideas of body parts and extremities), Locke then introduces the idea of extension, which is the idea of "the Space that lies between the Extremities of [the] solid coherent Parts [of a body]" (E II.xiii.11: 171). The idea of extension, then, appears to be a complex idea. And the idea of Body, also complex, is then characterized as the idea of "an extended solid thing" (E III.vi.21: 450; see also E III.vi.33: 460) – that is, as a combination of the ideas of extension, solidity, and substratum – while the idea of matter is nothing but a partial conception of body – that is, an idea composed of the ideas of solidity and substratum, without the idea of extension (E III.x.15: 498).[2]

The fact that the idea of body includes the idea of solidity is of some importance to Locke, for this distinguishes his view from the position taken by Descartes. As Descartes sees it, the idea of a body is no more than the idea of an extended substance (or substratum), and thus does not include the idea of solidity. Locke points out that Descartes's position rules out the very possibility of a vacuum by fiat, the idea of a vacuum being the idea of space (or extension) without body (E II.xiii.21: 177; E II.xiii.23: 178). By contrast, Locke holds that the question whether there is, or at least could be, a vacuum in nature is not only intelligible and substantive, but should also be answered in the affirmative.

Locke provides three arguments for the (possible or actual) existence of a vacuum. First, on the supposition that body is finite, Locke claims that if one were standing at the place beyond which there are no more bodies, it would still be possible to extend one's arm. If one did this, one would, by hypothesis, be extending a part of one's body in a space that is devoid of body, and such a space would, by definition, be a vacuum (E II.xiii.20: 175–176). Second, Locke argues that if God were to bring all motion to an end, so that all bodies were at rest, and if he were to annihilate one body, "the Space, that was filled by the parts of the annihilated Body, [would] still remain, and be a Space without Body" (E II.xiii.21: 176). So since it is possible, at least in principle, for a body among other bodies to be annihilated, it is possible for there to be a vacuum. This shows that Descartes's view that the essence of body is extension is mistaken. And, third, Locke sides with the atomists in thinking that the existence of motion proves the existence of a vacuum. For if there were no space devoid of body for a body to move into, motion would be impossible (E II. xiii.22: 177–178).

Bodies, then, being solid, extended substances, it may be asked what their properties and powers are, and what it is about them that accounts for these properties and powers. As Locke sees it, bodies possess motion (or rest) and shape, but also size, number, and texture. These he calls the "primary qualities" of bodies. But bodies also possess color, sound, taste, smell, and tangible properties (e.g., heat and cold, hard and soft). These he calls the "secondary qualities" of bodies (E II.viii.9–10: 134–135). Locke's view is that the secondary qualities of bodies depend on (result from) the primary qualities of their (insensible) parts, that it is by reason of these primary qualities that a body possesses the secondary qualities it has (E II.viii.23: 140–141). But as to how bodies come to have the particular primary and secondary qualities that they possess, Locke seems torn between mechanism and agnosticism.

Mechanism is the view that all (mental and corporeal) phenomena may be explained by the primary qualities of bodies (their size, motion, shape, number, and texture), oftentimes bodies that are not perceivable by means of the naked eye. In some places, Locke expresses confidence, not merely in the intelligibility of mechanism, but in its explanatory power and fruitfulness as a research program. For example, when Locke considers how the ideas of primary qualities are produced in our minds, he writes that because external bodies are not united to our minds, we perceive ideas of motion and shape (and other such qualities) by virtue of the fact that insensible corpuscles impinge on our bodies and that "some motion must be thence continued by our Nerves, or animal Spirits, by some parts of our Bodies, to the Brains or the seat of Sensation, there to *produce* [ideas] *in our Minds*" (E II.viii.12: 136). Notice Locke's use of "must" here. Locke seems to be saying that events happen in our minds as a direct result of the communication of the motion of insensible corpuscles of various shapes and sizes by impulse, and indeed that these events cannot happen in any other way. Mechanism, as Locke seems to suggest, is not merely the best explanation, but in fact the *only* possible explanation, for mental events. Similarly, Locke suggests that "if we discover the Figure, Size, Texture, and Motion of the minute Constituent parts of any two Bodies, we should know without Trial [i.e., without experiment] several of their Operations one upon another, as we do now the Properties of a Square, or a Triangle": we should know a priori, in particular, whether "*Rhubarb* will purge, *Hemlock* kill, and *Opium* make a Man sleep," whether silver will dissolve in *aqua fortis* and gold in *aqua regia*, and not vice versa (E IV.iii.25: 556). Like the mechanists of his day, Locke's confidence here is based on the view that the universe of material things is like a watch, that the explanation of the qualities of bodies is similar to the (purely mechanical) explanation of the behavior of gears and springs in a timepiece.

However, in other places, Locke is far more circumspect regarding the explanatory pretensions of mechanism. He tells us that we do not know "what figure, size, or motion of parts produce a yellow Colour, a sweet Taste, or a sharp Sound," that "we can by no means conceive how any *size, figure, or motion* of any Particles, can possibly produce in us the *Idea* of any *Colour,*

Taste, or *Sound* whatsoever" (E IV.iii.13: 545), and that although mechanism (or, as Locke calls it, "the corpuscularian Hypothesis") "is thought to go farthest in an intelligible Explication of the Qualities of Bodies [and] the Weakness of humane Understanding is scarce able to substitute another," it is doubtful whether "we shall ever be able to carry our general Knowledge . . . in this part much farther" (E IV.iii.16: 547–548). He claims that it is not only inconceivable how bodies operate on minds, but also no less inconceivable how minds operate on bodies: "How any thought should produce a motion in Body is as remote from the nature of our *Ideas*, as how any Body should produce any Thought in the Mind" (E IV.iii.28: 559). Indeed, Locke is so pessimistic about the possibility of a "perfect *Science* of natural Bodies" that he sees it as "lost labour to seek after it" (E IV.iii.29: 560).

Locke's optimism about the explanatory fruitfulness of mechanism seems to have been shattered by the recognition that several corporeal phenomena resist mechanistic explanation, the most important of which are gravity and cohesion. On the subject of cohesion, Locke points out that the most commonly accepted mechanistic explanation of the phenomenon, in terms of the pressure of ambient matter, is strikingly inadequate. For if the parts of a body cohere because of the ambient pressure of air, how is it then possible to account for the cohesion of the parts of air? If it is supposed that the cohesion of the parts of air is to be explained by the pressure of ambient ether, then how is it possible to account for the cohesion of the parts of *ether*? The problem of a vicious infinite regress looms (E II.xxiii.23: 308). Locke concludes that the proper explanation of cohesion is not merely unknown, but is "as incomprehensible, as the manner of Thinking, and how it is performed" (E II.xxiii.24: 309).

On the subject of gravity, Locke writes to Stillingfleet that, having become familiar with Newton's work, it has now become clear to him that the phenomenon "is not only a demonstration that God can, if he pleases, put into bodies powers and ways of operation above what . . . can be explained by what we know of matter, but also an unquestionable and every where visible instance, that he has done so" (W4: 467–468). Indeed, because of his realization that gravity resists mechanistic explanation, Locke altered one of the sections of the *Essay* in which he had previously evinced optimism in the explanatory power of mechanism. In the first three editions of the *Essay*, we read that bodies "*operate* upon another . . . manifestly by *impulse*, and nothing else." But in the fourth and fifth editions, the relevant passage says merely that impulse is "the only way which we can conceive Bodies operate in" (E II.viii.11: 135–136).[3] So, despite its intelligibility and fruitfulness (as compared to Scholastic science), Locke's considered view about the prospects of mechanism is almost certainly best captured by a section of *Some Thoughts Concerning Education*:

[I]t is evident, that by mere matter and motion, none of the great phaenomena of nature can be resolved: to instance but in that common one of gravity, which I think impossible to be explained by any natural operation of matter, or any other law of motion, but the positive will of a superior Being so ordering it. (W8: 184)

The conclusion to be drawn from this is that Locke is not a mechanist. He sees mechanism as more intelligible and fruitful than Scholastic science (inasmuch as there is a great deal it can and does explain that Scholastic science cannot explain), but he also recognizes that the mechanistic paradigm is incomplete and inadequate (inasmuch as there are important phenomena that cannot be explained mechanistically). As to how the latter phenomena are to be explained, Locke professes (a reasonable) agnosticism.

5.2 Spirit

As Locke sees it, we perceive primary and secondary qualities through sensation, but we also perceive mental operations (e.g., thinking, doubting, and willing) through reflection. Just as we cannot conceive of how a quality (e.g., solidity or color) could exist without being supported by something else that is itself without need of a support (i.e., a substratum), so we cannot conceive of how any mental operation could exist without being supported by a substratum (E II.xxiii.5: 297). It might then be thought that, for Locke, the idea of a spirit (or soul) is no more than the (Cartesian) idea of a thinking substance (i.e., a substratum). But this would be a mistake. Just as Locke finds himself opposed to the Cartesian thesis that the idea of body is the idea of an extended thing, so he finds himself opposed to the Cartesian thesis that the idea of spirit is the idea of a thinking thing. For Locke it is just as wrong to say that the essence of spirit is thinking as it is to say that the essence of body is extension.

Locke claims that the idea of spirit is complex, the result of combining three ideas: (i) the idea of thing or substratum, (ii) the idea of the power or ability to think (E II.xxiii.3: 297), and (iii) the idea of the power or ability to excite bodily motion by thought (i.e., by willing) (E II.xxiii.18: 306). For example, Locke writes that "our *Idea* of our Soul . . . is of a Substance that thinks [i.e., has the capacity to think], and has a power of exciting Motion in Body, by Will, or Thought" (E II.xxiii.22: 307–308). That there are bodies is something of which we are assured by sensation; that there are spirits is something of which we are assured by reflection (E II.xxiii.29: 312).

The fact that spirits, as Locke understands them, are things having the *power* to think (and will) entails that they do not need to be actually in the process of thinking (or willing) in order to exist. It is in this way that Locke's understanding of spirit differs from Descartes's. When Descartes claims that souls are (essentially) thinking things, he means that it is impossible for a soul to exist without (actually) thinking. As Locke sees it, this position is controverted by everyone's experience. In a metaphysical digression prominently placed in the very first chapter of Book II of the *Essay* (E II.i.9–20: 108–116), Locke insists, in particular, that "every drowsy Nod shakes their Doctrine, who teach, That the Soul is always thinking" (E II.i.13: 111). The argument is interesting, not only because it displays one of the many ways in which Locke distances himself from Descartes, but also because it reveals one of the basic assumptions of Locke's metaphysics of mind.

Locke assumes that a human being "cannot think at any time waking or sleeping, without being sensible of it" (E II.i.10: 109); that "'tis altogether as intelligible to say, that a body is extended without parts, as that any thing *thinks without being conscious of it*, or perceiving, that it does so" (E II.i.19: 115). The assumption is that it is impossible for one to think without being aware that one is thinking. Indeed, Locke goes so far as to suggest, more radically, that "thinking <u>consists in</u> being conscious that one thinks" (E II.i.19: 115 – underlining added). On this view, not only is self-consciousness required for consciousness, but to be conscious *is* to be self-conscious. (The significance of this assumption will become clear when we discuss Locke's theory of personal identity in Chapter 8.) Locke then uses this assumption to argue that we do not always think when we are asleep. For, when we are dreamlessly sleeping, we are not aware that we are thinking, and hence, by the assumption, we are not thinking at all (E II.i.12: 110). Locke concludes that thinking is not the essence of mind, but merely one of its operations or activities, in the way that motion is an activity, but not the essence, of body (E II.i.10: 108).

Surely the most important question about spirits, at least from the vantage point of Locke's contemporaries, is whether they are material or immaterial. Regarding this question, Locke's official position is agnosticism. In order to know whether spirits are immaterial, one would have to perceive whether the idea of spirit agrees with the idea of immateriality. As will become clear in Chapter 10, this sort of agreement is beyond our ability to perceive. Locke's statements about this are unequivocal. He writes:

> [One is] very far from certainly knowing what [one's] Soul is. 'Tis a Point, which seems to me, to be put out of the reach of our Knowledge: And he who will give himself leave to consider freely, and look into the dark and intricate part of each Hypothesis, will scarce find his Reason able to determine him fixedly for, or against the Soul's Materiality. (E IV.iii.6: 542)

> 'Tis past controversy, that we have in us something that thinks, our very Doubts about what it is, confirm the certainty of its being, though we must content our selves in the Ignorance of what kind of *Being* it is. (E IV.iii.6: 543)

According to Locke, the idea of matter is no more than the idea of solid substance (E III.x.15: 498), and the idea of something immaterial is the idea of something "without Solidity" (E II.xxiii.32: 314). So in saying that we do not know whether spirits are material, Locke is saying that we do not know whether spirits are *solid* substances. But it does not follow from this that Locke is agnostic about whether spirits are *extended*.

As it happens, Locke provides reasons to think that (finite) spirits are extended. (I omit the necessary modifier "finite" in what follows.) This is not something that Locke ever says explicitly, but it is surely a thesis to which he is logically committed. Recall that the idea of a spirit is the idea of a substance that is capable of thinking and also capable of exciting or causing bodily motion by an act of will. But experience teaches that one's own spirit "can think, will, and operate on [one's] Body, in the place where that is; but cannot operate on a Body, or in a place, an hundred Miles distant from it" (E II.xxiii.20: 307). Spirits, he tells us, "cannot operate, but where they are" (E II.xxiii.19: 306). It follows directly that every spirit is at a place, namely where the body on which it exercises its causal powers is. But place, for Locke, is a "Modification [i.e., mode] of Distance" (E II.xiii.9: 170), and distance is a "Modification of Space" (E II.xiii.4: 167) –that is, a mode of extension (E II.xiii.3: 167). So place is a mode of extension, and if every spirit is at a place, then every spirit is necessarily extended. Locke goes on to claim that every spirit "is certainly as capable of changing distance with any other Body, or Being, as Body it self; and so is capable of Motion" (E II.xxiii.19: 306–307). Indeed, one's spirit moves whenever one's body moves, and further, it must move (i.e., change place) if it departs one's body at the time of one's death (E II.xxiii.20: 307). Locke's conception of spirit, then, is not only different from Descartes's: it is radically at odds with the Cartesian picture of spirit, according to which soul is really distinct (i.e., can exist apart) from any body – that is, from any extended thing.[4]

There are passages in the *Essay* in which Locke seems to presuppose that spirits or souls are immaterial. These passages appear in his discussion of personal identity, about which more in Chapter 8. For example, Locke asks "Whether if the same thinking Substance (supposing immaterial Substances only to think) be changed, it can be the same Person" (E II.xxvii.13: 337). In a later section in the same chapter, he writes that "granting that the thinking Substance in Man must be necessarily suppos'd immaterial, 'tis evident, that immaterial thinking thing may sometimes part with its past consciousness, and be restored to it again" (E II.xxvii.23: 344). On a superficial reading of these texts, Locke is taking it for granted ("supposing," "granting") that spirits are immaterial. But this would be a mistake. Locke is doing no more than granting the immateriality of spirits *for the sake of argument* – that is, in order to show that personal identity does not reduce to identity of spirits: even if all spirits were immaterial, it would still be possible for distinct persons to share the same spirit and for the same person to be associated with distinct spirits.

The fact that Locke is agnostic about whether spirits are material or immaterial does not mean that he *takes no position* on the issue. As we will see, Locke distinguishes between knowledge and assent (or judgment), claiming that while the former consists in the *perception* of agreement between two ideas, the latter consists in the *presumption* of such an agreement (E IV.xiv.4: 653). All assent (or judgment), says Locke, is grounded in probability – that is, "the appearance of such an Agreement, or Disagreement, by the intervention of Proofs, whose connection is not constant and immutable, or at least is not perceived to be so, but is, or appears for the most part to be so" (E IV.xv.1: 654). Locke's agnosticism consists in the claim that we do not (indeed, cannot) *know* whether spirits are material or immaterial. But Locke's own *judgment* is that spirits are immaterial, and this judgment is squarely based on probability. As he puts it: "I agree the more probable Opinion is, that this consciousness is annexed to, and the Affection of one individual immaterial Substance" (E II.xxvii.25: 345).[5]

It is worth asking why Locke thinks that it is so much as *probable* that spirits are immaterial. Although he does not address this question directly, we can provide something in the way of an educated guess. Locke tells us that the basis of any probable conjecture concerning "[t]he Existence, Nature, and Operations of finite immaterial Beings without us; as Spirits, Angels, Devils, *etc.*" is "*Analogy*," by which Locke means a form of extrapolation from observed instances to unobserved instances on the assumption that nature is uniform (E IV.xvi.12: 665–666). And it is on the basis of analogical reasoning of this sort that Locke infers the existence, indeed a hierarchy, of finite immaterial spirits. He writes:

> Observing . . . gradual and gentle descents downwards in those parts of Creation, that are beneath Man, the rule of Analogy may make it probable, that it is so also in Things above us, and our Observation; and that there are several ranks of intelligent Beings, excelling us in several degrees of Perfection, ascending upwards towards the infinite Perfection of the Creator, by gentle steps and differences, that are every one at no great distance from the next to it. (E IV.xvi.12: 666)[6]

Locke's point here is that the observable parts of creation that are beneath human beings form a gently ascending hierarchy arranged by degree of perfection, and, following the rule of analogy, it is reasonable to infer that the unobservable parts of creation that lie between human beings and God *also* form a gently ascending hierarchy arranged by degree of perfection. On the assumption that immateriality is more perfect than materiality (material substance, but not immaterial substance, being divisible and corruptible), it follows that it is probable that the beings above human beings in the hierarchy are immaterial spirits.

This kind of reasoning establishes at most the probable existence of non-human finite immaterial spirits (e.g., angels and demons), but does not by itself establish that the substance that is capable of thinking and willing in human beings is immaterial. Still, the reasoning could be extended to cover human spirits, for it could be argued that human beings have more in common with angels than they do with the closest creatures that lie beneath them in the hierarchy (presumably, primates). And on this basis it might be concluded that human spirits are, more likely than not, immaterial.

But even if it is *probable* that human spirits are immaterial, Locke's views commit him to the thesis that it is *possible* that they are not. This is not just because, as Locke sees it, there is no necessary connection to be perceived between the idea of a human spirit (i.e., the idea of a substance that is capable of thinking thoughts and exciting bodily motion by acts of will) and the idea of immateriality, but because there is nothing to prevent an omnipotent God from endowing material things with the ability to think. In his proof of the existence of an immaterial and omnipotent God, Locke insists that material things *in or of themselves, by their own strength,* do not have the ability to produce thought (E IV.x.10: 623). The reason is that matter at rest is at best no more than a lump (E IV.x.17: 627), while matter in (unguided) motion can do no more than produce more (unguided) motion: "[Particles of matter] knock, impel, and resist one another, . . . and that is all they can do" (E IV.x.10: 624). But God himself, being able to do anything that is possible, can surely endow matter with the power of thought. In a famous passage, Locke writes:

> We have the *Ideas* of *Matter* and *Thinking*, but possibly shall never be able to know, whether any mere material Being thinks, or no; it being impossible for us, by the contemplation of our own *Ideas*, without revelation, to discover, whether Omnipotency has not given to some Systems of Matter fitly disposed, a power to perceive and think, or else joined and fixed to Matter so disposed, a thinking immaterial Substance: It being, in respect of our Notions, not much more remote from our Comprehension to conceive, that GOD can, if he pleases, superadd to Matter a Faculty of Thinking, than that he should superadd to it another Substance, with a Faculty of Thinking; since we know not wherein Thinking consists, nor to what sort of Substances the Almighty has been pleased to give that Power, which cannot be in any created Being, but merely by the good pleasure and Bounty of the Creator. For I see no contradiction in it, that the first eternal Being should, if he pleased, give to certain Systems of created senseless matter, put together as he thinks fit, some degrees of sense, perception, and thought: Though, as I think, I have proved . . . it is no less than a contradiction to suppose matter (which is evidently in its own nature void of sense and thought) should be that Eternal first thinking Being. (E IV.iii.6: 540–541)

Locke concludes that it is unjustified dogmatism to suppose that the substance that thinks in us *must* be immaterial. Given the lack of a necessary connection between the idea of spirit and the idea of immateriality, it would be straightforwardly inconsistent with God's omnipotence to suppose him incapable of superadding a faculty of thinking to matter.[7]

It was very difficult indeed for many of Locke's contemporaries to accept that, for all we know, the substance in us that thinks is material. Part of Stillingfleet's purpose, in his public letters admonishing the author of the *Essay*, was to savage this claim of Locke's and accuse him of impiety and irreligion. Though in his responses to Stillingfleet Locke defended his views in much the same terms as are found in the *Essay*, and in particular refused to retract the claim that we do not know that God has not endowed matter with the power to think, he was clearly stung and taken aback. And it is clearly in order to palliate further criticisms that Locke adds numerous references to immaterial spirits to the fourth and subsequent editions of the *Essay*. In some cases, these additions are unproblematic, and merely extend claims already made in the relevant context. But in other cases, it must be admitted that Locke's additions are at best infelicitous. A good example of this occurs in a passage that reads as follows in the first three editions:

> [B]y the simple *Ideas* we have taken from those Operations of our own Minds, which we experiment daily in our selves, as Thinking, Understanding, Willing, Knowing, and Power of beginning Motion, *etc.* co-existing in some Substance, we are able to frame *the complex* Idea *of a Spirit* . . . For putting together the *Ideas* of Thinking and Willing, or the Power of moving or quieting corporeal Motion, joined to Substance . . ., we have the *Idea* of Spirit. (E II.xxiii.15: 305)

In the fourth and fifth editions, the word "Spirit" is replaced with the phrase "immaterial Spirit." But this is unfortunate. The result of putting together the idea of substance with the idea of the power of thought and the idea of the power to cause bodily motion by willing is not the idea of an *immaterial* spirit – that is, a spirit *without solidity*: it is no more than the idea of a spirit *simpliciter*, as Locke tells us in no uncertain terms elsewhere in the *Essay*, as we have seen. What this shows us, I think, is not that Locke's views on the nature of spirit are inconsistent, but that Locke was human. Stung and wanting to make sure that future readers would not associate his position with (atheistic) materialism, Locke overreacted in a way that made a mess of passages in the *Essay* that were unproblematic as originally penned. This should not make us think any less of him; indeed, it should make us feel nothing but sympathy.

notes

1 Locke insists that the idea of solidity should be distinguished from both the idea of space and the idea of hardness, the latter idea (unlike the idea of solidity) presupposing a relation to our bodies, "that being generally call'd hard by us, which will put us to Pain, sooner than change Figure by the pressure of any part of our Bodies" (E II.iv.4: 125).

2 Notice that on Locke's official account of the ideas of extension and body, the idea of body is a constituent of the idea of extension, and the idea of extension is a constituent of the idea of body. This is an unfortunate consequence, and should be avoided. Perhaps the best cleaned-up version of Locke's theory would be this: (i) the idea of solidity is a combination of the ideas of filling space and impenetrability, (ii) the idea of extension is the idea of filling space (from which it follows that anything that is solid is extended), and (iii) the idea of body is a combination of the ideas of extension and impenetrability (i.e., solidity) and the idea of substratum.

Locke's description of the idea of body is not always consistent. In one passage, he describes it as the idea of "solid extended figured substance" (E

III.x.15: 498). This might be unproblematic, inasmuch as "Solidity cannot exist without . . . Figure" (E III.x.15: 498), and thus the fact that a substance is figured simply follows from the fact that it is solid. But in another passage, he characterizes the idea of body as the idea of "something that is solid, and extended, whose parts are separable and movable different ways" (E II.xiii.11: 171). And he uses the thought that it is essential to a body that its parts be separable and movable to distinguish the idea of body from the idea of (pure) space, the parts of which "are inseparable one from the other" (E II.xiii.13: 172). (See also E II.xxiii.3: 297, where Locke defines body as "a *thing* that is extended, figured, and capable of Motion.") Still, it is clear that the central ideas that constitute the idea of body are the ideas of impenetrability, extension, and substratum.

3   In the seventeenth century, as Locke was no doubt well aware, mechanists also struggled to explain other recalcitrant phenomena, such as magnetism and static electricity.

4   There is one passage in which Locke seems to equate materiality with extension and immateriality with lack of extension. In a passage we have already quoted, he writes that it is impossible for a person to know whether the soul is material. The passage continues: "Since on which side soever [a person] views [the soul], either as an unextended [i.e., immaterial] Substance, or as a thinking extended Matter; the difficulty to conceive either, will, whilst either alone is in his Thoughts, still drive him to the contrary side" (E IV.iii.6: 542). But this passage is anomalous, and does not fit with Locke's official position on the nature of matter and its relation to extension.

In a passage added to the fourth edition of the *Essay*, Locke writes: "[I]t may be conjectured, that created Spirits are not totally separate from Matter, because they are both active and passive. Pure Spirit, *viz.* God, is only active; pure Matter is only passive; those Beings that are both active and passive we may judge to partake of both" (E II.xxiii.28: 312). The conjecture here cannot be that finite spirits partake of both materiality and immateriality, for this would make them self-contradictory entities. The point, rather, is that it may be that finite spirits partake of both "pure spirit" and "pure matter" in being both active and passive. It does not follow from this that finite spirits are both material and immaterial.

5   This point is echoed elsewhere, both in the correspondence with Stillingfleet and in the following passage from the *Essay*: "I say not this, that I would any way lessen the belief of the Soul's Immateriality: I am not here speaking of Probability, but Knowledge; and I think not only, that it becomes the Modesty of Philosophy, not to pronounce Magisterially, where we want that Evidence that can produce Knowledge; but also, that it is of use to us, to discern how far our Knowledge does reach; for the state we are at present in, not being that of Vision, we must, in many Things, content our selves with Faith and Probability: and in the present Question, about the immateriality of the Soul, if our Faculties cannot arrive at demonstrative Certainty, we need not think it strange" (E IV.iii.6: 541–542).

6   Elsewhere, Locke writes: "That there should be more *Species* of intelligent Creatures above us, than there are of sensible and material below us, is probable to me from hence; That in all the visible corporeal Worlds, we see no Chasms, or Gaps. All quite down from us, the descent is by easy steps, and a continued series of Things, that in each remove, differ very little one from the other . . .

And when we consider the infinite Power and Wisdom of the Maker, we have reason to think, that it is suitable to the magnificent Harmony of the Universe, and the great Design and infinite Goodness of the Architect, that the *Species* of Creatures should also, by gentle degrees, ascend upward from us toward his infinite Perfection, as we see they gradually descend from us downwards: Which if it be probable, we have reason then to be perswaded, that there are far more *Species* of Creatures above us, than there are beneath" (E III.vi.12: 446–447).

7 Notice that Locke's claim that matter of itself cannot think is not logically inconsistent with the claim that God could give matter the power to think. To say that matter *of itself* cannot think is not to say that matter cannot think: it is to say that matter, if left to its own devices (in particular, without the assistance of a thinking substance more powerful than it) cannot produce thought. So Locke's proof of God's existence does not rest on any premise that is incompatible with the claim that God has the power to superadd to matter the faculty of thinking.

Some scholars think that there is a tension between Locke's mechanism and his insistence on the logical possibility of superaddition. For if God can superadd to matter the faculty of thinking, but matter of itself cannot produce thought by mechanical means, then it is possible, in principle, for matter to operate non-mechanically. Indeed, it would seem that we cannot know whether matter operates non-mechanically, and hence we cannot know whether mechanism is true. The scholars are right that the logical possibility of superaddition is incompatible with mechanism, but they are wrong in thinking that Locke is a mechanist. As I argued above, he is not. This is sufficient to dissolve the relevant tension.

further reading

Bennett, Jonathan, "Locke's Philosophy of Mind," *The Cambridge Companion to Locke*, edited by Vere Chappell. Cambridge: Cambridge University Press, 1994, pp. 89–114.

Downing, Lisa, "Locke's Ontology," in *The Cambridge Companion to Locke's "Essay Concerning Human Understanding"*, edited by Lex Newman. Cambridge: Cambridge University Press, 2007, pp. 352–380.

McCann, Edwin, "Locke's Philosophy of Body," in *The Cambridge Companion to Locke*, edited by Vere Chappell. Cambridge: Cambridge University Press, 1994, pp. 56–88.

Stuart, Matthew, "Locke on Superaddition and Mechanism," *British Journal for the History of Philosophy* 6 (1998): 351–379.

qualities

Locke's world is divided into substances, modes, and relations. Substances are things that do not depend for their existence on the existence of anything else, modes are things that depend for their existence on the existence of a single substance, while relations are things that depend for their existence on more than one substance. The question that will occupy us in this chapter is the place of corporeal qualities within Locke's ontology. In Chapter 7, we will discuss mental operations, with special attention to Locke's account of volition and freedom.

It is important at the outset to distinguish, as Locke does not always clearly do, between qualities and ideas that represent qualities. Squareness is a quality, a property that belongs to square-shaped substances and to no other substances. The *idea of squareness* differs from squareness itself in being something that is in (i.e., directly perceived by) the mind. As Locke famously writes: "Ideas *in the Mind, Qualities in Bodies*" (E II.viii.7–8: 134, section heading). But Locke's point goes further, for the distinction between ideas and what they represent applies not only when the represented things are in bodies, but also when they are in minds. So, for example, we need to be careful not to confuse belief (the mental operation) with *the idea of* belief, the idea that represents the mental operation. When we avoid confusion here, we are simply taking to heart Locke's general view that the world is not identical to our representation of it.

More has been written on Locke's theory of the qualities of bodies than about almost any other part of his metaphysics and epistemology. This is because Locke famously distinguishes, as does his friend and contemporary Robert Boyle, between "primary qualities" and "secondary qualities." The primary qualities of bodies, for Locke, include the following determinable properties, as well as their particular determinations: shape (or figure), motion/rest (or mobility), size (or bulk), number, extension, solidity, texture, and possibly place (or situation).[1] The secondary qualities of bodies include the

Locke, First Edition. Samuel C. Rickless.
© 2014 Samuel C. Rickless. Published 2014 by John Wiley & Sons, Ltd.

following determinable properties, as well as their particular determinations: color (and light), sound, taste, smell (or odor), hot and cold (or warmth).[2] It is clear that, as Locke sees it, these two kinds of qualities differ metaphysically. The question is how.

According to some scholars, secondary qualities are in the mind, while primary qualities are in bodies. According to others, primary qualities differ from secondary qualities in that the former are intrinsic or essential properties of bodies, while the latter are not. According to yet others, secondary qualities are textures, while primary qualities are not. Another group of scholars claims that the main difference between primary and secondary qualities is that the former, but not the latter, resemble the ideas we have of them. As we will see, none of these proposals makes the best sense of the relevant texts. For Locke, the criterion that fixes the distinction between primary and secondary qualities is that the latter, unlike the former, are relations between bodies and minds, relations that depend for their existence on the minds that perceive ideas of them. But it must be acknowledged that the relevant texts *are* confusing, and sometimes confused. Any interpretation of Locke's seemingly inconsistent pronouncements on the nature of the primary/secondary quality distinction should explain why this is so.

To understand the primary/secondary quality distinction, as well as the confusion among commentators understandably provoked by Locke's account of it, it helps to begin with Locke's official definition of a quality. Locke tells us that "the Power to produce any *Idea* in our mind, I call *Quality* of the Subject wherein that power is" (E II.viii.8: 134). But he also tells us that he calls colors, sounds, tastes, and so on "qualities" in order "to comply with the common way of speaking" (E II.viii.10: 135). This suggests the following interpretive hypothesis: Locke takes colors, sounds, tastes, and so on to be powers to produce ideas in our minds; wanting to comply with common parlance, Locke calls these features of bodies "qualities"; and so he finds it necessary to define "quality" as a power to cause ideas.

If qualities are powers to cause ideas, and features of bodies such as size, shape, motion, and number are primary qualities (and hence qualities), then it follows that size, shape, motion, number, and so on are powers to cause ideas. But this is a problem for Locke. For, within his theory, powers are relations (see Chapter 4). But, as is the case for Boyle, relations depend for their existence on their relata: once the relatum of a relation ceases to exist, the relation itself ceases to exist. As Locke says: "[I]f either [relatum] be removed, or cease to be, the Relation ceases, and the Denomination consequent to it, though the other receive in it self no alteration at all. *v.g. Cajus*, whom I consider to day as a Father, ceases to be so tomorrow, only by the death of his Son, without any alteration in himself" (E II.xxv.5: 321). So if size, shape, motion, number, and so on are powers in bodies to produce ideas in our minds, then size, shape, motion, number, and so on are relations between bodies and minds, relations that would cease to exist if minds ceased to exist. But Locke makes it quite clear that he thinks that the annihilation of all perceivers would *not* result in the annihilation of the size, shape, motion, number, and so on of bodies. He writes: "Solidity, and Extension, and the termination of it, Figure, with Motion and Rest, whereof we have the *Ideas*, would be really in the World as they are, whether there were any sensible Being to perceive them, or no" (E II.xxxi.2: 376). It therefore appears as if Locke's theory of qualities is mired in contradiction from the very start. In order to avoid such a contradiction, it is necessary to deny one or more of the following: (i) that size, shape, motion, number, and so on are powers in bodies to cause ideas in minds, (ii) that the power in A to cause effects in B is a relation between A and B, (iii) that relations depend for their existence on their relata, (iv) that size, shape, motion, number, and so on do not depend for their existence on minds.

Upon reflection it seems clear that Locke would accept (ii)–(iv) and deny (i). Locke's considered view is that size, shape, motion, number, and so on are *not* powers to cause ideas in minds. It follows that, according to Locke's official definition of "quality," such features of bodies are not qualities. Thus there is a real sense in which his calling such features "primary qualities" is a misnomer. There is some evidence for this interpretation. First, Locke never actually *says* that shape, size, motion, number, and so on are powers, though he says repeatedly that color, sound, taste, and so on are powers. And, second, as we have seen, Locke acknowledges that he calls such features as color, sound, and taste "qualities" in order to comply with the common way of speaking. It could, then, be that Locke thinks that the common way of speaking is misleading, that in some sense color, sound, taste, and so on should not be counted as "qualities" at all. If this is so, then Locke's view is that there is a sense of the word "quality" according to which color, sound, taste, and so on are not qualities. This sense cannot be the sense stipulated by the definition of a quality as a power to cause ideas, for it is plain that Locke thinks of color, sound, taste, and so on as powers of this sort. Although Locke does not speak to this question, it is reasonable to suppose that he takes qualities in the second, non-official sense to be modes of the substances in which they inhere. In *this* sense, size, shape, motion, number, and so on are qualities of bodies, but color, sound, taste, and so on are not: for color, sound, taste, and so on are *relations*, and hence not modes or properties of bodies.

The best way to resolve the apparent contradiction in Locke's theory of qualities, then, is to suppose that Locke is using the word "quality" in two different ways, with two different meanings that could be captured by two different subscripts:

Quality$_1$: mode
Quality$_2$: power to produce ideas in minds

Size, shape, motion, number, and so on are qualities$_1$, but not qualities$_2$; color, sound, taste, and so on are qualities$_2$, but not qualities$_1$. In other words, primary qualities are qualities in the first sense, but not in the second; secondary qualities are qualities in the second sense, but not in the first.

Resolving this conundrum is only the first step in resolving the general puzzle of Locke's views on the nature of qualities. The claim of Locke's that has most befuddled his readers is that primary qualities are to be sharply distinguished from secondary qualities. The problem is *not* that there is confusion over which features of bodies belong in which category: size, shape, motion, number, and so on (as well as their determinates) are to be classified as primary qualities, while color, taste, sound, and so on (as well as their determinates) are to be classified as secondary qualities. The problem is that Locke provides what appear to be different, and indeed mutually inconsistent, criteria or grounds for the distinction. Our task is to determine whether Locke is hopelessly muddled, or whether there are unfortunate but remediable confusions obscuring his essentially consistent position.

There are some who believe that, for Locke, the distinction between primary qualities and secondary qualities is that the former are in bodies, while the latter are in minds. This interpretation of the distinction originates in a passage in which Locke begins by describing primary qualities as "in Bodies" (E II.viii.9: 134) and then moves on to describe secondary qualities as being "in truth nothing in the Objects themselves" (E II.viii.10: 135). But this reading rests on a failure to parse Locke's archaic prose and punctuation correctly. Locke does not say that secondary qualities are "in truth nothing in the Objects themselves": what he says is that these qualities are "in truth nothing in the Objects themselves, but Powers to produce various Sensations in us by their *Primary Qualities*" (E II.viii.10: 135). That is, Locke's point is that secondary qualities are *nothing but* (i.e., nothing other than, no more than) powers to cause ideas, from which it follows *not* that secondary qualities are not in bodies, but that secondary qualities are powers that bodies have to produce ideas in our minds.

Perhaps the most popular interpretation of Locke's distinction is that primary qualities, unlike secondary qualities, are intrinsic or essential characteristics of bodies – that is, features that bodies *cannot* lose (without ceasing to be what they are). The main textual basis for this reading is the following passage:

> Qualities thus considered in Bodies are, First such as are utterly inseparable from the Body, in what estate soever it be; such as in all the alterations and changes it suffers, all the force can be used upon it, it constantly keeps; and such as Sense constantly finds in every particle of Matter, which has bulk enough to be perceived, and the Mind finds inseparable from every particle of Matter, though less than to make it self singly be perceived by our Senses. (E II.viii.9: 134–135)

Locke seems to be telling us here that what makes a quality *primary* is the fact that it is impossible for a body not to possess it, and indeed that it is impossible even to *imagine* a body that does not possess it. This suggestion certainly makes sense of Locke's classification of the determinables, solidity, extension, shape, motion, and so on, as primary qualities. For every body is solid and extended (and perhaps also figured and mobile) *by definition*.[3]

But there are two problems with this interpretation. The first is that it does not make sense of the fact that Locke classifies all *determinate* instances of the relevant determinables as primary qualities. Locke writes that "the <u>particular</u> *Bulk, Number, Figure, and Motion of the parts of Fire, or Snow* . . . may be called *real* [i.e., primary] *Qualities*" (E II.viii.17: 137 – underlining added); but according to the "essentialist" or "intrinsicalist" criterion, no *particular* size, number, shape, or motion could be a primary quality, because no *particular* size, number, shape, or motion is essential to (i.e., inseparable from) any body. As Locke is well aware, a body (e.g., the piece of wax discussed by Descartes at the end of the Second Meditation) can lose its particular size and shape without ceasing to be what it is, a plant/animal/human can gain or lose material particles (and so undergo alteration in the number of its parts) without ceasing to be the same plant/animal/human (E II.xxvii.4–6: 330–332), and a ball remains what it is whether it is resting in the bowler's hand or on its way to knocking over ninepins.

The second problem is that Locke lists *texture* as a primary quality (E II.viii.10: 135; E II.viii.14: 137). But the texture of a body consists in the arrangement (i.e., the relative position) of its parts, and thus by definition it is impossible for a partless body (i.e., an atom) to have a texture. So if there were such things as indivisible bodies (i.e., atoms), they could not have texture, and hence texture could not be a primary quality of body on the "essentialist" or "intrinsicalist" criterion. It is possible to get around this objection by supposing that Locke believes that matter is infinitely divisible and hence that atoms are impossible, but this would be an unreasonably dogmatic position for the epistemically modest Locke to hold. Indeed, it makes more sense to suppose that Locke is officially agnostic about the possibility of atoms. By contrast, Locke is not agnostic about the status of texture as a primary quality. All told, then, it is unlikely to be Locke's considered view that primary qualities are distinguished from secondary qualities by virtue of being essential or intrinsic to the bodies that have them.

Some interpreters take Locke to hold that secondary qualities, unlike primary qualities, are bodily textures. Some of what Locke writes understandably lends itself to this reading. Speaking of the white and red colors of porphyry (a particular kind of igneous rock), Locke writes that "whiteness or redness are not in it at any time, but such a texture, that hath the power to produce such a sensation [of white or red] in us" (E II.viii.19: 139). And later in the *Essay* Locke tells us that "the Active and Passive Powers of Bodies [presumably, including colors, sounds, tastes, etc.], and their ways of operating, [consist] in a Texture and Motion of Parts . . ." (E IV.iii.16: 547). But, for reasons already discussed, this cannot be Locke's considered view. For the textures of bodies, as Locke emphasizes, are primary qualities. So if colors, say, were textures, then they would be primary qualities, and so not secondary qualities. But it is a fixed point of any interpretation that Locke takes colors (sounds, tastes, smells, etc.) to be secondary qualities. It is therefore far more likely than not that Locke is speaking loosely when he says that secondary qualities 'consist in' textures/motions of parts. What he is almost surely trying to convey is that secondary qualities *depend on* (and, in that sense, are 'reduced to' or 'result from') the primary qualities (including textures) that are causally responsible for the ideas that represent them (see E II.viii.14: 137; E II.viii.17: 138; E II.viii.23: 141).[4]

Locke says something important about the difference between primary qualities and secondary qualities, a difference that some see as critical to the nature of the distinction. Locke writes: "the *Ideas of primary Qualities* of Bodies, *are Resemblances* of them, and their Patterns do really exist in the Bodies themselves; but the *Ideas, produced* in us *by* these *Secondary Qualities, have no resemblance* of them at all. There is nothing like our *Ideas,* existing in the Bodies themselves" (E II.viii.15: 137). This certainly looks like a firm criterion: what differentiates any primary quality P from any secondary quality S is that while P resembles the idea of P, S does not resemble the idea of S. And there is surely something to this. As we have seen, Locke thinks that a triangle has three sides, whether it exists in reality or in the mind. The idea and its object are therefore similar. By contrast, the idea of red, which is a kind of mental picture, does not resemble the secondary quality, red, which is nothing but a power to produce the idea of red in our minds.

However, there is one compelling reason to treat this (to Locke's mind, very real) difference between primary and secondary qualities as other than *criterial*, indeed, as a byproduct of the real criterion. For it is not in a vacuum that Locke informs us that P resembles the idea of P while S does not resemble the idea of S. This fact about resemblance and non-resemblance is an observation that Locke tells us "it is easie to draw" from the following claim:

> What I have said concerning *Colours* and *Smells*, may be understood also of *Tastes* and *Sounds, and other the like sensible Qualities;* which, whatever reality we, by mistake, attribute to them, are in truth nothing in the Objects themselves, but Powers to produce various Sensations in us, and *depend on those primary Qualities.* (E II.viii.14: 137)

So Locke thinks that some fact about resemblance *follows from* some fact about reality, namely that primary qualities are *real* whereas secondary qualities are not. This suggests that it is a fact about reality and non-reality, rather than a fact about resemblance and non-resemblance, that accounts for the distinction between primary and secondary qualities. But this raises two questions. First, what is the real/non-real distinction that appears to lie at the heart of Locke's primary/secondary quality distinction? And, second, why does Locke think that his observation about resemblance and non-resemblance is "easie to draw" from his observation about reality and non-reality?

Locke tells us that primary qualities, unlike secondary qualities, are real in that they "really exist in the Bodies themselves" (E II.viii.15: 137). This statement might suggest that, for Locke, to say that the roundness of a ball is real is to say that it does not merely *appear* to exist, but rather *really and truly* exists, in the ball. But this cannot be what Locke means by "really exist" because it is clear that he thinks that secondary qualities are *really and truly* powers possessed by bodies, powers that *really and truly* exist in the bodies that possess them. Perhaps it should not surprise us, then, that Locke treats the word "real" (and its cognate, "really") as a technical term in this context. He explicates its meaning in the following terms:

> The particular *Bulk, Number, Figure, and Motion of the Parts of Fire, or Snow, are really in them*, whether any ones Senses perceive them or no: and therefore they may be called *real Qualities*. (E II.viii.17: 137; see also E II. viii.23: 140)

> [Bulk, Figure, Number, Situation, and Motion/Rest] may be properly called *real Original*, or *primary Qualities*, because they are in the things themselves, whether they are perceived or no. (E II.viii.23: 141)

> Solidity, and Extension, and the termination of it, Figure, with Motion and Rest, whereof we have the *Ideas*, would be really in the World as they are, whether there were any sensible Being to perceive them, or no: And therefore those we have reason to look on, as the real modifications of Matter. (E II.xxxi.2: 376)

A quality is real, in Locke's sense, if its existence in a body is independent of the existence of any perceivers: a quality that would continue to exist even if there were no perceivers is real, whereas a quality that would cease to exist if all perceivers were annihilated is not real. The distinction between primary qualities and secondary qualities, at bottom, resolves into the distinction between real and non-real qualities of bodies: primary qualities are real, whereas secondary qualities are not (see also E II.xxiii.9: 300).

Notice now that Locke's way of stating his resemblance theses makes explicit mention of the real/non-real distinction:

> [T]he *Ideas of primary Qualities* of Bodies, *are Resemblances* of them, and their Patterns do <u>really</u> exist in the Bodies themselves; but the *Ideas, produced* in us *by* these *Secondary Qualities, have no resemblance* of them at all. (E II.viii.15: 137 – underlining added)

On first reading, it is easy to pass over the word "really," which appears to be there for emphasis and nothing else. But the fact that Locke uses the word in a technical sense casts this statement in a very different light. What Locke is telling us is this:

(1) Ideas of primary qualities resemble *real* qualities of bodies.
(2) Ideas of secondary qualities do *not* resemble *real* qualities of bodies.

Thesis (1) follows from the following assumptions:

(A1) For any primary quality P, the idea of P resembles P.
(A2) Every primary quality is real.

To understand why Locke accepts Thesis (2), we need to understand that Locke divides qualities into three categories, not two. In addition to primary qualities and secondary qualities, Locke allows for a third sort of quality, which we might call "tertiary." A tertiary quality is a "*Power* that is in any Body, *by* Reason of the particular Constitution of *its primary Qualities, to* make such a *change* in the *Bulk, Figure, Texture, and Motion of another Body*, as to make it operate on our Senses, differently from what it did before" (E II.viii.23: 140; see also E II.xxiii.9: 300). Among tertiary qualities, Locke counts the power of the sun to make wax white and the power of fire to make lead fluid (E II.viii.23: 140–141). The important thing about tertiary qualities is that they are like secondary qualities in being powers of bodies to produce ideas in our minds: the difference between them is that whereas secondary qualities are powers to produce ideas *directly*, tertiary qualities are powers to produce ideas *indirectly* – that is, powers to produce changes in bodies that then produce ideas. Tertiary qualities, then, are no more real than are secondary qualities: were perceivers to be annihilated, tertiary qualities, like secondary qualities, would cease to exist.[5]

Thesis (2), then, derives from the following assumptions:

(A2) Every primary quality is real.
(B1) No secondary or tertiary quality is real.
(B2) Every quality is either primary, secondary, or tertiary.
(B3) No idea of a secondary quality resembles any primary quality.

The argument is simple. By (B3), ideas of secondary qualities do not resemble primary qualities of bodies. But by (B1), (B2), and (B3) primary qualities are the *only* real qualities of bodies. Therefore, (2) ideas of secondary qualities do not resemble real qualities of bodies. So it is now easy to see why Locke tells us that it is "easie to draw" his observation about resemblance/non-resemblance from his observation about reality/non-reality: (i) the former observation is just the conjunction of (1) and (2), (ii) the latter observation is just the conjunction of (A2) and (part of) (B1), (iii) taking (A1), (B2), and (B3) for granted, the conjunction of (1) and (2) follows logically from the conjunction of (A2) and (B1). But the fact that (A2) and (B1) are, in this sense, more fundamental than (1) and (2) confirms the claim that Locke's distinction between primary qualities and secondary qualities rests, at bottom, on the real/non-real distinction, rather than on the resemblance/non-resemblance distinction. What makes it the case that triangularity, say, is primary is *not* that the idea of a triangle resembles the triangle, but rather that triangularity is not perceiver-dependent; and what makes it the case that redness, say, is secondary is *not* that the idea of red does not resemble the power in bodies to produce the idea of red in our minds, but rather that redness *is* perceiver-dependent.

Now Locke does not merely *state* the distinction between primary qualities and secondary qualities: he also *argues* for it. The three arguments Locke provides are less than persuasive, but what is perhaps most interesting about them is that they further confirm the claim that the real/non-real distinction is the heart of the primary/secondary quality distinction. The first argument focuses on color, the second on color and taste, and the third on heat and cold. In each case, Locke's conclusion is that the relevant quality is not real, and is therefore to be distinguished from such real qualities as size, shape, number, texture, mobility, and solidity.

Here is Locke's first argument:

> Let us consider the red and white colours in *Porphyre*: Hinder light but from striking on it, and its Colours vanish; it no longer produces any such *Ideas* in us: Upon the return of Light, it produces these appearances on us again. Can any one think any real alterations are made in the *Porphyre*, by the presence or absence of Light; and that those *Ideas* of whiteness and redness, are really in *Porphyre* in the light, when 'tis plain *it has no colour in the dark*? (E II.viii.19: 139)[6]

The reasoning here is clear:

    (1a) In the presence of light, porphyry is red and white.
    (2a) In the absence of light, porphyry has no color.
So, (3a) The presence or absence of light changes the color of porphyry. [1a, 2a]
    (4a) The presence or absence of light does not change any of the real qualities of porphyry.
So, (5a) The red and white colors of porphyry are not real qualities. [3a, 4a]

Here is Locke's second argument:

> Pound an Almond, and the clear white *Colour* will be altered into a dirty one, and the sweet *Taste* into an oily one. What real Alteration can the beating of the Pestle make in any Body, but an Alteration of the *Texture* of it? (E II.viii.20: 139)

The reasoning here is clear as well:

    (1b) Before it is pounded, an almond is white and sweet.
    (2b) After it is pounded, an almond is dirty-colored and oily-tasting.
So, (3b) Pounding an almond changes its color and taste.
    (4b) The only real quality that pounding a body (e.g., an almond) can change is its texture.
    (5b) Neither the color nor the taste of an almond is identical to its texture.[7]
So, (6b) Neither the color nor the taste of an almond is a real quality.

And here is Locke's third argument:

> *Ideas* being thus distinguished and understood, we may be able to give an
> Account, how the same Water, at the same time, may produce the *Idea* of
> Cold by one Hand, and of Heat by the other: Whereas it is impossible, that
> the same Water, if those *Ideas* were really in it, should at the same time be
> both Hot and Cold. (E II.viii.21: 139)

The reasoning here is more compressed. Spelled out, it looks like this:

(1c) At time T, water W produces the idea of cold by one hand, H1.
(2c) At time T, water W produces the idea of hot by another hand, H2.
(3c) If, at T, W produces the idea of F, then W is F.
So, (4c) At T, W is both hot and cold.
(5c) Hot and cold are opposite qualities.
(6c) It is impossible for the same thing to have opposite real qualities at
the same time.
So, (7c) Hot and cold are not real qualities.

It is beyond question that Locke's aim in all three of these arguments is to
show that color, taste, hot, and cold are not real qualities of bodies. Given that
he has already told us that size, shape, number, mobility, solidity, and texture
are real, it follows that there is an exclusive distinction between qualities of
the first kind and qualities of the second kind. This is precisely the distinction
between secondary qualities and primary qualities.

I said above that these arguments do not persuade. Why so? The first argument rests on two problematic premises. The first is that bodies have no color
in the dark. Nowadays, we tend to think that, even in the absence of light,
porphyry is still red and white, even if we cannot *see* its colors under these
circumstances. So premise (2a) is dubious. The second is that the presence or
absence of light does not change any of the real (i.e., perceiver-independent)
qualities of porphyry. Locke must be assuming that the presence or absence
of light can affect no more than the visibility of bodies. But this assumption
is an empirical claim that might well turn out to be false. For example, it
might turn out that light is a stream of particles that alters the texture of the
bodies on which it impinges, and if this were so then (4a) would be false.

The second argument rests on premise (4b), namely that the only real
quality that pounding a body can change is its texture. This is an odd claim,
as Locke must surely be aware of the fact that pounding an object can change
its shape. Still, this objection is not fatal to the argument, for (4b) could be
altered to say that the only real qualities that pounding a body can change
are its texture and shape, and premise (5b) could be altered to say that neither
the color nor the taste of an almond is identical to its texture or shape. Far
more serious is the fact that (5b), whether altered or unaltered, simply begs
the question against Locke's opponents. If the color (or taste) of an almond

were identical to its texture, then the almond's color (or taste) would be a real quality. Locke needs to provide an *independent* reason for thinking that colors and tastes are not textures, and it is difficult to imagine what this reason could be.

The dubious premise of the third argument is assumption (3c), that if a body produces in us the idea of F (at T), then it is F (at T). Locke infers from (3c) that a body that produces in us the idea of hot is hot, and that a body that produces in us the idea of cold is cold. But it is not at all clear that the assumption is true. In the absence of reasons to believe the contrary, it is reasonable to hold that it is possible for cold bodies to *feel* hot and that it is possible for hot bodies to *feel* cold. The fact that a body appears to us to have a certain quality does not entail that it actually possesses that quality. So here, too, Locke assumes what at least some of his opponents would quite reasonably be unwilling to grant him.

The vast majority of what Locke says therefore points to a philosophically respectable and consistent position on the issue of whether the qualities of bodies belong to two mutually exclusive categories. Secondary qualities are perceiver-dependent powers that bodies have to produce ideas in our minds, powers that depend on (derive from, are explained by) primary qualities, which are (not powers, but) perceiver-independent corporeal modes. Although Locke's arguments for the distinction (and, in particular, for the non-reality of secondary qualities) are not conclusive, the claim that there is such a distinction, one based on the reality/non-reality distinction, is not, as many think it is, shot through with confusion and inconsistency.

This does not, however, mean that Locke's distinction between primary qualities and secondary qualities is utterly clear and distinct. One main source of potential confusion is Locke's understanding of the nature of a power. We now tend to think of powers as dispositions. The fragility of a glass, we think, is the passive power or disposition to break when it is struck by a hard object. And a glass possesses this disposition if and only if it would break when placed under the right sorts of conditions (being struck at such-and-such a speed by an object with such-and-such degree of hardness). At least some of what Locke says suggests that this is how he views powers too. Fire, he tells us, has the power to make lead fluid (E II.viii.23: 141). He may mean by this, not that fire makes lead fluid no matter the circumstances, but rather that if lead were to be brought close enough to a fire, it would melt. Fire has such a power even when there is no lead in its vicinity, and so even when, in actual fact, it causes no lead to melt. Whether it has the power to melt lead seems to depend on the truth of a counterfactual proposition.

But if this is how Locke thinks of powers, then what he says about secondary qualities must strike any charitable reader as odd. As we have seen, Locke insists that objects do not have color in the dark. But if colors are powers (i.e., powers to produce ideas of color in our minds) and powers are dispositions, then it would seem that objects *do* have color in the dark. For the fact that a fire-engine has the disposition to produce an idea of red in our minds is just the fact that the fire-engine *would* produce such an idea *if* it we were placed in front of it in the light and with our (undamaged) eyes open. And the fire-engine possesses this disposition in the dark no less than it possesses this disposition when illuminated.

Understood in this way, Locke's position is incoherent. To render it coherent, something has to give. Some commentators think that Locke does not in fact think of powers as dispositions, but rather as causes. And there is textual evidence that favors this reading. As early as the drafts of the *Essay*, Locke treats qualities (in one sense) as "powers & capacitys" and then distinguishes between "actuall qualitys" and "potentiall qualitys," the former being "the causes of [simple ideas] that are in any thing. v.g the taste colour smell & tangible qualitys of all the component parts of a cherry" (Draft B, 61: 164–165), the latter being "the fitness [something] hath to change the simple Ideas of any other thing or to have its owne simple Ideas changed by any other thing. v.g. it is a potentiall quality of lead to be melted by fire & of fire to melt lead" (Draft B, 61: 165). Here the secondary qualities (taste, color, smell, and tangible qualities) of a cherry are classified both as qualities (in the relevant sense), and hence as *powers*, and as *actual* qualities – that is, as the causes of corresponding ideas. And the idea that powers to cause are themselves causes is echoed in the *Essay*, where Locke writes, for example, that "those *Ideas* of Whiteness, and Coldness, Pain, *etc.* [are] in us the Effects of Powers in Things without us, ordained by our Maker, to produce in us such Sensations" (E II.xxx.2: 372; see also E II.xxxi.2: 375), and that "the Paper I write on, having the Power, in the Light . . . to produce in me the Sensation, which I call White, it [i.e., the sensation] cannot but be the Effect of such a Power, in something without the Mind" (E II.xxxi.12: 383). If powers to cause are causes, as Locke suggests, then it becomes easy to understand why porphyry loses the power to cause the ideas of red and white in us when the lights are turned off: it ceases to possess the relevant power precisely because it ceases to cause the relevant ideas.

But although some passages suggest that this is the best way of understanding Locke's conception of power, the bulk of what Locke says about powers belies this interpretation. When Locke turns his attention to providing an analysis of the idea of power, he tells us that the mind comes by the relevant idea when it "considers in one thing the possibility of having any of its simple *Ideas* changed, and in another the possibility of making that change" (E II.xxi.1: 233). The latter sort of power, he says, is active, namely the ability "to make . . . any change," while the former sort of power is passive, namely the ability "to receive any change" (E II.xxi.2: 234). For an object O to have an active power to produce effect E, then, is for it to be *possible* for O to produce E; and for O to have a passive power to receive effect E is for it to be *possible* for O to receive E. But, if anything is clear to Locke, it is that possibility is not the same as actuality. From the fact that it is possible for O to produce (receive) E it does not follow that O is now actually producing (receiving) E. It therefore cannot be that powers to cause are causes.

How, then, in the face of this textual confusion, can we make the best sense of Locke's account of secondary qualities as powers to produce ideas in our minds? The answer is that we should take Locke at his word. Secondary qualities are powers, but powers are neither dispositions nor causes: they are possibilities of causing. To say that porphyry has the power to cause the idea of red in the light is to say that it is possible for porphyry to cause the idea of red in a perceiver when it is illuminated; to say that porphyry has the power to cause the idea of red in the dark is to say that it is possible for porphyry to cause the idea of red in a perceiver when it is not illuminated. Given that red is the power to cause the idea of red and that porphyry can cause the idea of red when illuminated but cannot cause the same idea when not illuminated, it follows directly, as Locke says (E II.viii.19: 139), that porphyry is red in the light but not red in the dark. It also follows, as Locke says (E II.xxxi.2: 376), that the sun would not be hot if all perceivers were annihilated, for it is impossible for the sun to produce ideas of heat if there are no minds around to perceive them.

In the end, the most serious problem with Locke's account of secondary qualities is expository. Primary and secondary qualities are discussed together as if they belonged to a single ontological category: quality. But primary qualities are modes and secondary qualities are relations. Secondary qualities are relations because (i) secondary qualities are powers (in bodies to cause ideas in minds) and (ii) powers are relations (between bodies and minds). Locke calls colors, tastes, smells, and so on "qualities" in order "to comply with the common way of speaking" (E II.viii.10: 135), but this accommodation of popular discourse within his general ontology of substances, modes, and relations adds unnecessary confusion to his metaphysics. Secondary qualities (e.g., red and sweet) are discussed along with primary qualities (e.g., round and solid) in a chapter devoted to simple ideas because the ideas that correspond to these qualities (the idea of red and the idea of round) are simple. This makes sense within Locke's larger project of ideational empiricism, but it results in the unhelpful assimilation within a single ontological category of entities that really belong to two completely different categories. In hindsight, it would have been better for Locke to have separated his theory of ideas from his account of what these ideas represent. That he does not do so conduces to confusion, but it is the sort of confusion that careful interpretation can enable us to avoid.

notes

1   Shape (or figure) and motion/rest (or mobility) are counted as primary qualities at E II.viii.9, 10, 14, 17, 22, 23, and 26; size (or bulk) at E II.viii.10, 14, 17, 23, and 26; number at E II.viii.9, 17, 22, 23, and 26; extension at E II.viii.9, 22, and 26; solidity at E II.viii.9 and 22; texture at E II.viii.10 and 14; place (or situation) at E II.viii.23. Particular determinations of these properties include particular

shapes, motions, sizes, numbers, lengths, textures, and places. The only primary quality determinable that does not allow for determinates is the quality of solidity. There is no such thing as a particular (degree or type of) solidity.

2 Color, sound, and taste are counted as secondary qualities at E II.viii.10, 14, 17 and 23; smell (or odor) at E II.viii.14, 17, and 23; hot/cold (warmth) at E II.viii.15, 16, 17, 21, 24 and 25; light at E II.viii.17, 24 and 25. Particular determinations of these properties include particular colors, sounds, tastes, smells, and degrees of temperature. It is not clear whether Locke thinks of light as a determinable quality that allows for determinates (e.g., types or kinds of light).

3 For Locke's definition of "body" (i.e., for his enumeration of the ideational components of the idea of body), see Chapter 5. Indeed, it is no coincidence that all the primary qualities mentioned more than once in E II.viii.9 (i.e., solidity, extension, figure, and mobility) are included at least once in the *Essay* among the qualities that define what bodies are.

4 Note also that the passage from E II.viii.19 is ambiguous. It *could* mean that whiteness and redness are nothing but textures. But it could also mean that whiteness and redness are not really in porphyry, but those textures that have the power to produce in us the ideas of white and red *are* really in porphyry. In light of how inconsistent Locke's position would be under the first reading, the second reading makes more sense. Concerning the importance of the distinction between a quality's being *in* a body and its being *really in* a body, see the main text below.

5 Tertiary qualities are therefore to be distinguished from powers that bodies have to change the primary qualities of other bodies. The latter powers, being unrelated to and independent of the existence of perceivers, are real, even as tertiary qualities themselves are not.

6 It is important to note that in the phrase "those *Ideas* of whiteness and redness" the word "*Ideas*" does not refer to mental entities that are immediate objects of perception, but rather refers to the *qualities* of whiteness and redness in porphyry. As we saw above, Locke tells us that he sometimes uses the word "idea" to refer to qualities of bodies (E II.viii.8: 134). This is a case in point. For if the word "*Ideas*" here referred to the ideas of red and white in our minds, then it would be self-evident that the "*Ideas* of whiteness and redness" are not real qualities of porphyry (for they are not even *qualities*!), and hence there would be no point in arguing for the claim, as Locke does.

7 Notice that Locke's second argument for the primary/secondary quality distinction does not get off the ground unless it is assumed that color and taste are not textures. This provides further reason to reject the thesis, discussed above, that Locke identifies secondary qualities with the textures of bodies.

further reading

Alexander, Peter, *Ideas, Qualities and Corpuscles: Locke and Boyle on the External World*. Cambridge: Cambridge University Press, 1985.

Jacovides, Michael, "Locke's Distinctions between Primary and Secondary Qualities," in *The Cambridge Companion to Locke's "Essay Concerning Human Understanding"*, edited by Lex Newman. Cambridge: Cambridge University Press, 2007, pp. 101–129.

Mackie, J.L., *Problems from Locke*. Oxford: Clarendon Press, 1976, chapter 1.

McCann, Edwin, "Locke's Distinction between Primary Primary Qualities and Secondary Primary Qualities," in *Primary and Secondary Qualities: The Historical and Ongoing Debate,* edited by Lawrence Nolan. Oxford: Oxford University Press, 2011, pp. 158–189.

Rickless, Samuel C., "Locke on Primary and Secondary Qualities," *Pacific Philosophical Quarterly* 78 (1997): 297–319.

Stuart, Matthew, "Locke's Colors," *Philosophical Review* 112 (2003): 57–96.

Wilson, Robert A., "Locke's Primary Qualities," *Journal of the History of Philosophy* 40 (2002): 201–228.

mental operations

I n Chapter 6, we focused on the properties and qualities of bodies. In this
chapter, we focus on the properties and qualities of minds, paying special
attention to Locke's account of volition and freedom.

7.1   Actions and Passions

As we saw in Chapter 5, for Locke a mind or spirit is a substance that is capable
of thinking and also capable of exciting bodily motion by willing. The mind
therefore has two main faculties: (i) the Understanding, which is the power of
"*Perception*, or *Thinking*," and (ii) the Will, which is the power of "*Volition*,
or *Willing*" (E II.vi.2: 128; E II.xxi.5–6: 236–237).[1] Locke tells us that, with
respect to the reception of simple ideas, whether from sensation or reflection,
"the *Understanding* is merely *passive*" (E II.i.25: 118). By this, Locke means
that it is not within the mind's power whether it will have the simple ideas
it perceives in these two ways. By contrast, the will is an active, not a passive,
power of the mind: it is not as a result of exercising its power of willing that
the mind receives ideas from without or from within, but it is as a result of
its exercising its power of willing that it acts upon its ideas.

Does Locke take it to follow from the fact that the understanding is passive
with respect to the sensitive or reflective perception of simple ideas that perceiving *as such* is not a mental *activity*? The texts may at first suggest a negative answer to this question. Locke clearly classifies perception, no less than
volition, as an "action of the mind" (E II.vi.2: 128) or "act of the Understanding" (E II.xxi.5: 236). From this it appears to follow that perception is a mental
action, though one that is sometimes involuntary (as in the case of the mind's
receipt of ideas from sensation or reflection).

However, in the fifth edition of the *Essay*, Locke clarifies matters by
explaining that the term "action," as he uses it, does not always refer to
actions. He writes:

Locke, First Edition. Samuel C. Rickless.
© 2014 Samuel C. Rickless. Published 2014 by John Wiley & Sons, Ltd.

I have said above, that we have *Ideas* but of two sorts of *Action*, viz. *Motion* and *Thinking*. These, in truth, though called and counted *Actions*, yet, if nearly considered, will not be found to be always perfectly so. For, if I mistake not, there are instances of both kinds [i.e., motion and thinking], which, upon due consideration, will be found rather *Passions* than *Actions*, and consequently so far the effects barely of passive Powers in those subjects, which yet on their account are thought *Agents*. (E II.xxi.72: 285)

Locke tells us that in the case of motion, if a body moves as a result of having been moved by another, then its motion counts as a passion; it is only when a body moves itself or another that we can properly speak of its motion as an action. Similarly, if a mind receives ideas from without, then its thinking counts as a passion; it is only when a mind brings ideas into view by its own choice that we can properly speak of its thinking as an action (E II.xxi.72: 285–286).

Strictly speaking, then, not all of the events Locke *calls* "actions" are actions. Some of these events are passions, metaphysically speaking. These passions include perception of ideas of sensation, as well as perception of ideas of reflection. Does it follow that all perception is passive? Or does Locke treat some forms of perception as active?

Locke notes that there are various modes of perception or ways of thinking, including (but not limited to) sensation, remembrance, recollection, attention, contemplation, reverie, study, dreaming, and ecstasy. Sensation is the perception of an idea derived from the senses; remembrance, the percep of an idea that recurs in the absence of sensation (with the consciousness of having had it before); recollection, the kind of remembrance that occurs when the remembered idea is "sought after by the mind, and with pain and endeavour found"; attention, the perception of an idea that is "taken notice of, and, as it were, registerd in the Memory"; contemplation, a particularly lengthy form of attention; reverie, the perception of an idea without attention; study, a particularly intense form of contemplation in which the mind is impervious to distraction; dreaming, the perception of an idea "not suggested by any external Objects, or known occasion"; and ecstasy (i.e., hallucination), the kind of dreaming that occurs with the eyes open (E II.xix.1: 226–227).

A cursory inspection of these modes of perception reveals that while some perceptions are involuntary, others are clearly voluntary. We have no control over whether we sense, remember, dream, or hallucinate; but we do have control over whether we attend, recollect, contemplate, or study. It follows that the former perceptions are passions, while the latter are actions.

In addition to the various modes or ways of perceiving or thinking of ideas, Locke discusses many other mental acts or operations, including doubting, believing, reasoning, knowing, willing (E II.i.4: 105), judging (E II.xix.2: 227), discerning (distinguishing) (E II.xi.1–3: 155–157), comparing (E II.xi.4–5: 157–158), composing (compounding, combining) (E II.xi.6–7: 158), and abstracting (E II.xi.9: 159). The significant question that Locke does not explicitly address concerning most of these mental operations is whether they count as exercises of the faculty of perception or exercises of the faculty of volition. Locke eventually defines knowledge as perception of an agreement or disagreement between two ideas (E IV.ii.15: 538), and so treats knowing as an exercise of the faculty of perception, while willing is clearly an exercise of the faculty of volition. But it is unclear how Locke would classify the remainder of the mental operations mentioned above. Indeed, if we consider the issue more closely, we see that it poses something of an embarrassment for Locke's mental economy.

It should be clear, for example, that discerning/comparing/composing/abstracting are things the mind does as a consequence of willing to discern/compare/compose/abstract. In this sense, these four mental operations are voluntary. But it does not follow, nor would Locke think it follows, that the four mental operations are themselves exercises of the faculty of volition. Indeed, they are not, for only willings themselves are exercises of this faculty. According to what appears to be Locke's official account of the mind as having two faculties, understanding and will, it would follow that discerning, comparing, composing, and abstracting are all modes of perception. But this, too, seems wrong. Distinguishing between two ideas (or comparing them, or combining them, or abstracting one from the other) is not a way of perceiving an idea, in the way that, say, attentively considering, studying, or recollecting an idea is a way of perceiving it. The same might be said of doubting, believing, reasoning, and judging. Judging, in particular, is defined as the presumption (rather than the perception) of an agreement or disagreement between ideas (E IV.xiv.3–4: 653). To make matters worse, Locke in one place characterizes volition as a mode of thinking – that is, as a mode of perception, though this is not consistent with his official distinction between perceiving and willing (see E II.xix.2: 227).

The best way out of this interpretive conundrum is to suppose that Locke does not mean the activities of the faculty of understanding to be limited to active perception and its various modes. Sometimes the mind performs mental acts that are not ways of perceiving. Included among these acts are the operations the mind performs on ideas, namely distinguishing, combining, comparing, and abstracting. But this requires us to think of thought as the genus, with perception as one of its many species. This is not strictly consistent with Locke's identification of perception with thought, but it seems the least theoretically disruptive way of reconciling the various things that Locke wants to say about what the mind can do.

Among the mind's operations, Locke includes what are ordinarily thought of as passions or affections. He writes: "The term *Operations* here, I use in a large sence, as comprehending not barely the Actions of the Mind about its *Ideas*, but some sort of Passions arising sometimes from them, such as is the satisfaction or uneasiness arising from any thought" (E II.i.4: 105–106). (This fits with Locke's telling us in the fifth edition – see the discussion of E II. xxi.72 above – that he uses the term "action" to refer to both actions and passions.) Locke makes clear that "satisfaction" is one of the many names we use to refer to pleasure, while "uneasiness" is one of the many names we use to refer to pain (E II.vii.2: 128).[2] In Hobbesian vein, Locke provides us with a brief analysis of a number of modes of pleasure and pain (including love, hatred, desire, joy, sorrow, hope, fear, despair, anger, and envy – E II.xx.4–13: 230–231), each of which counts as a passion (rather than an action). But Locke is not interested in the metaphysics of the passions, in the way that, say, his successor Hume is.

Locke's picture of the mind's properties, then, is this. The mind possesses both passive powers and active powers. When its passive powers are exercised, it experiences sensitive or reflective perceptions, conation (i.e., desire), or emotions/feelings (e.g., love, sorrow, fear). When its active powers are exercised, it voluntarily acts on ideas in various ways, whether by attending, recollecting, contemplating, studying, combining, separating, comparing, abstracting, knowing, judging, believing, doubting, reasoning, or, of course, willing. Perception is sometimes passive (sensation, reflection), sometimes active (attention, recollection, contemplation, study). All pleasures, pains, desires, emotions, and feelings are passive. And all other mental events (combining, separating, etc.) are active. Metaphysically, the active/passive distinction turns out to be a much better way of dividing up what happens in the mind than the perception/volition distinction, as Locke himself came to recognize in the fifth edition of the *Essay*.

7.2   Will and Willing

An event counts as an action *in the strict sense* only if it is voluntary. The mark of a passively received mental state (e.g., a sense perception or pain) is that it is involuntary. But what is it for an occurrence to be voluntary? And what is it for an occurrence to be involuntary?

Locke begins his discussion of (in)voluntariness by defining "will" and "willing." These definitions underwent significant revision in the second edition of the *Essay*, revisions that were retained (with one very minor alteration) in all subsequent editions. It is well worth our while to compare the two definitions, as they appear in the first and second editions:

> [W]e find in our selves a *Power* to begin or forbear, continue or end several, Thoughts of our minds, and motions of our Bodies, barely by the choice or preference of our Minds. This *Power* the Mind has to prefer the consideration of any *Idea*, to the not considering; or to prefer the motion of any part of the body to its rest, is that, I think, we call the *Will*; and the actual preferring one to another, is that we call *Volition*, or *Willing*. (E II.xxi.5: 236 – first edition)

> [W]e find in our selves a *Power* to begin or forbear, continue or end several actions of our minds, and motions of our Bodies, barely by a thought or

preference of the mind ordering, or as it were commanding the doing or not doing such or such a particular action. This *Power* which the mind has, thus to order the consideration of any *Idea*, or the forbearing to consider it; or to prefer the motion of any part of the body to its rest, and *vice versa* in any particular instance is that we call the *Will*. The actual exercise of that power, by directing any particular action, or its forbearance is that which we call *Volition* or *Willing*. (E II.xxi.5: 236 – second edition)

As should be plain, whereas the first edition passage defines the will as a power of *preferring*, the corresponding second edition passage defines the will as a power of *ordering/commanding* (in the case of the mind) and as a power of *preferring* (in the case of the body). In both editions, volition (or willing) is defined as the actual exercise of the relevant power: an actual instance of preferring according to the first, or an actual instance of ordering/commanding (directing) according to the second.[3]

That Locke went to this kind of trouble suggests that the difference between the definitions in the first and second editions was theoretically important to him. And, indeed, in the second and subsequent editions Locke explains why this is so. In a passage added to the second edition, Locke writes:

I must here warn my Reader that *Ordering, Directing, Chusing, Preferring,* etc. which I have made use of, will not distinctly enough express *Volition,* unless he will reflect on what he himself does, when he *wills.* For example, *Preferring* which seems perhaps best to express the Act of *Volition,* does it not precisely. For though a Man would prefer flying to walking, yet who can say he ever *wills* it? (E II.xxi.15: 240–241 – second edition)

Locke here points out that the terminology he uses in defining the will and volition is potentially misleading if one does not reflect properly on the relevant definienda. He insists, in particular, that it is *inaccurate* to describe willing as a kind of preferring, given that it is possible (and often actual) to prefer flying without willing to fly. Why this is becomes clearer when Locke, in a section entitled "*Will and Desire must not be confounded*," clarifies what he takes the state of preferring to be:

I have above endeavoured to express the Act of *Volition,* by *chusing, preferring,* and the like Terms, that signify *Desire* as well as *Volition,* for want of other words to mark that Act of the mind, whose proper Name is *Willing* or *Volition.* (E II.xxi.30: 249 – second edition)

The reason, then, why it is possible to prefer flying without willing to fly is that preferring (in the relevant sense) is a kind of *desiring* or *wanting*: I may *want* to fly even though I do not *will* to fly. Indeed, Locke provides two further examples in which "*Will* and *Desire* run counter" to establish that willing should not be confused with desiring: (i) a man may, under threat or duress, will to persuade a friend, even though he does not desire that his friend be persuaded; and (ii) a man with gout may desire the removal of his pain but, knowing that such removal will result in a worsening of his condition, not will such removal (E II.xxi.30: 250 – second edition).

By the time of the second edition, Locke realized that his definitions of the will and volition were ambiguous, and hence potentially misleading. In the first edition, the will is defined as the power to *prefer* considering an idea to not considering it, or to *prefer* the motion of a part of one's body to its rest. But Locke recognizes that the term "prefer" can also be used to mean "desire," and that desiring is not the same as willing (for it is possible to desire that p without willing that p, and it is possible to will that p without desiring that p). So Locke redefines the will as the power to *order* the consideration (or non-consideration) of an idea, or to *direct* the motion (or rest) of a part of one's body; and correspondingly redefines volition (or willing) as the exercise of this power, rather than as the exercise of the power of desire. To will, therefore, on Locke's view, is to command or direct one's own mind or body to act, or to forbear to act, in this or that particular way. And the will, for Locke, is just the power to will.[4]

7.3 Voluntariness and Involuntariness

Although Locke's definitions of the will and volition shift between the first and second editions of the *Essay*, his understanding of voluntariness and involuntariness remains constant. In all editions, Locke holds that an action is *voluntary* if and only if its performance is "consequent to" a volition to do so, and that an action is *involuntary* if and only if it "is performed without" a volition to do so (E II.xxi.7: 237 – first edition; E II.xxi.5: 236 – second edition). These characterizations require further refinement.

Strictly understood, Locke's account of voluntariness commits him to the view that it is sufficient for an action to be voluntary that it be preceded in time by a volition to perform it. But this is false, and it is reasonable to suppose that Locke would have recognized its falsity if he had had more time to think about the issue. Suppose that immediately after willing to drop his weapon, Joe suffers a bout of cowardly ideation (unconnected to his volition) that causes him to drop his weapon. It should be clear that Joe's dropping his weapon is not voluntary despite the fact that his action is preceded in time by the volition to perform it. What Locke should claim, then, is not that an action is voluntary whenever it is *consequent to* a volition to perform it, but rather that an action is voluntary whenever it is *caused by*[5] a volition to perform it. Correlatively, Locke should say that an action is *involuntary* whenever it is *not* caused by a volition to perform it (even if it is preceded by such a volition), rather than that an action is involuntary whenever it fails to be preceded by a volition to perform it.

7.4 Freedom, Necessity, and Determination of the Will

Locke's understanding of freedom and necessity also remains stable throughout the various editions of the *Essay*. Like his predecessor Thomas Hobbes, Locke takes freedom (or liberty) of action to be "the power a Man has to do or forbear doing any particular Action, according as its doing or forbearance has the actual preference in the Mind, which is the same thing as to say, according as he himself *wills* it" (E II.xxi.15: 241). Put generally, freedom of action is the power to do what one wills.[6] And put more particularly, freedom *with respect to a particular action A* is a dual ability consisting of (i) the ability to perform A if one wills to perform A, and (ii) the ability not to perform A if one wills not to perform A. For example, "a Man standing on a cliff, is at liberty to leap twenty yards downwards into the Sea . . . because he has a power to leap, or not to leap [as he wills]," but "if a greater force than his, either holds him fast [a case of restraint: E II.xxi.13: 240], or tumbles him down [a case of compulsion: E II.xxi.13: 240], he is no longer free in that case: Because the doing, or forbearance of that particular Action, is no longer in his power" (E II.xxi.27: 247–248). And an action is *necessary* when the relevant agent is not free with respect to it.[7]

Locke's theory of freedom is compatibilist: freedom, for Locke, is compatible (i.e., logically consistent) with determinism, and in particular with the thesis that every choice and every action is (deterministically and nonprobabilistically) caused by a motive or judgment. The fact that one's choices and actions are caused does not take away from one's *ability* to do what one wills. And, indeed, Locke insists that our volitions are determined. In the first edition, Locke assumes that volitions are determined by (the appearance or perception of) the greater good (E II.xxi.29: 251; E II.xxi.33: 256). The idea is that one wills or chooses only what one perceives to be good and avoids only what one perceives to be bad. This assumption makes sense of many of our choices. But as Locke recognizes in the second and subsequent editions (after having been prodded by his friend William Molyneux), weakness of will is possible; that is, there are possible circumstances in which persons fail to choose what they perceive to be good, and possible circumstances in which they choose and pursue what they perceive to be bad. For example, it can happen that a man is convinced that it is better to be rich than poor, and yet out of general contentment with his lot fails to pursue wealth; and it can happen that a drunkard continues to drink despite being aware of the fact that drinking will bring about the loss of his health, wealth, and future happiness (E II.xxi.35: 253).

Locke's acceptance of the possibility of weakness of will leads him to revise his account of what determines the will. In the second edition, Locke claims that the will is generally (i.e., for the most part) determined, not by perception of the good, but rather by the greatest and so most pressing uneasiness (or pain) in the want or lack of the good (E II.xxi.35: 253; E II.xxi.40: 257–258).

On this view, the man who realizes that wealth is better than penury will be driven to pursue his own enrichment only if he feels pain at the want of money; and the drunkard who realizes that it is better to save his liver will stop drinking only if he feels pain at the want of sobriety.

The will, then, is the power to order consideration of an idea or motion/ rest of one's body; willing is the exercise of this power; and freedom (of action) is the power to do what one wills. It is no surprise, then, that when Locke turns his attention to the debate over the existence and possibility of free will, his first conclusion is that freedom of the will is literally impossible. Indeed, the question of free will, literally taken, is "altogether improper," for "it is as insignificant to ask, whether Man's *Will* be free, as to ask, whether his Sleep be Swift, or his Vertue square." The reason is that "*Liberty*, which is but a power, belongs only to Agents, and cannot be an attribute or modification of the *Will*, which is also but a Power" (E II.xxi.14: 240). A power, being a relation (E II.xxi.19: 243), is not the kind of thing that is capable of having a power. Only agents – that is, substances – can have powers.

But Locke thinks that the question of free will is better understood, not as the question whether the will is free, but rather as the question "*Whether a Man be free to will.*" As he sees it, *this* is the question that "is meant, when it is disputed, Whether the *will* be free" (E II.xxi.22: 245). Though this question is significant in the way that the literally understood free will question is not, Locke sees it as ambiguous, and hence splits it into two further questions. The first question is whether human beings are ever free with respect to the act of willing, whether they are ever free to will-or-not-will, and, in particular, whether they can ever avoid willing one way or the other with respect to the performance of a particular action. The second question is whether human beings who will to perform action A (whatever A may be) are ever free with respect to the act of willing A. The difference between the questions is subtle, but significant. And, indeed, Locke splits them because he thinks that they should be answered differently.

Let us consider the first question. Matters are complicated by the fact that Locke's answer to it changed slightly from the first to the fifth edition, almost certainly because he came to realize that change was logically forced by the addition of E II.xxi.47 to the second edition. E II.xxi.47 defends what we might call "the doctrine of suspension." Recall that Locke claims that the will is ordinarily – that is, *for the most part* – determined by the greatest and most pressing uneasiness (E II.xxi.40: 257–258). But, as he emphasizes in E II.xxi.47, the will is *not always* determined by the greatest uneasiness. For the mind, he says, in most cases has "a power to *suspend* the execution and satisfaction of any of its desires" (E II.xxi.47: 263), and so "may suspend the act of [its] choice from being determined for or against" the action that its most pressing uneasiness is pushing it to perform (E II.xxi.56: 270). For example, a man whose most pressing uneasiness is driving him to drink has the power to avoid willing one way or the other with respect to the act of drinking. If he exercises this power, he enters a state of volitional suspension (in which he holds his will undetermined – E II.xxi.52: 267) during which he has time to reflect on the likely consequences of drinking. And if he so reflects, he may come to recognize that drinking is bad for him, a recognition that may engender an uneasiness at the lack of sobriety that is *more pressing* than the initial uneasiness at the lack of inebriation. If this happens, he will be able to leave his state of volitional suspension by permitting his will to be determined by the newly engendered uneasiness, and thereby choose to stay home rather than go to the pub. Indeed, for Locke, the power of suspension is quite literally a gift from God, the purpose of which is to make it possible for us to achieve happiness – that is, "the utmost Pleasure we are capable of" (E II.xxi.56: 271; E II.xxi.42: 258). Notice, however, that there will be cases in which humans *lack* the power to suspend willing, "as when the pain of the Rack, an impetuous *uneasiness,* as of Love, Anger, or any other violent Passion, running away with us, allows us not the liberty of thought, and we are not Masters enough of our own Minds to consider throughly, and examine fairly" (E II.xxi.53: 267–268).

To understand the impact of the doctrine of suspension on Locke's answer to the first question, it helps to begin with the answer he provides in the first edition. He writes:

> *Willing,* or Choosing being an Action, and Freedom consisting in a power of acting, or not acting, *a Man in respect of willing any Action in his power once proposed to his Thoughts cannot be free.* (E II.xxi.23: 245 – first edition)

This passage strongly suggests that Locke's answer to the first question is a resounding and unqualified "no." That is, once it is proposed to us to perform or to forbear performing a particular action, we do not have the power to avoid willing one way or the other with respect to its performance or nonperformance: it is necessary that we either will to perform the action or will not to perform it. The reason for this, Locke tells us, is that (i) it is necessary that the action be either performed or not performed, (ii) that it is necessary that if the action is performed, it is because we will to perform it, and (iii) that it is necessary that if the action is not performed, it is because we will not to perform it. Thus, whether the action is performed or not, "the act of volition" is "that which [we] cannot avoid." And if we are not able to avoid willing, then, according to Locke's definition of freedom, we are not free with respect of the act of willing (E II.xxi.23: 245–246).

Locke illustrates this thesis by means of a useful example. He writes:

> [A] Man that is walking, to whom it is proposed to give off walking, is not at liberty, whether he will *will,* or no: He must necessarily prefer one, or t'other of them; walking, or not walking. (E II.xxi.24: 246 – first edition)

In this sort of case, a man, while engaged in the process of walking at a particular time, considers whether to continue the process or stop the process at that time. Locke's thesis is that, under these circumstances, if the process continues, that must be because the walking man *wills* it to continue, while if the process stops, that must be because the walking man *wills* it to stop. So, whether the process continues or not, the walking man cannot avoid willing. And this seems eminently reasonable.

In the first edition, Locke assumes that all circumstances are similar to the walking man's circumstances in respect of whether willing is unavoidable. For, after describing the case of the walking man, he claims:

> and so it is in regard of all other Actions in our power; they being once proposed, the Mind has not a power to act, or not to act, wherein consists Liberty. (E II.xxi.24: 246)

But sometime after the first edition was published, Locke must have realized that this claim is false. For in the fifth edition, Locke adds an important qualification. The amended passage reads:

> and so it is in regard of all other Actions in our power so proposed, which are the far greater number. For considering the vast number of voluntary Actions, that succeed one another every moment that we are awake, in the course of our Lives, there are but few of them that are thought on or proposed to the *Will*, 'till the time they are to be done: And in all such Actions, as I have shewn, the Mind in respect of *willing* has not a power to act, or not to act, wherein consists Liberty. (E II.xxi.24: 246 – fifth edition)

The relevant qualification is this. Although *most* of the actions we perform upon consideration of the question whether to perform them involve the choice whether to presently continue or stop a process in which we are currently engaged, not all actions are of this kind. Sometimes it is proposed to us to initiate or forbear initiating a completely new action sometime in the future. This sort of action is not "thought on or proposed to the *Will*, 'till the time [it is] to be done," and so differs in this respect from the action in the walking man example. And with regard to *these* future actions, Locke's argument for the unavoidability of willing fails, and his conclusion is false, at least if the doctrine of suspension is true. For if one has and exercises the power to suspend willing to initiate some future action, one enters a state in which one neither wills to initiate the action nor wills not to initiate it. The possibility of such a state entails that premise (iii) of Locke's argument is false: it is not, in fact, necessary that if the action is not performed, it is because one wills not to perform it. Further, the conclusion of the argument is false as well: for if one can enter a state of volitional suspension (as seems possible with respect to future action initiations), then one can avoid willing the action's performance as well as its nonperformance. All of this fits with Locke's summary of his answer to the first question in a passage added to the fifth edition:

[I]n most cases a Man is not at Liberty to forbear the act of volition; he must exert an act of his *will*, whereby the action proposed, is made to exist, or not to exist. But yet there is a case wherein a Man is at Liberty in respect of *willing*, and that is the chusing of a remote Good as an end to be pursued. Here a Man may suspend the act of his choice from being determined for or against the thing proposed, till he has examined, whether it be really of a nature in it self and consequences to make him happy, or no. (E II.xxi.56: 270)

All of this strongly suggests that Locke revised his answer to the first question after having thought more carefully about the logical consequences of the doctrine of suspension inserted in the second edition. Locke initially inclines towards an unqualifiedly negative answer to the first question: it is *never* possible to avoid willing an action's performance or nonperformance. But, having acknowledged that it is possible to suspend willing the initiation of future actions (in order to consider whether such actions conduce to one's happiness), Locke later realizes that it is *sometimes* possible to avoid willing an action's performance or nonperformance. His considered (fifth edition) answer to the first question, then, is "most often no, but sometimes yes."

Let us now consider the second question, which is whether human beings who will to perform action A (whatever A may be) are ever free with respect to the act of willing A. Locke's answer to it is short, but also easily misunderstood:

[T]he next thing demanded is, *Whether a Man be at liberty to will which of the two he pleases, Motion or Rest.* This Question carries the absurdity of it so manifestly in it self, that one might thereby sufficiently be convinced, that Liberty concerns not the Will. For to ask, whether a Man be at liberty to will either Motion, or Rest; Speaking, or Silence; which he pleases, is to ask, whether a Man can *will*, what he *wills*; or be pleased with what he is pleased with. A Question, which, I think, needs no answer: and they, who can make a Question of it, must suppose one Will to determine the Acts of another, and another to determinate that; and so on *in infinitum*. (E II.xxi.25: 247)

It is easy to read Locke as saying that the question is absurd in the way that the original free will question is, and hence that the right answer to it must be negative. Locke tells us that it is not significant to ask whether the will is free, and hence concludes that it is absurd to suppose (i.e., necessarily false) that the will is free (because powers are not agents, and so cannot possess powers). But this is not the only way that questions can be absurd. If I ask you whether you are human, you might not unreasonably reply: "What an absurd question! Of course I'm human." From the fact that a question is absurd in *this* sense, it does not follow that the answer to it is a necessary falsehood. Indeed, what makes some questions absurd (including this one) is precisely that the answers to them are obvious truths!

Upon reflection, it should be evident that it is in the *latter* sense that Locke takes the second question to be absurd. For he tells us that the question reduces to the question "whether a Man can *will*, what he *wills*; or be pleased with what he is pleased with." And the answer to *this* question is clearly positive. That a man can will what he wills, that he can be pleased with what he is pleased with, follows directly from the axiomatic truth that actuality entails possibility – that is, that what *is* the case *can be* the case. It is precisely because the answer to it is obviously in the affirmative that Locke describes the question as "need[ing] no answer."

But why does Locke think that the second question reduces to the question whether one can will what one wills? The second question is whether someone who performs action A is *ipso facto* free with respect to the act of willing to perform A. Now, according to Locke's definition of freedom, to be free with respect to an act is (i) to be able to perform it if one wills to perform it, and (ii) to be able not to perform it if one wills not to perform it. It follows from this definition that to be free with respect to *the act of willing to perform A* is (i) to be able to will to perform A if one wills to will to perform A, and (ii) to be able not to will to perform A if one wills not to will to perform A. Given Locke's definition of freedom, then, the second question reduces to the question whether someone who performs A can will to perform A if she wills to will to perform A, and can will not to perform A if she wills not to will to perform A.

Locke acknowledges that it is possible to "make a Question" of his answer to the second question. Now, to make a question of something, in the relevant sense, is to raise an objection to it or to express a doubt about it.[8] So Locke's point at the end of E II.xxi.25 is that there are some who might doubt or object to his claim that the second question reduces to the question whether one can will what one wills. These doubters, Locke tells us, "must suppose one will to determine the Acts of another, and another to determinate that; and so on *in infinitum*." Why? Consider what is involved in willing to will to perform A. On one model (the doubters' model), willing to will is an act of one will determining the act of another will, and willing to will to will is an act of one will determining the act of a second will determining the act of a third will, and so on. On another model (Locke's model), willing to will to perform A is just the same as willing to perform A, and willing not to will to perform A is just the same as not willing to perform A. On the doubters' model, an infinite regress of wills beckons, and the question whether someone can will to perform A if she wills to will to perform A is less than obvious. On Locke's model, the infinite regress of wills collapses, and the question whether someone can will to perform A if she wills to will to perform A reduces to the question whether someone can will to perform A if she wills to perform A. This is why Locke thinks that the second question reduces to the question whether one can will what one wills.

So Locke divides the two questions (whether one is ever free with respect to the act of willing, and whether one is free with respect to the act of willing what one wills) because he thinks that they should be answered differently. In the case of most actions that one ever thinks of performing (i.e., those continuations or stoppings of processes that are proposed to the will at the time they are to be performed), one cannot avoid willing one way or the other, and so one is not free with respect to the act of willing. But when one considers initiating a future action and one's mind is not overwhelmed with pain or overcome by a violent passion, one has the power to suspend willing and one is therefore free to will or not to will. By contrast, one is always and obviously free to will to do what one wills to do. But this result is a trivial consequence of Locke's definition of freedom, conjoined with the view that willing to will reduces to willing, while willing not to will reduces to not willing.

Locke treats the power to suspend willing as "the source of all liberty" (E II.xxi.47: 263), "the hinge on which turns the *liberty* of intellectual Beings in their constant endeavours after, and a steady prosecution of true felicity" (E II.xxi.52: 266–267), and "the great inlet, and exercise of all the *liberty* Men have, are capable of, or can be useful to them, and that whereon depends the turn of their actions" (E II.xxi.52: 267). Why does he say this if he treats liberty generally as the power to do what one wills? After all, does one not retain *this* power, and so retain one's freedom of action, even if one loses the power to suspend willing? Locke's thought here is that freedom of action would not mean much if one lacked the power of suspension. For if one could do what one wills without being able to avoid willing, then, depending on the sorts of pressing uneasinesses under which one happens to labor, one might not be able to avoid choosing the worst options and living unhappily as a result. It is to the power of suspension, and not to any other mental faculty, that one owes one's ability to achieve happiness in the long run (at least when one is not overcome by pain or some destructive emotion). And the reason why this power is the source, hinge, and inlet of liberty is that it is itself the source of a particular instance of freedom of action, namely freedom in respect of the act of willing.

7.5   A Problem

Suppose, then, along with Locke, that with respect to most proposed future action initiations one has the power to suspend willing. If one exercises this power, then one suspends the prosecution of one's desires – that is, one holds one's will undetermined (E II.xxi.52: 267). Suspension, then, is an act of the mind, and indeed a *voluntary* act: if one holds one's will undetermined, it is because one wills that one's will remain undetermined. But what determines *this* act of will? Locke's view is that all acts of will are determined by the most pressing uneasiness, except in those cases in which one exercises the power to suspend willing. So, in most cases, one's volition that one's will remain undetermined is itself determined by the most pressing uneasiness, presumably uneasiness at the lack of one's will being undetermined. But then, in such cases, one is the creature, rather than the master, of one's own uneasinesses. Of course, as Locke also holds, we have the power to suspend willing, and so have the power to suspend willing one way or the other with respect to whether one's will shall remain undetermined. But when this power is exercised, it is also exercised voluntarily: if one suspends willing in respect of whether one's will shall remain undetermined, then this is because one wills that one's will remain undetermined in respect of whether one's will shall remain undetermined. And again, it seems possible to voluntarily suspend *this* act of willing, in which case one wills that one's will remain undetermined in respect of whether one's will shall remain undetermined in respect of whether one's will shall remain undetermined. An infinite regress of voluntary suspensions of ever greater complexity beckons.

It must be admitted that this is a problem for Locke, one that he never recognizes and so never addresses. What renders the problem particularly irksome is that it is precisely because of an infinite regress of this sort that Locke rejects the doubters' objection to his answer to the second question. As far as I can tell, there is no satisfactory solution to it that does not itself abandon one or more of the central pillars of Locke's theory of freedom and motivation. Still, its failure on the whole does not detract much from its admirable complexity and sophistication. Locke's theory of freedom is by far the most elaborate and engaging of those provided by his predecessors and contemporaries, and clearly repays careful examination.

notes

1 This division mirrors the main division of mental faculties to be found in the work of Descartes, Malebranche, and Berkeley.
2 Other names for pleasure include "delight" and "happiness." Other names for pain (in its varying degrees) include "trouble," "torment," "anguish," and "misery" (E II.vii.2: 128–129).
3 See E II.xxi.28: 248: in the first edition, volition is characterized as "the *preferring* the doing any thing, to the not doing of it"; in the second edition, volition is defined as "an act of the Mind directing its thought to the production of any Action, and thereby exerting its power to produce it." And in the second edition of E II.xxi.30, Locke writes that "*Volition* is nothing, but that particular determination of the mind, whereby, barely by a thought, the mind endeavours to give rise, continuation, or stop to any Action, which it takes to be in its power."
4 It is not clear whether it makes sense to conceive anything (including the mind) as ordering *itself* to do something. Locke must be thinking that it is possible to distance oneself from oneself sufficiently to allow for this kind of self-directed command. Perhaps the way to do this is to conceive of the mind as divided, as on some (most likely, mistaken) models of self-deception it is.
5 And, perhaps, to avoid deviant causal chains, only caused *in the right way* by.
6 "[W]e can scarce tell how to imagine any Being freer, than to be able to do what he *wills*" (E II.xxi.21: 244).
7 Locke concludes that "*Voluntary . . . is not opposed to Necessary*" (E II.xxi.11: 239), for it is possible to stay in a locked room because one wills to stay there, in which case one's stay is both voluntary and necessary (E II.xxi.10: 238).
8 *Oxford English Dictionary*, "question," Phrases (b).

further reading

Chappell, Vere, "Locke on the Freedom of the Will," in *Locke's Philosophy: Content and Context*, edited by G.A.J. Rogers. Oxford: Oxford University Press, 1994, pp. 101–121.

Chappell, Vere, "Power in Locke's *Essay*," in *The Cambridge Companion to Locke's "Essay Concerning Human Understanding"*, edited by Lex Newman. Cambridge: Cambridge University Press, 2007, pp. 130–156.

LoLordo, Antonia, *Locke's Moral Man*. Oxford: Oxford University Press, 2012, chapter 1.

Lowe, E.J., *Locke*. New York: Routledge, 2005, chapter 5.

Magri, Tito, "Locke, Suspension of Desire, and the Remote Good," *British Journal for the History of Philosophy* 8 (2000): 55–70.

Rickless, Samuel C., "Locke on the Freedom to Will," *Locke Newsletter* 31 (2000): 43–67.

Yaffe, Gideon, *Liberty Worth the Name: Locke on Free Agency*. Princeton, NJ: Princeton University Press, 2000.

relations

R elations are things that depend for their existence on more than one substance. The *husband* relation connects a male individual with his spouse; the *whiter* relation connects two substances that differ in whiteness; the *servant* relation connects an individual to her or his master. As Locke says: "[T]here can be no Relation, but betwixt two Things, considered as two Things" (E II.xxv.6: 321). So if either one of these things ceases to exist, then any relation that depends on them for its existence also ceases to exist:

> *The nature* therefore *of Relation*, consists in the referring, or comparing two things, one to another; from which comparison, one or both comes to be denominated. And if either of those things be removed, or cease to be, the Relation ceases, and the Denomination consequent to it, though the other receive in it self no alteration at all. *v.g. Cajus*, whom I consider to day as a Father, ceases to be so to morrow, only by the death of his Son, without any alteration made in himself. (E II.xxv.5: 321)

This conception of relation is coherent as far as it goes, and fits well with Locke's conception of entities as divided into the general categories of substance, mode, and relation. But it does suffer from one conspicuous drawback, which is that *some* relations do not relate one substance *to another*, but rather relate one substance *to itself*. Among relations of this sort we find any relation of the form *same F* (where F is a term for a kind of thing). So, for example, I am the same person as myself, but a different person from anyone else. The *same person* relation therefore does not relate me to another substance, but rather relates me to myself. Locke does say that "[t]here must always be in relation two *Ideas*, or Things, either in themselves really separate, <u>or considered as distinct</u>" (E II.xxv.6: 321 – underlining added). But this does not help the cause much, given that when I think of myself as related to myself by the relation of personal identity, I do not *consider* myself as distinct from myself any more than I *am* distinct from myself.[1]

Locke, First Edition. Samuel C. Rickless.
© 2014 Samuel C. Rickless. Published 2014 by John Wiley & Sons, Ltd.

Leaving this problem to one side, Locke does not devote much effort to discussing the nature of relations in general. Rather, he focuses on particular relations of either metaphysical or moral significance. In Book II of the *Essay*, Chapter xxvi is devoted to *cause and effect* (and other relations of time and space), Chapter xxvii to *identity and diversity* (including personal identity), and Chapter xxviii to four types of relation (proportional, natural, instituted, and moral – with particular emphasis on the latter).

Locke's conception of the nature of causation is not well developed, but anticipates the far more influential conception articulated by his intellectual successor, David Hume. Hume famously claims that the concept of a cause is the concept of something that is temporally prior to and constantly conjoined with its effect. But Locke, too, claims that the idea of causation derives from the perception of a thing of one type being regularly followed by a thing of another type:

> That which produces any simple or complex *Idea*, we denote by the general name *Cause*; and that which is produced, *Effect*. Thus finding, that in that Substance which we call Wax, Fluidity, which is a simple *Idea*, that was not in it before, is constantly produced by the Application of a certain degree of Heat, we call the simple *Idea* of Heat, in relation to Fluidity in Wax, the Cause of it, and Fluidity the Effect. (E II.xxvi.1: 324)[2]

Far more interesting, from the point of view of later philosophical developments, are Locke's views on the nature of identity and diversity, and on the nature of moral relations.

8.1 Identity and Diversity

Locke claims that we form the idea of the relations of identity and diversity by comparing the idea of a thing, say X, existing at one time with the idea of a thing, say Y, existing at another time. What it is for X to be identical to Y (that wherein identity *consists*) is determined by two self-evident principles: (P1) that "it [is] impossible for two things of the same kind, to be or exist in the same instant, in the very same place," and (P2) that "[it is impossible for] one and the same thing [to exist] in different places" (E II.xxvii.1: 328). From P2, Locke infers directly that "one thing cannot have two beginnings of Existence" (for if X were to come into existence at place P1 and also at different place P2, then X would exist in two different places, which is impossible). And from P1, Locke infers directly that "two things [of the same kind cannot have] one beginning [of Existence]" (for if X and numerically distinct Y were of the same kind and came into existence in the same place, then two different things of the same kind would exist at the same time and place, which is impossible). Identity, for Locke, is therefore determined by *kind* and by *origin*. If X is of the same kind as Y, then X is numerically identical to Y if and only if X and

Y have the same origin (in space and time); if X and Y have the same origin, then X is numerically identical to Y if and only if X and Y belong to the same kind. Importantly, Locke allows that it is possible for two things to exist in the same place and time; but the two things must be of different kinds.

The case of a statue made out of a lump of clay is a good illustration of this principle. Imagine the lump (call it "Larry") molded into a statue (call it "Steve"). Although some philosophers might be tempted to say that Larry is identical to Steve, others, including Locke, conceive it possible for Larry and Steve to be numerically distinct, even though they exist in the same place at the same time, as long as Larry belongs to the kind "lump of clay" but not to the kind "statue," and Steve belongs to the kind "statue" but not to the kind "lump of clay."

Because the *kind* of thing to which a given entity belongs partially determines its identity over time, Locke emphasizes that the absence of confusion with regard to ascriptions of identity depends on having "precise Notions of the things to which [identity] is attributed" (E II.xxvii.1: 328). For the conditions of identity will depend on whether the relevant X that is being claimed to be identical to Y is a statue or a piece of clay, a collection of material particles or a living body, a human being or a person.

Locke therefore considers the main kinds of things that there are: substances, modes, and relations. Within the first category, Locke distinguishes between three sorts of substances: (i) God, a substance that exists at all places and times, (ii) finite spirits, and (iii) bodies. (Interestingly, Locke's principle of individuation suggests that it might be possible for a finite spirit to exist in the same place and time as a numerically distinct, living human body.) Locke claims that there should be no difficulty applying the concept of identity to God and to finite spirits, God being the only substance without a beginning in time, and one finite spirit X being identical to a finite spirit Y if and only if X and Y both came into existence at the same time and place. The same thing is true for modes and relations, each mode M1 (relation R1) being identical to mode M2 (relation R2) if and only if M1 and M2 (R1 and R2) have the same origin (E II.xxvii.2: 329).

The interesting, and potentially confusing, question, for Locke, is under what conditions body X counts as numerically identical to body Y. Here it turns out to matter what *kind* of body is at issue. Locke takes there to be three kinds of bodies: (i) simple bodies (i.e., atoms, or particles of matter), (ii) compound inanimate bodies (i.e., masses of matter), and (iii) compound animate bodies (plants, animals, and humans). The individuation of atoms is uncomplicated: atom A1 is identical to atom A2 if and only if A1 and A2 both came into existence at the same time and place. The individuation of masses of matter is completely determined by the individuation of their constituents, mass M1 being identical to mass M2 if and only if the atoms constituting M1 are identical to the atoms constituting M2 (no matter how those atoms might be arranged). By contrast, the individuation of a living human body depends *not* on the individuation of the atoms or masses that compose it at any time and place, but rather on the individuation of its *life*, namely an organization (or "disposition") of parts that is designed to distribute nourishment (E II. xxvii.4: 330–331). Thus, "the Identity of the same [living body] consists . . . in nothing but a participation of the same continued life" (E II.xxvii.6: 331). Locke recognizes, then, that the very same living body (plant, animal, or human) can continue to exist even as the atoms and masses of matter that constitute it differ from one moment to the next, indeed that the mass of matter that constitutes a living body at time T1 might have *no* atoms in common with the mass of matter that constitutes the *same* living body at time T2. Finally, regarding the category of human beings in particular, Locke takes pains to establish that sameness of finite spirit (or soul) is not sufficient for sameness of human being; for if it were sufficient, then transferring the soul of Heliogabalus into one of his hogs would, as we know it does not, turn the hog into a human being (E II.xxvii.6: 332).

Having discussed the individuation of modes, relations, and five kinds of substances (God, finite spirits, atoms, masses of matter, and living bodies), Locke turns his attention to the individuation of *persons*. Given that he has already discussed all the sorts of things there are in the world (substances, modes, and relations), it is at least initially unclear in which of these three categories Locke takes persons to belong. Scholarly opinion divides on the issue, some commentators taking Locke to hold that persons are modes, others taking him to hold that persons are substances. The truth, as I see it, is that Lockean persons must be substances. For Locke tells us that (the idea of) a person is (the idea of) a "thinking intelligent Being, that has reason and reflection, and can consider it self as it self, the same thinking thing in different times and places" (E II.xxvii.9: 335); so persons are beings that possess powers (the power to reason, the power to reflect, the power to consider itself as itself), and hence, given that "*Powers* belong only to *Agents*, and *are Attributes only of Substances*" (E II.xxi.16: 241), persons must count as Lockean substances.

But if (finite) persons are substances, then they are clearly neither atoms (for they are, if material, surely compound) nor masses of matter (for, again if material, they can lose and gain atoms without ceasing to exist). One question, then, is whether (finite) persons are living bodies or finite spirits (or perhaps some combination of the two). If a person is a living body, then its principle of individuation will be the same as the principle of individuation for living bodies; whereas if a person is a finite spirit, then its principle of individuation will be the same as the principle of individuation for finite spirits. However, as Locke methodically argues, the principle of individuation for persons differs both from the principle of individuation for living bodies and from the principle of individuation for finite spirits.

Locke makes four points, backed by four separate types of thought-experiment. First, he argues that sameness of living body is not *necessary* for sameness of person; for it is possible to conceive (and hence, for Locke, it is possible) that X is the same person as Y despite the fact that X's living body is numerically distinct from Y's living body. We may suppose, for example, that I am "conscious of any of the Actions of *Nestor*" at the siege of Troy; in that case, says Locke, I am "the same Person with *Nestor*," though it is clear that Nestor's living body is numerically distinct from mine, having begun to exist many years before mine did (E II.xxvii.14: 340). Similarly, Locke tells us that "if *Socrates* and the present Mayor of *Quinborough* agree [in identity of consciousness], they are the same Person" (E II.xxvii.19: 342). Locke also imagines a (now famous) case in which consciousness of past actions is transferred from one living body to another:

> [S]hould the soul of a Prince, carrying with it the consciousness of the Prince's past Life, enter and inform the Body of a Cobler as soon as deserted by his own Soul, every one sees, he would be the same Person with the Prince, accountable only for the Prince's Actions: But who would say it was the same Man? (E II.xxvii.15: 340)

Imagine, then, that the relevant transfer of consciousness takes place at T1. Locke's hypothetical is meant to establish that the person in the prince's body before T1 is numerically identical to the person in the cobbler's body after T1, even as the prince's body before T1 is numerically distinct from the cobbler's body after T1. If Locke is right, and conceivability is a guide to possibility, then sameness of personhood does not require sameness of living body.[3]

Locke is not shy to point out that this result pays interesting theological dividends. For the fact that it is possible for X to be the same person as Y despite the fact that X and Y do not have the same living body entails that it is possible for a person to be resurrected after death "in a Body not exactly in make or parts the same which he had [on Earth]" (E II.xxvii.15: 340). And this result is desirable, because the disintegration of a person P's living body B after death entails that resurrection *may* require the attachment of P to a living body that is numerically distinct from B.[4]

Second, Locke argues that sameness of living body is not *sufficient* for sameness of person; for it is possible to conceive (and hence, for Locke, it is possible) that X is a numerically distinct person from Y despite the fact that X's living body is numerically identical to Y's living body. Locke imagines a situation in which Socrates while awake does not partake of the same consciousness as Socrates while asleep, a situation in which waking Socrates is not conscious of any of sleeping Socrates's past actions or thoughts, and sleeping Socrates is not conscious of any of waking Socrates's past actions or thoughts (E II.i.11: 110). In this hypothetical scenario, Locke tells us, "[i]f the same *Socrates* waking and sleeping do not partake of the same *consciousness*, *Socrates* waking and sleeping is not the same Person," even though the living body of Socrates waking is numerically identical to the living body of Socrates sleeping (E II.xxvii.19: 342).[5]

Third, Locke argues that sameness of soul (or finite spirit) is not *necessary* for sameness of person (at least for all we know). Here Locke distinguishes between two possibilities: that the soul is material and that it is immaterial.

Locke's own view is that "the more probable Opinion is, that . . . conscious-ness is annexed to, and the Affection of one individual immaterial Substance" (E II.xxvii.25: 345). But, as he sees matters, it cannot be ruled out that God has "given to some Systems of Matter fitly disposed, a power to perceive and think" (E IV.iii.6: 540). So Locke divides the question of the necessity of same-ness of soul for sameness of personhood into two: (assuming souls are material) whether sameness of person requires sameness of *material* soul; and (assuming souls are immaterial) whether sameness of person requires sameness of *imma-terial* soul.

Suppose, then, that the soul is material. In that case, it would surely be a material compound, a mass of matter rather than an atom. But it is already clear from Locke's examination of the identity conditions of living bodies that sameness of living body does not require sameness of mass of matter, for one of the hallmarks of living bodies is that they persist through the loss and acquisition of atoms (and hence, through change of mass of matter). Similarly, Locke says, those who take the soul to be material "conceive personal Identity preserved in something else than Identity of [material] Substance; as animal Identity is preserved in Identity of Life, and not of [material] Substance" (E II.xxvii.12: 337). That is, sameness of person no more requires sameness of mass of matter than it requires sameness of living body.

Suppose, now, that the soul is immaterial. Here Locke is careful not to state unequivocally that sameness of personhood does not require sameness of immaterial soul. But he does claim that this is true *for all we know*. Locke would like to be able to imagine a hypothetical situation in which X is the same person as Y, though X's immaterial soul differs from Y's immaterial soul. Such a situation would be one in which Y is (or could be) conscious of some action or thought of X's. So the imaginability of the relevant hypothetical situ-ation depends on whether it is possible to imagine consciousness being trans-ferred from one immaterial soul to another. If the nature of immaterial substances were somehow incompatible with such transfers of consciousness, then Locke could not run a thought-experiment like the others against the relevant necessity claim. Still, Locke points out that nothing that we know of immaterial substances, should such things exist, rules out transfers of con-sciousness from one to another. He then concludes that "if the same con-sciousness . . . can be transferr'd from one thinking Substance to another, it will be possible, that two thinking Substances may make but one Person" (E II.xxvii.13: 338).

Fourth, Locke argues that sameness of soul (or finite spirit) is not *sufficient* for sameness of person (at least for all we know). Here again, the question divides into two, depending on whether one conceives of the soul as material or as immaterial. The first question is whether it could happen that two persons share the same material soul. Although Locke does not address the issue directly, it is clear what his answer would be. For Locke holds that it is conceivable for two persons (e.g., Socrates waking and Socrates sleeping) to share the same living body. By the same token, it should be conceivable (and so, possible) for two persons to be connected to the same mass of matter, and hence to the same material soul.

The second question is whether it could happen that two persons share the same immaterial soul. Locke argues that this could happen in principle if a soul could be "wholly stripp'd of all the consciousness of its past Existence, and lose it beyond the power of ever retrieving again" (E II.xxvii.14: 338). Then, discussing the case of a person who was convinced that his soul is the same as Socrates's soul, Locke insists that no one would say that this person, "being not conscious of any of *Socrates's* Actions or Thoughts, could be the same Person with *Socrates*." Similarly, Locke writes that even if one's soul were numerically identical to the soul of "*Nestor* or *Thersites*, at the siege of *Troy*," one could not "conceive [oneself] the same Person with either of them" if one had "no consciousness of any of the Actions [of either]" (E II.xxvii.14: 339).[6]

It follows from Locke's four points that sameness of living body or soul (whether material or immaterial) is (at least for all we know in the case of immaterial substance) neither necessary nor sufficient for sameness of person. And this entails that persons are neither living bodies nor souls, nor are they combinations of living bodies and souls. If persons are substances, as it seems they must be, then they are *sui generis*, and Locke's earlier claim (at E II. xxvii.2: 329) that God, finite spirits, and bodies are the only substances of which we can think is an overstatement.

Locke's four arguments reveal what he appears to treat as necessary and sufficient for sameness of person, namely sameness of *consciousness*. He tells us that "in [consciousness] alone consists *personal Identity*" (E II.xxvii.9: 335), that "*personal Identity* consists . . . in the Identity of *consciousness*" (E II. xxvii.19: 342), and that "*self* is . . . determined . . . only by Identity of consciousness" (E II.xxvii.23: 345); that "the same consciousness being preserv'd . . ., the personal Identity is preserv'd" (E II.xxvii.13: 338); that "consciousness . . . unites Existences, and Actions . . . into the same Person" (E II.xxvii.16: 340), and indeed "[n]othing but consciousness can unite remote Existences into the same Person" (E II.xxvii.23: 344). If the consciousness of X is the same as the consciousness of Y (as in the case of the prince and the cobbler), then X is the same person as Y; while if the consciousness of X differs from the consciousness of Y (as in the case of Socrates waking and Socrates sleeping), then X is a different person from Y.

It is not immediately clear what Locke takes this consciousness to be. Many have taken Locke to be identifying consciousness with memory. This is a natural interpretation of the text, given his explicit identification of consciousness with "a present representation of a past Action" (E II.xxvii.13: 337), and given how easily he slips from talk of consciousness to talk of memory, and vice-versa. For example, Locke treats the existence of "intervals of Memory and Forgetfulness" taking their turns regularly by day and night as sufficient for numerical distinctness of persons (E II.xxvii.23: 345); argues that any thought or action "which I cannot recollect [i.e., remember]" will not belong to me (E II.xxvii.24: 345); and treats irreversible total amnesia ("wholly los[ing] the memory of some parts of [one's] life, beyond a possibility of retrieving them") as sufficient for the existence of "distinct incommunicable consciousness at different times," and hence sufficient for numerical distinctness of persons (E II.xxvii.20: 342). Moreover, Locke often treats the fact of consciousness "reaching back" or "extending backwards" as sufficient for personal identity, where it is clear that such backwards reaching and extending is a matter of being conscious of (i.e., remembering) a past action or thought.[7]

Relying on these passages, memory theorists attribute to Locke the view that X is the same person as Y if and only if X remembers (or can remember) an action or thought of Y. But this would be to overread the relevant passages, all of which signal quite clearly that Locke takes the existence or possibility of recollection as *sufficient*, but not *necessary*, for personal identity. Indeed, given that Locke is surely well aware that identity is a symmetrical relation (if X is identical to Y, then Y is identical to X) while potential or actual recollection is not (it is not true that if X can or does remember a thought or action of Y, then Y can or does remember a thought or action of X), it would be very odd indeed for him to *identify* sameness of consciousness with the fact of (potential or actual) recollection. And, in an often overlooked passage, Locke himself underlines the point, writing that "it is by the consciousness [any intelligent being] has of its present Thoughts and Actions, that it is *self* to it *self* now, and so will be the same *self* as far as the same consciousness can extend to Actions past or to come" (E II.xxvii.10: 336 – underlining added).

What, then, is that consciousness, the sameness of which Locke appears to treat as both necessary and sufficient for sameness of person? Locke tells us that consciousness "is inseparable from thinking" and "always accompanies thinking" (E II.xxvii.9: 335), that it is "hard to conceive, that any thing should think, and not be conscious of it" (E II.i.11: 110), that it would be unintelligible to say "that any thing *thinks without being conscious of it*," and that "thinking consists in being conscious that one thinks" (E II.i.19: 115). Consciousness, in Locke's sense, is therefore a second-order mental operation (perception of perceiving or willing) that either invariably accompanies or constitutes every first-order mental operation (perception or volition). For example, if I am looking at a flower, I (first-order) perceive a number of ideas (of color, shape, and other qualities). Because I have the power of reflection, I (second-order) perceive the very act of (first-order) perception by which I perceive the flower. This very act of second-order perception is what consciousness of perceiving the flower amounts to. Moreover, as Locke tells us earlier in the *Essay*, reflection (which involves the perception of mental acts) is the source of simple ideas, ideas that represent the mental acts perceived. So consciousness, as Locke conceives of it, produces in the mind ideas of the mental activities of which one is conscious. So if I am perceiving, and thus also conscious of perceiving, a flower, that very consciousness issues in an idea that represents my act of perceiving the flower.

It follows from Locke's understanding of the nature of consciousness that X has the same consciousness as Y if and only if X and Y engage in the second-order act of perceiving the same first-order act of perception or volition. And because this second-order act is both necessary and sufficient for the production of an idea of that act, it also follows that X has the same consciousness as Y if and only if X and Y have a reflective idea that represents a second-order act of perceiving the same first-order act of perception or volition.

Let us consider briefly how this would work in a typical case of diachronic identity. Suppose that at the age of five X perceives a model sailboat in a fountain in the Tuileries Gardens in Paris. This first-order act of perception (call it "P1") is accompanied by a second-order act (call it "P2") of perceiving the first-order act of perception, a second-order act that itself produces an idea that represents that very second-order act. Later, at the age of forty-eight, Y engages in a second-order act (call it "P3") that represents P1, at which time Y also invariably perceives an idea of P3. According to Locke, this is the sort of event that is required for X and Y to possess the same consciousness. Notice that it is neither necessary nor sufficient for X to count as having the same consciousness as Y that X and Y engage in the same first-order or second-order act of perception. Locke emphasizes this when he writes that "the same Consciousness [is not] the same individual Action, . . . but [rather] a present representation of a past Action" (E II.xxvii.13: 337). This is important, because it is clear that a person at time T1 is not capable of engaging in a first- or second-order perceptual act that is numerically identical to an act engaged in by a person at T2. Each perceptual act is particular to its time and place, and cannot be identified with any perceptual act engaged in at a different time or place. Locke's genius here is to see the possibility of representing the same particular perceptual act at different times and places.[8]

With a clear understanding of the relation of sameness of consciousness in hand, we should now consider exactly how Locke conceives of the connection between this relation and the relation of personal identity. I said above that Locke appears to treat sameness of consciousness as both necessary and sufficient for sameness of person. But Locke's view is a bit more refined than this. For although there are clearly passages that point to *actual* identity of consciousness as constituting personal identity, there are also many passages that suggest that *potential* identity, rather than *actual* identity, of consciousness is what personal identity consists in. Here are a few representative instances (with the relevant modal language underlined):

And as far as this consciousness <u>can</u> be extended backwards to any past Action or Thought, so far reaches the Identity of that *Person*. (E II.xxvii.9: 335 – underlining added)

For as far as any intelligent Being <u>can</u> repeat the *Idea* of any past Action with the same consciousness it had of it at first, and with the same consciousness it has of any present Action; so far it is the same *personal self*. (E II.xxvii.10: 336 – underlining added)

For it is by the consciousness it has of its present Thoughts and Actions, that it is *self* to it *self* now, and so will be the same *self* as far as the same consciousness <u>can</u> extend to Actions past or to come. (E II.xxvii.10: 336 – underlining added)

For whatsoever any Substance has thought or done, which I <u>cannot</u> recollect, and by my consciousness make my own Thought and Action, it will [not] belong to me. (E II.xxvii.24: 345 – underlining added)

Locke's point in these passages is that the key to personal identity is not the fact of *having* the same consciousness, but rather the fact of *being capable of having* the same consciousness. Of course, if X *actually has* the same consciousness as Y, then (because actuality entails possibility) X *can have* the same consciousness as Y. Thus, *actual* identity of consciousness is sufficient for personal identity if *potential* identity of consciousness is. But *actual* identity of consciousness is not necessary for personal identity: it is possible for X to be the same person as Y even if X and Y do not have the same consciousness, as long as X and Y *can* have the same consciousness. Locke therefore misspeaks when he writes that someone who is "not conscious of any of *Socrates's* Actions or Thoughts, could [not] be the same Person with *Socrates*" or that no one who has "no consciousness of any of the Actions either of *Nestor* or *Thersites*, [can] conceive himself the same Person with either of them" (E II.xxvii.14: 339). It would have been more accurate for Locke to have said, instead, that it is because one *cannot* be conscious of the thoughts or actions of Socrates, Nestor, or Thersites that one is not the same person as any of them.

Of course it stands to reason that Locke should have held that *potential*, rather than *actual*, identity of consciousness is what personal identity consists in. It may well be that I do not now represent to myself any of the actions or thoughts I had when I was writing the previous chapter of this book. But surely no one, least of all Locke, would want to say that I am not the person who wrote the previous chapter. What matters, surely, is that I am *able to* represent the relevant actions or thoughts, and this I can surely do, either by sheer effort of will or by simply re-reading the previous chapter and recapturing the thought processes in which I was previously engaged.

There has been some controversy among Locke scholars about the best way of interpreting his use of "can" in the passages just quoted. When Locke says that an intelligent being "will be the same *self* as far as the same consciousness <u>can</u> extend to Actions past or to come," what sense of "can" does Locke have in mind? Logical possibility? Physical possibility? Metaphysical possibility? The answer, I believe, is the latter. Consider first whether Locke's use of "can" means *logical* possibility. In that case, Locke would be saying that X is the same person as Y as long as it is logically possible for X to have the same consciousness as Y. But a proposition's being logically possible consists in its not being self-contradictory. So Locke would be saying that X is the same person as Y as long as it is not self-contradictory for X to have the same consciousness as Y. The problem with this, as Locke would surely have been aware, is that it is not *self-contradictory* for *any* person to have the same consciousness as any *other* person: by no means does the proposition that I have the same consciousness as Nestor entail a contradiction. So if Locke were using "can" in the sense of logical possibility, then he would be advocating the absurdity that every person is identical to every other person. Surely this is not what Locke was trying to say.

Could Locke's use of "can," then, mean *physical* possibility? A proposition is physically possible if it is consistent with the laws of nature. Physical possibility differs from logical possibility, because although everything that is physically possible is logically possible, not everything that is logically possible is physically possible: it may be logically possible (because not self-contradictory) for me to hop over the Empire State building, but it is certainly not physically possible for me to do so. If Locke's use of "can" meant *physical* possibility, then he would be telling us that what makes X the same person as Y is the fact that it is consistent with the laws of nature for X and Y to have the same consciousness. On this view, if the laws of nature precluded the possibility of my being conscious of the actions or thoughts of the five-year-old boy who once walked the Tuileries Gardens in 1969, then I would not be the same person as that boy. But this is surely not Locke's view. For Locke believes in the Day of Judgment, "when every one shall *receive according to his doings, the secrets of all Hearts shall be laid open*" (E II. xxvii.26: 347). And on the Day of Judgment, Locke thinks, the persons God judges will have been resurrected, most likely with new, and surely incorruptible, bodies. But because resurrection is a miracle – that is, an act contrary to the laws of nature – it follows that it would be contrary to the laws of nature for a person on the Day of Judgment to have the same consciousness as any person now living. So, if Locke's use of "can" meant physical possibility, then Locke would be committed to the (from his point of view, false) proposition that no person on the Day of Judgment could be identical to any person now living.

The only reasonable interpretation, it seems to me, is to suppose that Locke's use of "can" means *metaphysical* possibility. A proposition is metaphysically possible if it is consistent, not with the laws of logic or with the laws of physics, but rather with the laws of metaphysics. It should be clear, first, that the laws of metaphysics differ from the laws of logic. Although it is clearly *logically* possible, Locke's view is that "we [do not conceive] it possible, that two things of the same kind should exist in the same place at the same time" (E II.xxvii.1: 328). But the possibility that two things of the same kind exist in the same spatio-temporal location is not ruled out by the laws of nature. So Locke must be thinking of the impossibility of co-locating two things of the same kind as a third kind of impossibility, distinct from both logical possibility and physical possibility. This is presumably the kind of impossibility at issue in the claim that it is impossible that Locke should have been a cat, namely *metaphysical* impossibility.

Locke's theory of personal identity, then, is this: X is the same person as Y if and only if it is metaphysically possible for X and Y to have the same consciousness – that is, if and only if it is metaphysically possible for X and Y to have a second-order perception of the same first-order action (perception or volition).

Having put forward the theory that personal identity consists in potential identity of consciousness, Locke then notes that the theory has important moral consequences, owing to the fact that personhood is forensic (i.e., connected to law):

> Person . . . is a Forensick Term appropriating Actions and their Merit; and so belongs only to intelligent Agents capable of a Law, and Happiness and Misery. This personality extends it *self* beyond present Existence to what is past, only by consciousness, whereby it becomes concerned and accountable, owns and imputes to it *self* past Actions, just upon the same ground, and for the same reason, that it does the present. (E II.xxvii.26: 346)

Locke's idea here is that punishment or reward is just if and only if it is deserved, and desert depends on personal identity, in the following sense: X deserves punishment or reward for an action committed by Y if and only if X is the same person as Y. As Locke rephrases the point: "In this *personal Identity* is founded all the Right and Justice of Reward and Punishment" (E II.xxvii.18: 341). It would be a mistake to suppose, as some have done, that Locke thinks of X's being justly deserving of reward or punishment as *definitive* or *criterial* of personal identity: it is not that being justly deserving of reward or punishment is what personal identity *consists in*. But Locke thinks that the inference from the idea of being justly punished (or rewarded) to the idea of being guilty (or responsible), and the inference from the idea of being guilty (or responsible) to the idea of being the same person as the person who performed the relevant action, are self-evident (see E IV.xvii.4: 673). It is on this basis that Locke insists that waking Socrates is not accountable for the actions of sleeping Socrates: "[T]o punish *Socrates* waking, for what sleeping *Socrates* thought, and waking *Socrates* was never conscious of, would be no more of Right, than to punish one Twin for what his Brother-Twin did, whereof he knew nothing, because their outsides were so like, that they could not be distinguished" (E II.xxvii.19: 342).[9]

There is, however, potential theoretical tension between Locke's theory of the nature of personal identity and his account of its forensic significance. Locke himself mentions one objection on this score:

> But is not a Man Drunk and Sober the same Person, why else is he punish'd for the Fact he commits when Drunk, though he be never afterwards conscious of it? (E II.xxvii.22: 343)

The problem stems from the fact that (enlightened) human systems of justice punish sober Socrates for the past actions of drunk Socrates. Assuming that the actions that (enlightened) human systems of justice treat as deserving of punishment are justly punished, and assuming (along with Locke's theory of personal identity) that sober Socrates is not the same person as drunk Socrates (for the same reason that waking Socrates is not the same person as sleeping Socrates), it follows that it is sometimes just to punish one person for the actions of another. But this result contradicts the forensic nature of personhood, according to which it is always unjust to punish one person for the actions of another.

In reply, Locke acknowledges that it may well be that the sober person is not (and, we may presume, could never be) conscious of any of the drunk person's actions, in which case the sober person and the drunk person are numerically distinct. But he insists that it might still be appropriate for human systems of justice to punish the sober person for the actions of the drunk person, because "they cannot distinguish certainly what is real, what counterfeit; and so the ignorance in Drunkenness . . . is not admitted as a plea" (E II.xxvii.22: 344). The problem, as Locke sees it, is that it is practically impossible to determine whether the sober person who claims not to be conscious (or not to be capable of being conscious) of any of the drunk person's actions is telling the truth. If ignorance were admitted as a plea, the threat of punishment would no longer deter criminal behavior, given that all potential perpetrators would know, before the fact, that such a plea would be sufficient for acquittal. Locke is therefore willing to accept the existence of occasional instances of injustice, given that the consequences of admitting ignorance as a plea would be far more deleterious than the consequences of not doing so. But he is confident that God will rectify these injustices on the Day of Judgment, a day when "no one shall be made to answer for what he knows nothing of" (E II.xxvii.22: 344).

Potentially more serious than this objection are the famous charges of circularity and internal inconsistency later leveled at Locke's theory by Joseph Butler, George Berkeley, and Thomas Reid. Butler writes:

> And one should really think it self-evident, that consciousness of personal identity presupposes, and therefore cannot constitute personal identity, any more than knowledge, in any other case, can constitute truth, which it presupposes.[10]

Butler's charge is that Locke's theory of personal identity is circular. For Butler takes Locke to be saying that personal identity consists in (i.e., is constituted by) consciousness, that the consciousness that is supposed to constitute personal identity is consciousness *of personal identity*, and hence that the consciousness that is supposed to constitute personal identity presupposes, and hence cannot constitute, personal identity.

Butler's circularity criticism fails, however. For although some of what Locke writes might be read to suggest as much, Locke's considered view is that the consciousness that constitutes personal identity is not consciousness *of personal identity*, but rather consciousness *of a person's actions or thoughts*. It is true that Locke writes that *"personal Identity* consists . . . in the Identity of *consciousness"* (E II.xxvii.19: 342). But he does not here (or anywhere) say (or imply) that X is the same person as Y if and only if X is (or can be) conscious *of being the same person as* Y. What Locke means is no more than that X is the same person as Y if and only if X can be conscious of some thought or action of Y. This account of personal identity is no more circular than the obviously non-circular theory according to which X is the same person as Y if and only if X approves of some thought or action of Y.

Easily the most serious objection to Locke's theory of personal identity, an objection that has spawned numerous and interesting Lockean alternatives to Locke's own theory, derives from Berkeley and Reid. Though Berkeley was the first to notice the potential difficulty, Reid's objection is more colorful:

> Suppose a brave officer to have been flogged when a boy at school for robbing an orchard, to have taken a standard from the enemy in his first campaign, and to have been made a general in advanced life; suppose, also, which must be admitted to be possible, that, when he took the standard, he was conscious of having been flogged at school, and that, when made a general, he was conscious of his taking the standard, but had absolutely lost the consciousness of his flogging. These things being supposed, it follows, from Mr. Locke's doctrine, that he who was flogged at school is the same person who took the standard, and that he who took the standard is the same person who was made a general. Whence it follows, if there be any truth in logic, that the general is the same person with him who was flogged at school. But the general's consciousness does not reach so far back as his flogging; therefore, according to Mr. Locke's doctrine, he is not the person who was flogged. Therefore the general is, and at the same time is not, the same person with him who was flogged at school.[11]

Reid's charge is that Locke's theory of personal identity is internally inconsistent. For it follows from the theory that the general (who is conscious of some of the officer's actions) is the same person as the officer, and that the officer (who is conscious of some of the boy's actions) is the same person as the boy. But the relation of personal identity is transitive: *if* X is the same person as Y and Y is the same person as Z, *then* X is the same person as Z. Consequently, it follows that the general is the same person as the boy. Unfortunately, the general is not conscious of having been flogged as a boy, and we may suppose further that the general has lost all consciousness of *any* of the boy's actions. From this, Reid charges, it follows from Locke's theory that the general is *not* the same person as the boy. Consequently, Locke's theory entails that the general is, and is not, the same person as the boy. But this is a contradiction, and any theory that entails a contradiction is internally inconsistent.

Influential as this criticism has been, it is relatively easy to see why it too fails, though it must be admitted that Locke's poor choice of words is at least partly responsible for its continued appeal. Reid is surely right that Locke's theory of personal identity entails both that the general is the same person as the officer and that the officer is the same person as the boy. For if person X is actually conscious of some of the actions of person Y, then, as Locke sees matters, X is the same person as Y. Reid is surely also right that personal identity is transitive, and hence that Locke's theory entails that the general is the same person as the boy. But Reid errs in supposing that Locke's theory commits him to the view that the general is *not* the same person as the boy. As Reid describes the case, "the general's consciousness does not reach so far back as his flogging." However, as we have already seen, Locke's view is *not* that the general's not being *actually* conscious of the boy's actions is sufficient for the general to count as a different person from the boy, but rather that personal distinctness in the case requires that it be metaphysically impossible for the general to be conscious of the boy's actions. But even if it is *physically* impossible for the general to be conscious of the boy's actions, the relevant consciousness is not *metaphysically* impossible. For example, at the Day of Judgment it would, at least in Locke's eyes, be possible for God to restore consciousness of the boy's actions to the newly deceased general. Locke's theory therefore escapes from Reid's objection unharmed. That it appears to be vulnerable to such an objection stems from Locke's unfortunate failure to distinguish clearly between *actual* and *potential* consciousness.[12]

There is one passage in Locke's chapter on personal identity that interpreters have found it very difficult to make sense of, given everything else to which Locke commits himself. Locke claims that, for all we know, it could happen that "one intellectual Substance [might] have represented to it, as done by it self, what it never did, and was perhaps done by some other Agent" (E II. xxvii.13: 338). But he goes on to say that although it is, for all we know, *possible* for an intellectual substance to make this sort of mistake, God will guarantee that such a mistake never actually occurs:

> And that it never is so, will by us, till we have clearer views of the Nature of thinking Substances, be best resolv'd into the Goodness of God, who as far as the Happiness or Misery of any of his sensible Creatures is concerned in it, will not by a fatal Error of theirs transfer from one to another, that consciousness, which draws Reward or Punishment with it. (E II.xxvii.13: 338)

The problem with the passage is this. Locke assumes that if consciousness were transferred from one intellectual substance (or soul) to another, it would draw reward or punishment with it. But, as he affirms shortly after, "[i]n this *personal Identity* is founded all the Right and Justice of Reward and Punishment" (E II.xxvii.18: 341). So if consciousness were transferred from soul S1 to soul S2, the person attached to soul S1 (call this person "P1") would be identical to the person attached to soul S2 (call this person "P2"). As Locke also says: "[T]he same consciousness being preserv'd, . . . the personal identity is preserv'd" (E II.xxvii.13: 338). But then why would it be contrary to God's goodness for him to allow for such a transfer? If P2 were punished for an action committed by P1, then there would be no contravention of Locke's principle that no person is justly punished for the actions of another. Indeed, it seems no more problematic to punish P2 for the actions of P1 than it would be to punish the cobbler who is conscious of the prince's past actions for the prince's past actions.

The best interpretation of this passage, I believe, is to suppose that Locke means us to focus, not on the punishment of *persons*, but rather on the punishment of *souls*. Souls, after all, are thinking beings, capable of pleasure and pain. Given that punishment is the causation of pain for breach of a law (E II.xxviii.5: 351), it is possible to punish a soul just as much as it is possible to punish a person. Locke's question in the relevant passage is not whether God would permit a *person* who mistakenly represents himself as having done what a different *person* did to be punished for it, but rather whether God would permit a *soul* who mistakenly represents itself as having done what a different *soul* did to be punished for it. His answer to *this* question is: no. For although the *person* attached to the former soul might well be identical to the *person* attached to the latter soul, the relevant souls are numerically distinct (by hypothesis), and it is generally unjust to punish any *substance* for the actions of another. However, satisfying as this interpretation may be in some respects, it should be noted that it does not sit well with Locke's claim that *all* the right and justice of punishment is founded in *personal* identity. If Locke's statements are to be rendered mutually consistent, it would be best to read this claim as an overstatement, and to suppose that what he should have said, on reflection, is that all the right and justice of punishment is founded in identity of *personhood or thinking substance*.

8.2 Moral Relations

Having discussed the relations of identity and diversity, Locke briefly outlines four categories of relations, with special attention to moral relations. Locke focuses on these relations, both because they are of special significance given the rest of our interests and purposes and because they give him yet another chance to explain how we can acquire ideas of such relations on the basis of comparison and combination of simple ideas of sensation and reflection.

The first category consists of proportional relations, namely relations "depending on the Equality and Excess of the same simple *Idea*, in several Subjects," as in the case of "*Whiter, Sweeter, Bigger*," and so on (E II.xxviii.1: 349). The second category consists of natural relations, namely relations concerning "the Circumstances of . . . origin or beginning," as in the case of "*Father* and *Son, Brothers*, [and] *Country-men*" (E II.xxviii.2: 349). The third category consists of instituted (or voluntary) relations, namely relations "whereby any one comes by a Moral Right, Power, or Obligation to do something," as in the case of *"General"* (one who has the power to command an army), *"Citizen"* (one who has a right to certain privileges in a given society), or *"Army"* (those who are obligated to obey their commanding officers). The third category is distinct from the second, Locke tells us, by virtue of the fact that instituted relations, unlike natural relations, are "alterable, and separable from the Persons, to whom they have sometimes belonged, though neither of the Substances, so related, be destroy'd" (E II.xxviii.3: 350). For example, it is possible for a person who is now a general to cease to be a general (think: court-martial or dishonorable discharge), so being a general is an instituted relation; by contrast, it is not possible for a father to cease to be a father as long as he and his son remain alive, so being a father is a natural relation.

The most interesting category for Locke's purposes is the fourth, which comprises moral relations, namely relations that concern "the Conformity, or Disagreement, Men's voluntary Actions have to a Rule, to which they are referred, and by which they are judged of" (E II.xxviii.4: 350). The most important moral relations are moral goodness and moral badness, in the case of which the relevant rule is a law "whereby Good or Evil [i.e., pleasure or pain, in the form of reward or punishment] is drawn on us, from the Will and Power of the Law-maker" (E II.xxviii.5: 350).

Locke also distinguishes three sub-categories within the category of moral relations, depending on three kinds of law: corresponding to the divine law (or law of God) are duties and sins; corresponding to the civil law (or law of political societies) are innocent actions and criminal actions; and corresponding to the law of opinion (or law of fashion) are virtues and vices (E II.xxviii.8–10: 352–354). Locke claims that divine law is "the only true touchstone of *moral Rectitude*" (E II.xxviii.8: 352), and we may infer from this that Locke thinks it possible and coherent to criticize both the laws of political societies (e.g., a law that takes from the poor to give to the rich) and the law of fashion (e.g., dueling conventions) as morally bad from the divine standpoint. As to how one might come to knowledge of divine law, Locke says that it is "promulgated to [men] by the light of Nature, or the voice of Revelation" (E II.xxviii.8: 352). As examples of divine laws discovered by the light of nature (i.e., either because they are self-evident or because they self-evidently follow from self-evident principles), Locke lists *"Where there is no Property, there is no Injustice"* and *"No Government allows absolute Liberty"* (E IV.iii.18: 549–550), along with all the conditional ("if–then") principles that connect consecutive ideas in the following chain: *"Men shall be punished,—God the punisher,—just Punishment,—the Punished guilty—could have done otherwise—Freedom—self-determination"* (E IV.xvii.4: 673).

We will look at Locke's moral theory in more detail in Chapter 11. But in the meantime, it is worth noticing that Locke's theory of morality is firmly ensconced in the natural law tradition. According to this tradition, an action is right or wrong (a duty or a sin) depending on whether it conforms or disagrees with God's law, which is natural inasmuch as it is accessible to human reason. This raises the question of whether Locke's theory is a version of the divine command theory of morality. If it is, then it is vulnerable to objections that target divine command theories generally, the most important of which derives from Plato's *Euthyphro*. The problem is that the claim that actions are right because God commands us to perform them reverses the proper order of explanation: the truth, so the objection goes, is that God commands us to perform actions because they are right (otherwise God's commands would be arbitrary). Below, we will consider whether Locke has the (or, at least, some) theoretical resources to meet this objection.

It should also be noted that Locke's theory of virtue and vice, like his theory of causation, anticipates Hume's elaboration of it. Locke's view is that an action is called "virtuous" if praised (or approved) by one's fellows and "vicious" if blamed (or disapproved) by them (E II.xxviii.10–12: 353–357). If the claim that a relation to one's sentiments (e.g., approval and disapproval) defines virtue and vice is characteristic of sentimentalism, then Locke is a sentimentalist (indeed, arguably the *first* modern sentimentalist). That Locke is not generally well known for his sentimentalism most likely derives from the brevity of his discussion of the matter, rather than from his failure to adhere to the doctrine.

notes

1   The consequence is that there may be no neat way of distinguishing, within Locke's ontology, between modes and relations. It is unclear, for example, whether personal identity should be thought of as a mode or as a relation.

2   Notice that the term "idea" in this passage refers to *qualities* of corporeal substances (heat, fluidity), not to mental representations of such qualities or to mental representations produced by such qualities. This is in keeping with Locke's statement that he uses the word "idea" to refer to qualities whenever he applies the word to things that are *in* corporeal substances (see E II.viii.8: 134).

3   Locke also writes: "Could we suppose . . . the same consciousness acting by Intervals two distinct Bodies: I ask . . . Whether . . . there would not be one Person in two distinct Bodies, as much as one Man is the same in two distinct clothings" (E II.xxvii.23: 344).

4   This result caused grumblings among the hierarchy of the Anglican Church, many of whom followed orthodox religious teaching to the effect that the body of a person after resurrection is numerically identical to his body prior to resurrection. This is one of the issues that comes up in Locke's correspondence with Stillingfleet.

5   Locke also writes: "Could we suppose two distinct incommunicable consciousnesses acting the same Body, the one constantly by Day, the other by Night; . . . I ask . . . Whether the *Day* and the *Night-Man* would not be two as distinct Persons, as *Socrates* and *Plato*" (E II.xxvii.23: 344).

6   Locke also imagines a day-man/night-man case in which the same man with the same immaterial soul experiences "intervals of Memory and Forgetful-

ness" taking turns "by Day and Night." In such a situation, says Locke, "you have two Persons with the same immaterial Spirit" (E II.xxvii.23: 345). Here again, Locke's point is that sameness of immaterial substance is not sufficient for sameness of person.

7 For example, Locke writes that "as far as this consciousness can be extended backwards to any past Action or Thought, so far reaches the Identity of that *Person*" (E II.xxvii.9: 335); and that "whatever has the consciousness of present and past Actions, is the same Person to whom they both belong" (E II.xxvii.16: 340).

8 Notice also that the relation of sameness of consciousness, as I have just described it, unlike the relation of (potential or actual) remembering, is symmetrical. This is as it should be. At the same time, the description of sameness of consciousness I have given renders it easy to understand why Locke slips so easily from consciousness-talk into memory-talk. For when the time at which Y experiences (the idea of) P2 is later than the time at which X experiences (the idea of) P2, Y counts as remembering P1 (as long as Y is conscious of having engaged in P1 before).

9 Note that, for the sake of internal consistency, Locke should really be saying that the reason why waking Socrates is not justly punishable for the actions of sleeping Socrates is not that waking Socrates "was never" conscious of any of the actions of sleeping Socrates, but that it is (metaphysically) impossible for waking Socrates to be conscious of any of the actions of sleeping Socrates.

Note also that the conceptual relation between the idea of desert and the idea of personhood has theological consequences that derive from its moral consequences. For, as we saw above, it is part of Christian doctrine (to which Locke subscribes) that, after their deaths, God will reward the righteous and punish the unrighteous on the Day of Judgment.

10 Joseph Butler, *The Works of Joseph Butler, LL. D.* London: William Tegg, 1867, 264.

11 See Thomas Reid, *Philosophical Works*, with notes and supplementary dissertations by Sir William Hamilton. Hildesheim: Georg Olms Verlagsbuchhandlung, 1967, 351. Berkeley's version runs as follows: "Let us then suppose that a Person hath Ideas, and is conscious during a certain Space of Time, which we will divide into three equal Parts, whereof the later Terms are marked by the Letters, A, B, C. In the first part of Time, the Person gets a certain Number of Ideas, which are retained in A: during the second part of Time, he retains one Half of his old Ideas, and loseth the other Half, in place of which he acquires as many new ones. And in the third Part, we suppose him to lose the Remainder of the Ideas acquired in the First, and to get new ones in their stead, which are retained in C, together with those acquired in the second Part of Time . . . The Persons in A and B are the same, being conscious of common Ideas by Supposition. The Person in B is (for the same Reason) one and the same with the Person in C. Therefore the Person in A, is the same with the Person in C, by that undoubted Axiom, *Quae conveniunt uni tertio conveniunt inter se* [things that are equal to a third thing are equal to each other]. But the Person in C hath no Idea in common with the Person in A. Therefore Personal Identity doth not consist in Consciousness" (George Berkeley, *Alciphron* VII.viii, in *The Works of George Berkeley, Bishop of*

Cloyne, vol. 3, edited by A.A. Luce and T.E. Jessop. London: Thomas Nelson, 1950, 299).

12 Consider the following examples: "I ask then, Whether *Castor* and *Pollux*, thus, with only one Soul between them, which thinks and perceives in one, <u>what the other is never conscious of, nor is concerned for</u>, are not two as distinct Persons, as *Castor* and *Hercules*; or, as *Socrates* and *Plato* were?" (E II.i.12: 111); "[W]ould any one say, that [one who was persuaded his had been the soul of Socrates], <u>being not conscious of</u> any of *Socrates*'s Actions or Thoughts, could be the same Person with *Socrates*?" (E II.xxvii.14: 339); "But he, <u>now having no consciousness of</u> any of the Actions either of *Nestor* or *Thersites*, does, or can he, conceive himself the same Person with either of them?" (E II.xxvii.14: 339); "And to punish *Socrates* waking, for what sleeping *Socrates* thought, and waking *Socrates* <u>was never conscious of</u>, would [not be] Right" (E II.xxvii.19: 342); "no one shall be made to answer for what <u>he knows nothing of</u>" (E II.xxvii.22: 344).

further reading

Alston, William P. and Jonathan Bennett, "Locke on People and Substances," *Philosophical Review* 97 (1988): 25–46.

Atherton, Margaret, "Locke's Theory of Personal Identity," in *Midwest Studies in Philosophy VIII: Contemporary Perspectives on the History of Philosophy*, edited by Vere Chappell. Minneapolis: University of Minnesota Press, 1983, pp. 273–293.

Bolton, Martha Brandt, "Locke on Identity: The Scheme of Simple and Compounded Things," in *Individuation and Identity in Early Modern Philosophy*, edited by Kenneth F. Barber and Jorge J.E. Gracia. Albany, NY: State University of New York Press, 1994, pp. 103–131.

Chappell, Vere, "Locke and Relative Identity," *History of Philosophy Quarterly* 6 (1989): 69–83.

Chappell, Vere, "Locke on the Ontology of Matter, Living Things and Persons," *Philosophical Studies* 60 (1990): 19–32.

Garrett, Don, "Locke on Personal Identity, Consciousness, and 'Fatal Errors,'" *Philosophical Topics* 31 (2003): 95–125.

LoLordo, Antonia, *Locke's Moral Man*. Oxford: Oxford University Press, 2012, chapter 2.

Mattern, Ruth, "Moral Science and the Concept of Persons in Locke," *Philosophical Review* 89 (1980): 24–45.

Thiel, Udo, *The Early Modern Subject: Self-Consciousness and Personal Identity from Descartes to Hume*. Oxford: Oxford University Press, 2011, chapters 3–6.

Uzgalis, William, "Relative Identity and Locke's Principle of Individuation," *History of Philosophy Quarterly* 7 (1990): 283–297.

Winkler, Kenneth P., "Locke on Personal Identity," *Journal of the History of Philosophy* 29 (1991): 201–226.

Yaffe, Gideon, "Locke on Ideas of Identity and Diversity," in *The Cambridge Companion to Locke's "Essay Concerning Human Understanding"*, edited by Lex Newman. Cambridge: Cambridge University Press, 2007, pp. 192–230.

language

The main purpose of Locke's *Essay* is epistemological, to "search out the *Bounds* between Opinion and Knowledge" (E I.i.3: 44) – that is, to determine what can be known, what can at best be assented to (on the basis of probability), and what cannot be either known or assented to. One of Locke's main theses is that the human understanding is limited, and that we should all "sit down in a quiet Ignorance of those Things, which, upon Examination, are found to be beyond the reach of our Capacities" (E I.i.4: 45). Unfortunately, as Locke sees it, philosophers, both past and present, believe that it is possible to know propositions that, as it happens, the human understanding cannot know. Such philosophers, he tells us, engage in endless and fruitless disputes, epitomized by the method of disputation held up as the model of philosophical investigation by the Scholastics. Such wrangling leads many to skepticism, the belief that nothing can be known, in part because no consensus has yet been reached, even on the very important questions of morality and religion. It also has the power to introduce controversy where none should exist – for example, as we will see, regarding the nature and proper bounds of species or sorts of substances.

Originally, Locke thought that he could address these matters without having to provide a theory of the nature, function, purpose, and meaning of language. But, upon reflection, he realized that the failure to understand the semantic features of language can lead to the kind of imperfection and abuse that represent obstacles to the acquisition of knowledge. In the *Epistle to the Reader*, Locke famously writes that he thinks of himself as *"an Under-Labourer in clearing Ground a little, and removing some of the Rubbish, that lies in the way to Knowledge."* What is less well understood is that the "rubbish" of which Locke speaks here consists in *"the learned but frivolous use of uncouth, affected, or unintelligible Terms, introduced into the Sciences, and there made an Art of,"* that the chief obstacle to the acquisition of knowledge involves the use of *"[v]ague and insignificant Forms of Speech, and Abuse of Language"* involving *"hard or misapply'd Words, with little or no*

Locke, First Edition. Samuel C. Rickless.
© 2014 Samuel C. Rickless. Published 2014 by John Wiley & Sons, Ltd.

meaning" (E: 10). So, as part of his campaign to determine what can and cannot be known, Locke found it necessary to develop a philosophy of language, indeed an even broader "semiotics" or *"Doctrine of Signs . . .*, the business whereof, is to consider the Nature of Signs, the Mind makes use of for the understanding of Things, or conveying its Knowledge to others" (E IV.xxi.4: 720). This is the aim and purpose of Book III of the *Essay*, titled "Of Words."

9.1   Language and Meaning

In Locke's ontology, words are *"articulate Sounds"* (E III.i.1: 402; E IV.xxi.4: 724). This account of words makes sense of vocal utterances, of course, but it seems notably unsatisfying with respect to its account of inscriptions. Marks on paper (or pixels on a screen, for that matter) are not articulate sounds, and yet they are (token) words nonetheless. Locke seems blissfully unaware of, or unconcerned with, this issue. A charitable interpreter might reasonably suppose that if this issue had been brought to Locke's attention, he would have extended his account of words to cover inscriptions as well as utterances.[1]

The fundamental thesis of Locke's philosophy of language is that *"Words in their primary or immediate Signification, stand for nothing, but the* Ideas *in the Mind of him that uses them"* (E III.ii.2: 405). Locke uses many linguistic devices to pick out the relation of signification, including "signifies," "is a sign of," "stands for," "is a mark of," "marks," "is used for," "is applied to," "expresses," "is put for," "intimates." From our point of view, this list of words and phrases comes across as a semantic grab-bag. Philosophers of language distinguish nowadays between the sense (or meaning) of a word and its referent (or extension). The word "bachelor," we want to say, has a sense, roughly the property of being an eligible, unmarried, adult, male human being. The sense of a word is what one grasps when one understands the word. But we also want to say that the word "bachelor" refers to or picks out actual bachelors, and that the extension of the word "bachelor" is the set of all those individuals picked out by the word. Because actual bachelors are not properties (or whatever else senses or meanings might be), the referent of "bachelor" is not identical to its sense. This allows us to say, for example, that the proposition that bachelors are unmarried is *about* the referent (or extension), but not *about* the sense (or meaning), of the word "bachelor." Philosophers of language mark the different relations that a word bears to its sense and to its referent by saying that a word "expresses" its sense and "refers to" or "stands for" its referent. But for Locke, the expressions "expresses" and "stands for" are interchangeable: they are both used to pick out the relation of signification.

What does Locke think the relation of signification amounts to? Because he does not answer this question explicitly, various theories of Lockean signification have been proposed. On one theory (inspired by Gottlob Frege), to say that X signifies Y is to say that the meaning of X is Y. On another theory (inspired by the late Scholastic philosophy of language that Locke imbibed in his youth at Oxford), to say that X signifies Y is to say that X makes Y known to the cognitive power. On this view, the range of Y can include both the sense and referent of X. On yet another theory (inspired by the Stoics, Hobbes, and the Port-Royal logicians, Antoine Arnauld and Pierre Nicole), to say that X signifies Y is to say that X indicates Y (in much the way that smoke indicates fire). None of these theories is persuasive. Locke's semiotic theory is a theory of signs, *all* signs, not just linguistic signs. For Locke, there are two main sorts of signs: words and ideas. Words signify, but so do ideas (E III.iii.11: 414; E IV.v.2: 574). Ideas are needed as signs of "the Things, the Mind contemplates" because those things "are none of them, besides [the mind itself], present to the Understanding," while words are needed as "Signs of our *Ideas*" in order to "communicate our Thoughts to one another, as well as record them for our own use" (E IV.xxi.4: 720–721). Assuming, as Locke appears to assume, that the relation of signification that obtains between words and ideas does not differ in its nature from the relation of signification that obtains between ideas and things-in-the-world, it cannot be right to say that signification is meaning or making known or indication; for ideas don't *mean* objects, not all the things we think about by means of ideas can be known, and ideas do not always indicate the objects they signify.

Signification, as Locke makes plain in a few places, is nothing more than the relation of *representation*. For example, Locke writes that the nature of general words and ideas is that of "signifying or representing many particulars" (E III.iii.11: 414), and that things can be present to the mind only when "something else, as a Sign or Representation of the thing it considers, should be present to [the mind]" (E IV.xxi.4: 721). Moreover, Locke explains that the definition of a word consists in an explication of its meaning or signification by means of "*several other not synonymous Terms*" (E III.iv.6: 422), and then argues that "*the Names of Simple* Ideas, and those only, *are incapable of being defined*" on the grounds that "the several Terms of a Definition, signifying several *Ideas*, they can altogether by no means represent an *Idea*, which has no Composition at all" (E III.iv.7: 422). Here it is plain that Locke is simply equating the claim that a definition cannot *signify* a simple idea with the claim that a definition cannot *represent* a simple idea.

Representation is a very general relation, and Locke means it to be. Words can represent ideas, ideas can represent things-in-the-world, words can represent things-in-the-world, but also ideas can represent other ideas, ideas can represent themselves, and things-in-the-world can represent other things-in-the-world (as when, for example, a member of Parliament represents or "stands for" her constituency). To represent something is to stand in for it, to serve as a proxy for it: representation is not a narrowly semantic, cognitive, or causal relation. However, in the case of the relation between words and their meanings, the relation of representation can subserve a semantic function. And this appears to be how Locke conceives of it: when a word represents (stands for, expresses, is a sign of) an idea in the mind of the word's user, the idea counts as the word's meaning.

There are several reasons for thinking that for Locke the ideas that words signify or represent count as their meanings. First, there is the fact that Locke says as much explicitly. For example, Locke writes that "[t]he meaning of Words [are] only the *Ideas* they are made to stand for by him that uses them" (E III.iv.6: 422), that "when any term stands for a simple *Idea*, that a Man has never yet had in his Mind, it is impossible, by any Words, to make known its meaning to him" (E III.iv.14: 427), that "[h]e that hath Names without *Ideas*, wants meaning in this Words, and speaks only empty sounds" (E III.x.31: 506), and that "[w]hen a Man makes use of the *name* of *any simple* Idea, which he perceives is not understood, or is in danger to be mistaken, he is obliged . . . to declare his Meaning, and make known what *Idea* he makes it stand for" (E III.xi.14: 515). Second, knowing that what makes a word intelligible by one who hears it is the fact that the hearer can grasp its meaning, Locke identifies a word's intelligibility with the possibility of grasping the idea its user has annexed to it. For example, Locke writes that "[w]ords having naturally no signification, the *Idea* which each stands for, must be learned and retained by those, who would exchange Thoughts, and hold intelligible Discourse with others," and that "Names standing for any simple *Ideas*, which another has not Organs or Faculties to attain" are "not intelligible at all" (E III.ix.5: 477). These remarks presuppose that the idea signified by a word is identical to its meaning. Third, knowing that communication is possible only when the hearer grasps the meaning of the words used by the speaker, Locke explains that communication depends on the fact that words signify ideas in the minds of their users: "[I]t was farther necessary, that [Man] should be *able to use these Sounds, as Signs of internal Conceptions*; and to make them stand as marks for the *Ideas* within his own Mind, whereby they might be made known to others, and the Thoughts of Men's Minds be conveyed from one to another" (E III.i.2: 402). So here again, Locke presupposes that a word's ideational significatum should be identified with its meaning. And, fourth, knowing that definitions are designed to explicate the meanings of words, Locke points out that what definitions do is to set out the ideas users associate with those words: "[T]he meaning of any Term is then shewed, or the Word defined when by other Words, the *Idea* it is made the Sign of, and annexed to in the Mind of the Speaker, is as it were represented, or set before the view of another; and thus its Signification ascertained" (E III.iv.6: 422).

Interestingly, however, Locke's fundamental thesis presupposes a further distinction between immediate and (though he does not use the term) mediate signification. Locke's thesis is not that words *mediately* signify ideas in the minds of their users, but rather that words *immediately* signify those ideas. But what is the mediate/immediate signification distinction? Again, Locke does not answer this question explicitly, and so we are left to reconstruct how he would have answered it if he had put his mind to it. Here it helps to look at other contexts in which Locke draws a similar immediate/mediate distinction. As we will see in Chapter 10, in his discussion of the degrees of knowledge Locke distinguishes between the *immediate* perception of agreement (or disagreement) between ideas and the *mediate* perception of such agreement (or disagreement). Immediate perception of ideational agreement happens "without the intervention of any other [idea]" (E IV.ii.1: 530–531), while mediate perception of ideational agreement happens "by the Intervention of other *Ideas* (one or more, as it happens) . . . which serve to shew the Agreement of any two" (E IV.ii.2–3: 532). Thus, perception of the agreement between idea X and idea Z is mediate when, for example, it is by means of the perception of the agreement between X and another idea Y and the perception of the agreement between Y and Z that the agreement between X and Z is perceived. Using this understanding of mediacy as a model, it is reasonable to suppose that when Locke says that X mediately signifies Z, what he means is that there is a set of intervening objects {Y1, Y2, . . . Yn} such that X signifies Z by virtue of the fact that X signifies Y1, Y1 signifies Y2, . . ., Yn-1 signifies Yn, and Yn signifies Z.[2] If this is right, then Locke's claim that X immediately signifies Z is just the claim that it is not by virtue of any such mediating chain of significations that X signifies Z.[3]

It is in *this* sense of "immediate" that Locke thinks of the idea that a user annexes to her use of a word as its *immediate* signification. When I use the word "white," on Locke's view, the word signifies or represents the idea or sensation of white in my mind, and it does so without signifying anything else that itself signifies that idea (and without signifying anything else that itself signifies something that signifies that idea, etc.). But this brings up the question whether Locke thinks of words as having mediate signification in addition to immediate signification. The answer here is surely that he does. For, as we have seen, ideas represent or signify just as words do. So when a word immediately signifies an idea that itself immediately signifies a thing (or many things, or a sort), then the word comes to mediately signify the thing (or many things, or the sort). It is no surprise, then, to find Locke talking of names representing particulars by (immediately) representing ideas that themselves (immediately) represent those particulars. For example, Locke speaks of children using the names *"Nurse"* and *"Mamma"* to represent ideas of particular persons, ideas that "represent only those Individuals" (E III.iii.6: 411). In this sort of situation, the names "nurse" and "mamma" mediately signify the particular nurse and the particular mamma of which a child is thinking when he uses those terms. And mediate signification extends to general names as well as to particular names. "Words become general," Locke tells us, "by being made the signs of general *Ideas*: and *Ideas* become general [by abstraction, and thereby] are made capable of representing more Individuals than one" (E III.iii.6: 410–411). So a general term, such as "human," signifies an abstract idea, an idea that itself signifies a large number of human beings; and hence the term "human" mediately signifies all human beings.

Because words, both particular and general, mediately signify things-in-the-world, it makes sense to identify the mediately signified objects in these circumstances as the *referents* of those words. In this respect, though not in all, Locke's philosophy of language comes to resemble Frege's. For Frege, words have both sense (*Sinn*) and reference (*Bedeutung*). The sense of a word is what one grasps when one understands it; the referent of a word is what the word picks out in the world, by virtue of satisfying the requirements embodied in its sense. With this understanding of the sense-reference distinction in mind, we can say, correctly, that, for Locke, the idea that a word immediately signifies counts as its sense, while the entity that the word mediately signifies by virtue of being represented by its sense counts as its referent. But there are two main differences between Locke's theory of meaning and Frege's. First, according to Frege, the sense of a word is an objective entity existing in a "third realm" separate both from the realm of ideas and from the realm of sensible objects; for Locke, by contrast, the sense of a word is a subjective entity existing in the mind of its user. Second, according to Frege, the sense of a word is a way of presenting (a mode of presentation of) its referent; for Locke, by contrast, the sense of a word is no more than a sign or representation of, and hence not a *way of representing*, its referent (or extension).

Although Locke states his fundamental thesis as a general truth governing all words, he is well aware that the thesis is subject to important exceptions. The first major exception concerns the class of syncategoremata. The Scholastics distinguished between categorematic terms and syncategorematic terms: the former are terms for entities belonging to the 10 Aristotelian categories: substance (e.g., horse), quantity (e.g., four-foot), quality (e.g., white), relative (e.g., double), somewhere (e.g., in the market-place), sometime (e.g., yesterday), being in a position (e.g., is-sitting), having (e.g., has-shoes-on), acting (e.g., cutting), and being acted upon (e.g., being-cut); the latter are terms that cannot serve as subjects or predicates, but serve to bind categorematic terms or sentences into larger sentences or verbal propositions (e.g., quantifiers, such as "all," "some," and "no"; logical connectives, such as "and," "or," and "if-then"; and the copula, "is"). Locke calls syncategorematic terms "particles," and theorizes that, unlike categorematic terms, particles do not immediately signify ideas, but rather (immediately) signify mental acts of joining or separating (of ideas or propositions): "Besides Words, which are names of *Ideas* in the Mind, there are a great many others that are made use of, to signify the *connexion* that the Mind gives to *Ideas, or Propositions, one with another*" (E III.vii.1: 471). For example, Locke claims that the copula "is" signifies the mental act of joining ideas in an affirmation (affirmative proposition), while the negative copula "is not" signifies the mental act of separating ideas in a denial (negative proposition) (E III.vii.1: 471; E IV.v.5–6: 575–576). The second major exception concerns "negative or privative Words" or "*negative Names*," such as "nothing," "ignorance," "barrenness" (E III.i.4: 403), "insipid," and "silence" (E II.viii.5: 133). These words, Locke tells us, "denote positive *Ideas* . . . with a signification of their absence" (E II.viii.5: 133), and "cannot be said properly to belong to, or signify no *Ideas*: for then they would be perfectly insignificant Sounds; but they relate to positive *Ideas*, and signify their absence" (E III.i.4: 403). Thus, the word "insipid" denotes, but signifies the absence of, the idea of taste, and the word "silence" denotes, but signifies the absence of, the idea of sound. Understandably, these exceptions to Locke's fundamental thesis render his entire philosophy of language much less vulnerable to counterexamples. Moreover, unlike Fregean theories, which do not make room for mental acts of unification as the senses of words, the first exception makes it possible for Locke's theory to account for propositional unity.

In addition to a theory of signification of words, Locke offers a theory of the signification of sentences as well as a theory of truth. As Locke sees it, a proposition "consists in joining, or separating Signs" (E IV.v.5: 576). And because there are two sorts of signs – ideas and words – Locke distinguishes between two kinds of propositions – mental and verbal. In the case of mental propositions, "the *Ideas* in our Understandings *are* without the use of Words *put together, or separated* by the Mind" via affirmation or denial; in the case of verbal propositions, "*Words* the signs of our *Ideas* [are] *put together or separated in affirmative or negative Sentences*" (E IV.v.5: 575–576). On this view, every verbal proposition represents, and so signifies, a corresponding mental proposition. For example, the verbal proposition "snow is white," which consists in the affirmative joining of the word "snow" with the word "white" by means of the copula "is," signifies the mental proposition that snow is white, which itself consists in the affirmative joining of the idea of snow (signified by the word "snow") with the idea of white (signified by the word "white") by means of the mental act of affirmation (signified by "is"). This too corresponds to Frege's account of the sense of sentences; for Frege holds that a sentence is a grammatical string of words, and that the sense expressed by a sentence is a thought (*Gedanke*), itself composed of the senses expressed by the various parts of the sentence.

Truth, as Locke understands it, is "nothing but *the joining or separating of Signs, as the Things signified by them, do agree or disagree one with another*" (E IV.v.2: 574). Again, then, given that there are two kinds of signs – ideas and words – there are two kinds of truth – mental truth and verbal truth (or "truth of words"). Mental truth obtains "[w]hen *Ideas* are so put together, or separated in the Mind, as they, or the Things they stand for do agree, or not"; verbal truth consists in "the affirming or denying of Words one of another, as the *Ideas* they stand for agree or disagree" (E IV.v.6: 576). So truth in general consists in the agreement between joined significata or the disagreement between separated significata: when the relevant significata are the entities signified by words (i.e., ideas), the truth is verbal, and when the relevant significata are the entities signified by ideas, the truth is mental. Thus, mental truth consists in the truth of a mental proposition, while verbal truth consists in the truth of a verbal proposition. The theory, such as it is, is clear, neat, and completely consistent.

The question is sometimes raised, whether Locke has a theory of meaning. The answer must surely be that he does, assuming that meaning is something that is understood, defined, and communicated, and that it is tied in the way Locke does to the truth-conditions of sentences and propositions. Locke's theory of meaning is part of a larger theory of signification or representation. As theories of meaning go, it is not particularly sophisticated and ignores pragmatic features of language use that some of his successors (such as Berkeley) made more of. But it is clear and its connections to the theory of ideas well thought out. It also plays an important role in Locke's explanation for past mistakes in speculative and natural philosophy, as well as the continued prevalence of disagreement and disputes among philosophers. It is to this explanation that we now turn.

9.2   The Imperfections and Abuses of Language

As Locke sees matters, language is *imperfect* in the performance of any of its functions if its signification or meaning is, through no fault of its user, "doubtful" or "uncertain," and hence not understood by those to whom it is addressed. Language is *abused* when its imperfection is the result of *"willful Faults and Neglects"* (E III.x.1: 490).

Locke claims that words, and the verbal propositions they constitute, serve two main functions: (i) "for the recording of our own Thoughts," and (ii) "for the communicating of our Thoughts to others" (E III.ix.1: 476). With respect to the first of these functions, Locke says, language is not susceptible of imperfection (and hence not susceptible of abuse), as long as a language user "constantly use[s] the same sign for the same *Idea*: for then he cannot fail of having his meaning understood" (E III.ix.2: 476). But with respect to the second of these functions, language is susceptible of both imperfection and abuse. Part of the main point of Book III of the *Essay* is to identify and suggest cures for the main imperfections and abuses of language.

According to Locke, successful communication between speaker and hearer requires that the hearer grasp exactly what the speaker's words immediately signify: "To make Words serviceable to the end of Communication, it is necessary . . . that they excite, in the Hearer, exactly the same *Idea*, they stand for in the Mind of the Speaker" (E III.ix.6: 478; see also E III.ii.8: 408, E III.iii.3: 409, E III.vi.45: 467, and E III.ix.4: 476–477).[4] Communication therefore fails when the hearer fails to grasp the idea immediately signified by the speaker's use of a word or phrase. This happens in one of two main ways: (i) when the relevant idea is extremely complex and/or the signification of the word cannot be adjusted or rectified by means of a stable external standard, or (ii) when such a standard exists but either can only be known with great difficulty or cannot be known at all (E III.ix.5: 477).

Locke claims that the names of mixed modes (but not the names of sensible qualities, simple modes, or substances) are vulnerable to the first kind of linguistic imperfection. The reason is that these words signify ideas of great complexity, and when this happens "it is not easy for Men to form and retain that *Idea* so exactly, as to make the Name in common use, stand for the same precise *Idea*, without any the least variation" (E III.ix.6: 478). Thus it can happen that the idea that I associate with the word "justice" is not the same as the idea that you associate with the word. And when this happens, communication breaks down because the idea excited in you by my use of "justice" is not the same as the idea that the word immediately signifies for me. This problem is then exacerbated by the fact that names of mixed modes are (for the most part) mere "assemblages of Ideas put together at the pleasure of the Mind, pursuing its own ends of Discourse, and suited to its own Notions" (E III.ix.7: 478), and hence not created with any archetype (or external standard of potential rectification) in view.

Locke then claims that the names of substances (but not the names of qualities or modes) are vulnerable to the second kind of linguistic imperfection. This is because they have what Locke calls a "double *reference* in their ordinary use" (E III.ix.12: 482). Sometimes the names of substances "are referred to a supposed real Essence of each Species of things," and sometimes "they are only design'd to be Pictures and Representations in the Mind, of Things that do exist, by *Ideas* of those qualities that are discoverable in them" (E II.xxxi.6: 378). The phrase "double reference" may mislead here. Locke does not mean by "reference" what Frege means by "Bedeutung." Locke is pointing to a different linguistic phenomenon. The problem is that speakers who use names of substances, such as "gold," suppose that these words (immediately) signify something in the world that is distinct from the complex ideas actually expressed by those words. They suppose, for instance, that the word "gold" (immediately) signifies a particular internal constitution (what Locke calls the "real essence" of gold) or substantial form that is causally responsible for all the observable properties of those items to which the word is customarily applied (yellowness, fusibility, malleability, heaviness, fixedness, solubility in aqua regia, etc.). Alternatively, they suppose that the word "gold" (immediately) signifies all of these observable properties themselves. What Locke means by "P refers X to Y" is that P supposes that X (immediately) signifies Y (see E III.x.18: 500). And in the case of the names of substances, Locke's main thesis is that both of the suppositions embodied in the "double reference" are mistaken. And this mistake leads to the doubtful and uncertain signification that Locke takes to lie at the heart of unsuccessful communication.

Locke claims that the real essence of any (sort of) substance is unknown, and quite possibly unknowable by human minds (though it is surely known by God, who is omniscient, and possibly by "Spirits of a higher rank than those immersed in Flesh," such as angels) (E II.xxxi.6: 378–380; E III.vi.9: 444–445; E III.xi.23: 520).[5] But anything that is unknown cannot serve as a standard by which to categorize substances by means of general names, and thus those who mistakenly "refer" their substance-terms to real essences can easily end up talking past each other, thinking that they are signifying the same thing with the same substance-term, but all the while associating completely different complex ideas with, and hence assigning completely different meanings to, that term. And something similar obtains when speakers suppose (again, mistakenly) that their substance-terms (immediately) signify the observable properties of the relevant sort of substance. The problem here is that every kind of substance has an "almost infinite" number of observable properties and powers, and consequently different speakers end up associating different sets of properties and powers with the same substance-term depending on which of the almost infinite number of such properties they happen to notice or think about. And when this happens, communication breaks down as a result of doubtful signification. For example, one person may associate "gold" with no more than "Colour and Weight," while another adds "Solubility in *Aqua Regia*" or "Fusibility" or both, and yet others add "Ductility [i.e., malleability] or Fixedness, *etc.* as they have been taught by Tradition, or Experience." As Locke points out, no one set of qualities or powers counts as *the* "right signification of the Word *Gold*," and hence "the complex *Ideas* of Substances, in Men using the same Name for them, will be very various; and so the significations of those names, very uncertain" (E III.ix.13: 482–483).

These linguistic imperfections are natural outcomes of facts about linguistic signification as Locke sees them. Communication failure can happen even though neither speaker nor hearer is responsible or blameworthy for its occurrence. But Locke also thinks that some speakers can and should be held responsible for the negligent or willful exploitation of linguistic imperfections. By and large, Locke is thinking of the Scholastics here. In a chapter devoted exclusively to "the Abuse of Words," Locke excoriates "the Schoolmen and Metaphysicians" for engaging in the following forms of blameworthy linguistic malfeasance: (i) "the using of Words, without clear and distinct *Ideas*; or, which is worse, signs without any thing signified" (E III.x.2: 490), as in the case of the "Gibberish" represented by the use of terms such as "*substantial Forms, vegetative Souls, abhorrence of a Vacuum,* [and] *intentional Species*" (E III.x.14: 497); (ii) "*Inconstancy* in the use of [words]," – that is, "the same Words . . . used sometimes for one Collection of simple *Ideas*, and sometimes for another" (E III.x.5: 492); (iii) "an *affected Obscurity*, by either applying old Words, to new and unusual Significations; or introducing new and ambiguous Terms, without defining either; or else putting them so together, as may confound their ordinary meaning" (E III.x.6: 493); (iv) "*the taking* [words] *for Things*," particularly in the case of names for substances (E III.x.14: 497); (v) "*the setting* [words] *in the place of Things, which they do or can by no means signify*" (E III.x.17: 499); and (vi) speakers' imagining of "*so near and necessary a connexion between* [*names and their signification*], that they forwardly suppose one cannot but understand what their meaning is; and therefore one ought to acquiesce in the Words delivered" (E III.x.22: 503).

Looking back at the imperfections and abuses, Locke hypothesizes that "the greatest part of the Disputes in the World, [are or may be] meerly Verbal, and about the Signification of Words" (E III.xi.7: 511), and that the interminable wrangling and disputation of the Scholastics could be brought to a halt if only all conversational participants took sufficient care to avoid imperfections and abuses via careful definition of terms, including the reduction of complex significata to a determinate list of simple ideas that are susceptible of rectification by presenting the same object to the senses of different persons under similar circumstances (E III.xi.7: 511; E III.xi.14: 515). In this way, disputes about whether extension is sufficient for corporeality (E III.x.15: 498), about whether all human beings are rational animals and all rational animals are human beings (E III.vi.26: 453), about whether a bat is a kind of bird (E III.xi.7: 511), and about whether ice and water are different species (E III.vi.13: 447), can all be seen to be avoidable. For though they appear to be about the nature of things, they are about the meanings of words and no more. Careful enumeration of the simple ideas that make up the complex ideas (immediately) signified by the words "body," "human," "bat," "bird," "ice," and "water" is sufficient to resolve the disputes that constitute the sort of *"Rubbish, that lies in the way to Knowledge"* of which Locke speaks in his *Epistle to the Reader*.

The main remedy for the imperfections and abuses of language is therefore careful definition of terms. But here, Locke thinks, philosophers are prone to error if they do not accept the fundamental thesis of his philosophy of language, namely that the immediate signification of a (categorematic) term used by a speaker is the idea that the term immediately signifies. Many of Locke's contemporaries, in their rush to define terms, defined every (categorematic) term under the sun.[6] And yet, as Locke emphasizes, some such terms – that is, the names of simple ideas – are indefinable.[7] For definition, he tells us, is *"the shewing the meaning of one Word by several other not synonymous Terms"* (E III.iv.6: 422). And by the fundamental thesis, every one of those "not synonymous terms" (immediately) signifies an idea, and thus every definition must itself (immediately) signify a complex idea. But if a definition is correct, then its (immediate) signification must be the same as the (immediate) signification of the definiendum. Given that no complex idea is identical to any simple idea, it follows that no definition of a term that (immediately) signifies a simple idea can be correct (E III.iv.7: 422). And thus in defining our terms, it is important, Locke thinks, that we define only terms that (immediately) signify modes and substances.[8]

9.3 Nominal Essence, Real Essence, and Classification

In his chapter on the names of substances (E III.vi) and elsewhere, Locke emphasizes not only that the immediate signification of a substance-term for a speaker is the complex idea composed of those ideas the speaker associates with her use of the term, but also that the immediate signification of a substance-term for a speaker is *not* the real essence of the substance. As we have seen, the real essence of a substance is the internal constitution that is responsible for all of the substance's observable properties, particularly those that conform to the idea of that substance. Locke's main point is that real essence is unknown (and quite possibly unknowable by human beings), and hence cannot serve as the relevant substance-term's immediate signification. As Locke also argues, real essence is not what we use to classify substances into classes (whether for scientific purposes or for more quotidian purposes).

Locke contrasts a substance's *real essence* with its *nominal essence*, claiming that in the case of substances real essence differs from nominal essence, whereas in the case of (mixed) modes (and relations) real essence and nominal essence coincide (E III.v.14: 436–437).[9] One question that has attracted a great deal of attention among Locke scholars is what Locke thinks the real essence of a substance *is*, and whether, in particular, he thinks that the real essence of a substance should be identified with the substance's *substratum*.

Some scholars think that Locke takes the real essence of a substance to be numerically identical to its substratum. The main reason for taking this position is that much of what Locke says about real essence he also says about substratum, and vice versa. The real essence of a substance is unknown (E III. vi.9: 444); but the substratum of a substance is unknown too (E II.xxiii.2: 295). As to the real essences of substances, "we only suppose their Being" (E III.vi.6: 442; also E III.iii.15: 417); but we also "accustom our selves, to suppose some *Substratum*" (E II.xxiii.1: 295). We think of the real essence of a substance as that upon which the substance's qualities depend (E III.vi.2: 439), as that from which those qualities flow (E III.vi.3: 440) or result (E IV.iii.11: 545), and as the foundation and source of those qualities (E III.vi.3: 440); but we also think of a substance's substratum as that in which the substance's qualities subsist, and as that from which those qualities result (E II.xxiii.1: 295). Finally, we think of a substance's real essence as the cause of the union of the substance's qualities (E III.vi.6: 442; E IV.iv.12: 568); but we also think that the cause of the union of those qualities is the substance's substratum (E II.xxiii.6: 298; E III.vi.21: 450).

And yet Locke carefully avoids claiming that a substance's substratum is identical to the substance's real essence. The main reason for this, I think, is that Locke cannot consistently believe that such an identity holds. Most of the properties of a substance are secondary qualities, powers the substance has to produce ideas of certain kinds in our minds. These qualities depend on the primary qualities of the substance's insensible parts (or, as Locke says, "if not upon them, upon something yet more remote from our Comprehension" (E IV.iii.11: 544)), qualities such as "size, figure, and texture" (E IV.iii.11: 545). Locke identifies these primary qualities of a substance's parts as the substance's real essence or constitution (E IV.iii.11–13: 545; E III.vi.9: 444). But these primary qualities (or whatever qualities more remote from our comprehension that explain the presence of the substance's secondary qualities), like all properties or accidents, cannot exist unsupported, and must therefore inhere in some substratum, presumably the substratum of the relevant substance.[10] So if the real essence of a substance were identical to its substratum, then the real essence of a substance would inhere in and support itself. But this is impossible, for nothing can serve as its own support.

The more reasonable interpretive hypothesis, then, is that the real essence of a substance (whatever it may be) is numerically distinct from the substance's substratum. It follows, then, that Locke's description of the properties of real essences and substrata is a little sloppy. There is no harm in saying that both real essences and substrata, though numerically distinct, are both supposed and yet unknown. But it cannot be that the real essence of a substance and its substratum are *both of them* that on which the qualities of the substance depend, that from which these qualities flow, and that which accounts for their union. I suspect that if Locke had been apprised of this controversy, he would have articulated the following more careful position, namely that the qualities of a substance inhere in, and depend for their existence on, the substance's substratum; that the fact that the qualities inhere in and depend on a single thing is what accounts for their union; but that these very same qualities flow from or result from a single source, namely the substance's real essence.

It must be admitted that Locke's discussion of essence is confusing. One question that naturally arises is whether Locke thinks that essences belong to *substances* or to *sorts (or species) of substances*. Sometimes Locke speaks of the essences of *sorts* of substances:

[I]t is evident, that the *Essences of* the *sorts, or* (if the Latin word pleases better) *Species* of Things, are nothing else but these abstract *Ideas*. (E III. iii.12: 414)

But it being evident, that Things are ranked under Names into sorts or *Species*, only as they agree to certain abstract *Ideas*, to which we have annexed those Names, the *Essence* of each *Genus*, or Sort, comes to be nothing but that abstract *Idea*, which the General, or *Sortal* . . . Names stands for. (E III.iii.15: 417)

The measure and boundary of each Sort, or *Species*, whereby it is constituted that particular Sort, and distinguished from others, is that we call its *Essence*, which *is* nothing but that *abstract* Idea *to which the Name is annexed*: So that every thing contained in that *Idea*, is essential to that Sort. (E III.vi.2: 439)

At the same time, Locke appears to deny that *individual* (particular) substances have essences:

But there is nothing I have, is essential to me. (E III.vi.4: 440)

So that if it be asked, whether it be *essential* to me, or any other particular corporeal Being to have Reason? I say no; no more than it is *essential* to this white thing I write on, to have words in it. (E III.vi.4: 441)

[B]ut there is no individual parcel of Matter, to which any of these Qualities are so annexed, as to be *essential* to it, or inseparable from it. (E III.vi.6: 442)

And yet sometimes Locke is happy to attribute essences to individual (particular) things:

> *First, Essence* may be taken for the very being of any thing, whereby it is, what it is. And thus the real internal, but generally in Substances, unknown Constitution of Things, whereon their discoverable Qualities depend, may be called their *Essence* . . . And in this sense [the word] is still used, when we speak of the *Essence* of particular things, without giving them any Name. (E III.iii.15: 417)

It might be thought that the solution to this conundrum is to suppose that Locke means that *nominal* essences belong to *sorts* but not to *particulars*, and that *real* essences belong to *particulars* but not to *sorts*. But this hypothesis contradicts Locke's claim that he has "often mentioned a *real Essence*, distinct in Substances, from those abstract *Ideas* of them, which I call their [i.e., the substances'] *nominal Essence*" (E III.vi.6: 442). Thus in at least some cases, Locke speaks of particulars as having nominal essences. And it also does not fit well with Locke's (apparent) claim that particulars do not have real essences.

The answer, I believe, is that Locke is speaking somewhat archly when he denies that particulars have real essences and intimates that nominal essences belong only to sorts. Properly set out, his view is this. Nominal essences, in the first instance, belong to *sorts*; but nominal essences can, in the second instance, belong to *particulars*. The nominal essence of a sort of substance (e.g., gold) is a set of observable qualities (e.g., yellow, malleable, weighty, fusible) picked out by a set of ideas (e.g., the idea of yellow, the idea of malleability, the idea of fusibility) associated with the name of that substantial sort (i.e., "gold"). We can then say that a particular substance (call it "Rock") partakes of that nominal essence, and belongs to the relevant sort, inasmuch as it possesses all the qualities in the relevant set. By contrast, real essences, in the first instance, belong to *particulars*; but each real essence to which a particular belongs is relative to a *sort*. Thus, there is no real essence of Rock "considered barely in [itself]" (E III.vi.5: 441). But Rock has a real essence relative to any nominal essence of which it partakes: "None of these [qualities] are essential . . . to any Individual whatsoever, till the Mind refers it to some Sort or *Species* of things; and then presently, according to the abstract *Idea* of that sort, something is found *essential*" (E III.vi.4: 440). So, relative to the nominal essence <yellow, malleable, fusible>, Rock has a real essence, namely whatever internal constitution is responsible for its yellowness, malleability, and fusibility. But this real essence of Rock might well differ from the real essence of Rock that is relative to the nominal essence <yellow, malleable, fusible, ductile>. For it is not clear that the same internal constitution is responsible for the yellowness, malleability, and fusibility of Rock as is responsible for Rock's yellowness, malleability, fusibility, *and ductility*.

The distinction between nominal essence and real essence is relevant to Locke's discussion of the classification of substances into sorts, under names that signify those sorts. As against the Scholastics, who, following Aristotle, hold that a substance is properly classified in accordance with its substantial form, and as against corpuscularians and atomists who might hope to classify substances in accordance with their real essences, Locke argues that a substance is properly classified in accordance with its nominal essence. What makes something human, rather than an ape, what makes something gold, rather than lead, what makes something a watch, rather than a clock, is determined by the qualities signified by the ideas we take the words "human," "gold," and "watch" to signify.

Locke offers four arguments for the claim that the classification of substances into sorts is not determined by their real essence (or putative substantial form). The first argument depends on two premises: first, "[t]hat we find many of the Individuals that are ranked into one Sort, called by one common Name, and so received as being of one *Species*, have yet Qualities depending on their real Constitutions, as far different one from another, as from others, from which they are accounted to differ *specifically*" (E III.vi.8: 443); and, second, that real essence, by definition, is "the foundation of all those Properties [of a substance], that are combined in, and are constantly found to co-exist with the *nominal Essence*" (E III.vi.6: 442). The reasoning is simple. According to the first premise, we will find ourselves ranking X and Y as belonging to the same sort, S, and then later discovering that X and Y differ in their properties (e.g., X is soluble in aqua regia, but Y is not; X turns blue when heated, but Y turns red when heated). (Locke thinks this happens all the time. In chemistry, for example, one often seeks in vain "for the same Qualities in one parcel of Sulphur, Antimony, or Vitriol, which [one has] found in others" (E III.vi.8: 443).) But, by the second premise, "it is . . . impossible, that two Things, partaking exactly of the same real *Essence*, should have different Properties" (E III.iii.17: 418), and hence from the fact that X and Y differ in their properties it follows that the real essence of X is numerically distinct from the real essence of Y. Therefore, it is not the fact that X and Y share the same real essence that accounts for their being classified in the same sort, S.

The second argument for the claim that we do not classify substances according to their real essence (or substantial form) also depends on two premises: first, that the basis on which we classify anything must be known (or, at least, knowable); and, second, that we cannot know the real essence (or substantial form) of any substance, whether material (E III.vi.9: 444–445) or spiritual (E III.vi.11–12: 445–447).[11]

The third argument establishes that classification is not based on real essence (or substantial form) even if the latter is actually knowable. Locke points out that ordinary "ignorant and illiterate" people classified substances into sorts long before scientists "troubled themselves about *Forms* and *Essences*," and concludes that real essence (or substantial form) could not be the basis for "the more or less comprehensive [sortal] terms" they have bequeathed us (E III.vi.25: 452).

The fourth argument is based on a thought-experiment. First, Locke claims that we would all agree that ice and water are "two distinct *Species* of Things." But, second, he imagines "an *English-man*, bred in *Jamaica*, who, perhaps, had never seen nor heard of *Ice*, coming into *England* in the Winter [and finding] the Water he put in his Bason at night, in a great part frozen in the morning." Such an Englishman, claims Locke, might well, and with reason, call the substance in his basin "harden'd Water," and then "[i]t would not to him be a new *Species*, no more than congealed Gelly, when it is cold, is a distinct *Species*, from the same Gelly fluid and warm; or than liquid Gold, in the Fornace, is a distinct *Species* from hard Gold in the Hands of a Workman" (E III.vi.13: 447–448). But if real essence were the basis of our classification of substances into sorts, then we would have to say that either those who treat ice and water as different species are wrong or those (such as the hypothetical Jamaican-bred Englishman) who treat ice and water as belonging to the same species are wrong. And yet this is not something that we want to say. Locke concludes that the classification of ice and water cannot depend on the real essence of these substances.

How good are these arguments? The answer is that none is persuasive. Consider the first and the third. Locke claims that we often find ourselves sorting two substances in the same category and only to discover later that the substances differ in their observable properties/powers. But Locke then assumes that the discovery of these differences has no impact on our classificatory scheme. This may be true for the "ignorant and the illiterate." But the scientist typically treats these differences as evidence that she is dealing with substances that, though superficially similar, really belong in different scientific categories. What we originally think of as three instances of vitriol may, after further experiment, be classified as zinc sulfate, ferrous sulfate, and copper sulfate.[12] So the evolution of science since Locke's day disproves his classification hypothesis. As for the second argument, although there is something laudable about Locke's epistemic modesty, it turns out that scientific investigation is able to uncover a great deal more about the internal constitution of substances than Locke ever thought possible. And the fourth argument, interestingly enough, is really the description of the first step in the discovery that ice and water are isomers, rather than substances belonging to completely different scientific categories.

notes

1 Locke sometimes speaks of words as remaining the same "when written" (E IV.iii.19: 550). In the same section, Locke claims that geometrical diagrams more closely correspond to geometrical figures than "any Words or Sounds whatsoever." This suggests that he may be contrasting words with sounds, thinking of them in this particular context as inscriptions.

I am passing over some tricky issues here. Locke is a nominalist, for he endorses the view that "all things that exist are only particulars" (E III.iii.6:

410). So Locke would refuse to accept the type-token distinction, assuming that types are universals. More likely he would treat resembling inscriptions as inscriptions of the same word, and resembling articulate sounds as articulations of the same word. The tricky question would be to explain how a particular utterance and a particular inscription can both instantiate the same word if they do not resemble each other. Of course, it is possible for an inscription to *represent* an utterance (and vice versa), but this would be to suggest that inscriptions *signify* utterances, and, as we will see, this is something Locke would almost surely want to deny.

2 This account of mediate signification also works, of course, when the set of intervening objects is a singleton. In such a case, X mediately signifies Z when X signifies Z by virtue of the fact that there is something, namely Y, such that X signifies Y and Y signifies Z.

3 Some scholars think that the immediate/mediate distinction is not important in the case of signification because Locke largely stops invoking the distinction as Book III of the *Essay* progresses. But this view understates the number of times Locke appeals to the distinction in Book III (see, e.g., E III.i.6: 404; E III.ii.1: 405; E III.ii.2: 405; E III.ii.4: 406; E III.ii.6: 407; E III.ii.7: 407; E III.iv.1: 420; E III.iv.2: 421; E III.ix.13: 482; and E III.ix.18: 487). The fact that Locke appeals to the distinction in so many places, both earlier and later in Book III, strongly suggests that he finds it important and does not merely drop it.

4 This claim raises problems for Locke, for elsewhere he says that it "could never be known" whether the idea produced in one person's mind by a violet is the same as the idea produced in another person's mind by a marigold (E II. xxxii.15: 389). But in that case, it could never be known whether a speaker and hearer are communicating successfully, because, as Locke puts it, "one Man's Mind could not pass into another Man's Body, to perceive, what Appearances were produced by those Organs." Locke finesses this problem by claiming that he is "nevertheless very apt to think, that the sensible *Ideas*, produced by any Object in different Men's Minds, are most commonly very near and undiscernibly alike" (E II.xxxii.15: 389). It is most likely that Locke would count ideas X and Y as being the same (for purposes of communication) if X and Y resemble each other in this sense.

5 For more on real essence, see Section 9.3 below.

6 Locke targets Scholastics, Cartesians, and atomists for criticism, noting, for example, that all of them provide definitions of terms such as "motion" and "light." For the Scholastics (Thomas Aquinas, following Aristotle), motion is defined as "[t]*he Act of a being in Power, as far forth as in Power*"; for the atomists, motion is defined as a "*passage from one place to another*"; and for the Cartesians, motion is defined as "*the successive Application of the parts of the* Superficies *of one Body, to those of another*" (E III.iv.8–9: 422–423). Locke discusses Scholastic and Cartesian/atomist definitions of "light" at E III.iv.10: 423–424.

7 By parity of reasoning, Locke should argue that terms that signify simple mental acts (such as affirming and denying) are also indefinable.

8 And presumably relations too, because ideas of relations are complex (see Chapter 4).

9 This latter claim is confusing, because the real essence of a mode (or relation) is a complex of *properties*, whereas the nominal essence of a mode-term (or

relation-term) is a complex of *ideas* that signify those properties. Locke mitigates (or perhaps compounds) the problem by sometimes talking of nominal essence as the set of properties signified by a complex of ideas, rather than as the complex of ideas itself. For example, at E III.vi.26: 453, the nominal essence of "man" is characterized as an abstract idea, and at E III.vi.7: 443, the nominal essence of a sort is characterized as what the name for the sort (immediately) signifies; but at E III.vi.2: 439, Locke claims that the nominal essence of gold, namely its "Qualities, and all [of its] other Properties," depends on its real essence. More careful editing of the *Essay* would have avoided this sort of confusion.

10 It might be thought that the substratum that supports the primary qualities of a substance's insensible parts is numerically distinct from the substratum that supports the primary qualities and secondary qualities of the substance itself. For example, if we suppose that gold is made of atoms, we might suppose that the substratum that supports atomic mobility is distinct from the substratum that supports the mobility of gold itself. Nothing that Locke explicitly says rules this option out. But it is unlikely that he would have favored it, for one of the main functions of substratum is to explain the *union* of all of a substance's properties. So if a substance were to have a multiplicity of substrata, the union of its properties would be left unexplained.

11 With respect to this argument, the only difference between real essence and substantial form is that whereas we have at least an obscure conception of the former (as that internal constitution responsible for a substance's observable properties), "we have scarce so much as any obscure, or confused Conception" of the latter, which is "wholly unintelligible" (E III.vi.10: 445).

12 And what we originally think of as a blue-white metal, a yellow metal, and a black metal may, after further experiment, be classified as different allotropes of antimony.

further reading

Ashworth, E.J., "Locke on Language," *Canadian Journal of Philosophy* 14 (1984): 45–73.

Atherton, Margaret, "Locke on Essences and Classification," in *The Cambridge Companion to Locke's "Essay Concerning Human Understanding"*, edited by Lex Newman. Cambridge: Cambridge University Press, 2007, pp. 258–285.

Ayers, Michael, *Locke: Epistemology and Ontology*, 2 vols. London: Routledge, 1991, vol. 2, pp. 15–90.

Bolton, Martha Brandt, "The Relevance of Locke's Theory of Ideas to his Doctrine of Nominal Essence and Anti-Essentialist Semantic Theory," in *Locke*, edited by Vere Chappell. Oxford: Oxford University Press, 1998, pp. 214–225.

Frege, Gottlob, *Translations from the Philosophical Writings of Gottlob Frege*, edited and translated by Peter Geach and Max Black. Oxford: Blackwell, 1952.

Guyer, Paul, "Locke's Philosophy of Language," in *The Cambridge Companion to Locke*, edited by Vere Chappell. Cambridge: Cambridge University Press, 1994, pp. 115–145.

Kretzmann, Norman, "The Main Thesis of Locke's Semantic Theory," *Philosophical Review* 77 (1968): 175–196.

Lennon, Thomas M., "Locke on Ideas and Representation," *The Cambridge Companion to Locke's "Essay Concerning Human Understanding"*, edited by Lex Newman. Cambridge: Cambridge University Press, 2007, pp. 231–257.

Losonsky, Michael, "Language, Meaning, and Mind in Locke's *Essay*," in *The Cambridge Companion to Locke's "Essay Concerning Human Understanding"*, edited by Lex Newman. Cambridge: Cambridge University Press, 2007, pp. 286–312.

Mackie, J.L., *Problems from Locke*. Oxford: Clarendon Press, 1976, chapter 3.

Ott, Walter, *Locke's Philosophy of Language*. Cambridge: Cambridge University Press, 2004.

Owen, David, "Locke on Real Essence," *History of Philosophy Quarterly* 8 (1991): 105–118.

Stanford, Kyle P., "Reference and Natural Kind Terms: The Real Essence of Locke's View," *Pacific Philosophical Quarterly* 79 (1990): 78–97.

knowledge and belief

Although Locke wrote the *Essay* in fits and starts over a period of almost 20 years, it was always designed to build to a well thought-out climax: a complete anti-dogmatic and anti-skeptical theory of knowledge consistent with, and indeed in some ways driven by, his theory of ideas. Locke's theory of knowledge, unlike his theories of ideas, anti-innatism, qualities, freedom, personal identity, and real essence, never really caught on, most likely in part because it does not capture many of our intuitions about knowledge. For Locke is a *necessitarian* about knowledge, in the sense that he takes all genuine knowledge to be of necessary truths; whereas for most working epistemologists nowadays, a great deal of our knowledge is of contingent matters.

Locke is mainly concerned to articulate an epistemology that avoids the Scylla of dogmatism and the Charybdis of skepticism. He sees himself as a humble, commonsense epistemologist who, unlike the dogmatists of Scholasticism, Cartesianism and Epicurean atomism, insists that there is much about the world that we do not (indeed, cannot) know, but also, unlike Pyrrhonian and Academic Skeptics, insists that we are all capable of acquiring a good deal of knowledge, particularly in the domains of religion and ethics. For its time, Locke's theory is deeply original and well repays careful consideration.

I begin by discussing (i) Locke's official account of the nature of knowledge, and the distinction he draws between knowledge and judgment (belief, assent), (ii) his seemingly tripartite division of knowledge into intuitive, demonstrative, and sensitive, and (iii) the anti-dogmatic and anti-skeptical aspects of his epistemology. I then consider (iv) how this theory applies to claims of divine revelation, including those made by religious "enthusiasts."

10.1 The Official Account of Knowledge

Locke defines knowledge as *"the perception of the connexion and agreement, or disagreement and repugnancy of any of our Ideas"* (E IV.i.1: 525). This

Locke, First Edition. Samuel C. Rickless.
© 2014 Samuel C. Rickless. Published 2014 by John Wiley & Sons, Ltd.

account of knowledge requires further elucidation. First, the definition is ambiguous as stated. Does Locke mean that knowledge is the perception of agreement or disagreement between two ideas, or does he mean that knowledge is the perception of agreement or disagreement between one idea and something else that is not an idea? Second, what does Locke mean by "perception"? Does the term "perception" in this context mean what it means in other contexts in which it appears in the *Essay* (e.g., in E II.ix, a chapter titled "*Of Perception*")? Third, what does Locke mean by "agreement" and "disagreement"?

Locke also draws connections between knowledge, propositions, and truth. In his correspondence with Stillingfleet, Locke writes that "every thing which we either know or believe, is some proposition" (W4: 357). And in the *Elements of Natural Philosophy*, Locke claims that knowledge "consists in the perception of the truth of affirmative or negative propositions" (W3: 329). This raises the question of whether this understanding of knowledge is consistent with Locke's official account of knowledge as the perception of ideational agreement or disagreement.

Let us begin by disambiguating Locke's official definition of knowledge. At first, it might appear that Locke allows that some forms of knowledge involve perception of agreement between an idea and an extra-mental thing, for he tells us that there are four main kinds of agreement, the fourth of which is "of *actual real Existence* agreeing to any *Idea*" (E IV.i.7: 527). But on reflection this cannot be correct as an interpretation of Locke's theory of knowledge. There are two main reasons for this. First, in some places Locke makes it clear that "our Knowledge consist[s] in the perception of the Agreement, or Disagreement of any two *Ideas*" (E IV.ii.15: 538). Second, Locke tells us that agreement can be perceived in two main ways, the first of which involves *immediate* perception of agreement "of two *Ideas*" (E IV.ii.1: 530), and the second of which involves the *mediate* perception of agreement "of two *Ideas*" (E IV.ii.2: 531) (more on this below). So the best interpretation of Locke's statement about the perception of actual real existence agreeing to any idea is that he is thinking of a situation in which there is perception of agreement between one idea (e.g., the idea of a particular chair) and *the idea of existence*.

The next issue is what Locke means by "perception" in the claim that knowledge is the perception of ideational (dis)agreement. It might be thought that Locke uses "perception" to refer to the mental operation that is discussed in the *Essay* chapter on simple ideas of reflection and in the *Essay* chapter devoted to "perception." But this cannot be right. In these chapters, Locke tells us that perception is one of the "two great and principal Actions of the Mind . . . which are so frequent, that every one that pleases, may take notice of 'em in himself" (E II.vi.2: 128), that it is "the first faculty of the Mind, exercised about our *Ideas* . . . and is by some called Thinking in general" (E II.ix.1: 143), and that it is "that, which *puts the distinction betwixt the animal Kingdom, and the inferior parts of Nature*" (E II.ix.11: 147). In this sense, perception is the most basic faculty that distinguishes sentient from non-sentient beings, and thus all forms of mental activity, including knowledge and faith (or belief), are properly classified as modes of perception (E II. vi.2: 128). But the perception that partly constitutes knowledge is not merely the mental operation of thinking in general. Locke distinguishes knowledge from belief (or judgment), claiming that whereas knowledge is *perception* of ideational (dis)agreement, belief (or judgment) is *presumption* of such (dis)agreement (E IV.xiv.4: 653) (more on this below). But presumption is a mode of thinking in general, so if Locke were thinking of the perception involved in knowledge as the operation of thinking, then judgment would end up being classified wrongly as just another mode of knowledge.

The perception of ideational (dis)agreement that defines knowledge is therefore not just the mental operation of thinking in general that Locke sometimes calls "perception." Rather, it must be a particular mode of thinking, a mode that is numerically distinct from the mode of thinking Locke calls "presumption." Locke says that one *presumes* an agreement between ideas when one "takes [one's] *Ideas* to agree" (E IV.xiv.3: 653). Knowledge, as Locke understands it, is supposed to involve a mode of thought that goes beyond mere presumption or "taking." This mode of thought, which Locke calls "perception," is factive: whenever one *perceives* an agreement between X and Y, X and Y really do agree. By contrast, presumption is a non-factive faculty: from the fact that one *presumes* an agreement between X and Y, it does not follow that X and Y really do agree. Beyond this, Locke tells us precious little about the nature of perception, as contrasted with presumption. When one perceives an agreement, one *sees* that the agreement holds, and there is not much more to it than that.

Locke tells us somewhat more (though perhaps not as much as would be optimal) about the nature of ideational (dis)agreement, and what he says requires clarification. The official view appears to be that there are four kinds of agreement: identity, relation, co-existence (in the same subject), and real existence (E IV.i.3: 525). But Locke quickly clarifies that, in fact, given that identity and co-existence are relations, there are two main kinds of agreement: (i) relation (including identity and co-existence), and (ii) real existence (E IV.i.7: 527).

When Locke comes to discuss the general category of agreement in relation, what he says is surprisingly uninformative (E IV.i.5: 526). So some reconstruction of his views about this kind of agreement is in order. Locke speaks of the idea of the three angles of a triangle agreeing *in bigness* with the idea of two right angles (E IV.ii.2: 532), of the idea of an obtuse triangle agreeing *in equality* (i.e., in identity of area) with the idea of an acute triangle (E IV.iii.3: 539), and, implicitly, of the agreement in relation between the idea of right (or property) and the idea of justice (E IV.iii.18: 549), as well as the disagreement in relation between the idea of government and the idea of absolute liberty (E IV.iii.18: 550). Locke's mathematical examples could, in principle, be regimented as special cases of agreement in respect of *identity*. For example, what Locke describes as the idea of the three angles of a triangle agreeing in bigness with the idea of two right angles could be redescribed as the idea of the sum of the three angles of a triangle agreeing in identity with the idea of the sum of two right angles. But such a redescription is not available in Locke's moral examples: there is no reasonable way of redescribing the agreement Locke thinks obtains between the idea of property and the idea of justice as an agreement in identity between two other ideas. What *can* be said about the moral examples is that the relevant ideas are necessarily connected: the idea of property is necessarily connected to the idea of justice inasmuch as "[w]here there is no Property, there is no Injustice," and the idea of government is necessarily disconnected from the idea of absolute liberty inasmuch as "[n]o Government allows absolute Liberty" (E IV.iii.18: 549–550).

The hallmark of agreement in respect of relation, then, is the existence of a necessary connection.[1] Such a connection clearly holds in the case of the two sorts of agreement in relation that Locke singles out for special consideration: identity and co-existence (in the same subject). When the idea of white agrees in respect of identity with the idea of white, it is clearly necessarily connected to itself (E IV.i.4: 526); and when the idea of fixedness (i.e., "a power to remain in the Fire unconsumed") agrees in respect of co-existence (in the same subject) with the idea of gold, the two ideas are also necessarily connected, at least inasmuch as the first idea "always accompanies, and is join'd with" the second (E IV.i.6: 527). The existence of a necessary connection also seems to be the hallmark of agreement in respect of real existence. For example, Locke makes clear that he thinks that he knows that he exists and that God exists, and that he perceives his own existence immediately and the existence of God mediately (E IV.iii.21: 552–553). This presupposes that perception of his own existence requires perception of an agreement between the idea of himself and the idea of existence, and perception of God's existence requires the perception of an agreement between the idea of God and the idea of existence. The agreement in both cases clearly requires a necessary connection between the two ideas (see E IV.vii.7: 594), inasmuch as it is impossible to think of oneself as not existing and (as Locke tries to show) one's own existence guarantees God's existence.[2]

For Locke, then, knowledge is the perception (rather than the presumption) of a necessary (dis)connection (or (dis)agreement) between two ideas. How, if at all, is this account to be reconciled with Locke's claim that knowledge is the perception of the truth of affirmative or negative propositions? The answer is to be found in Locke's theory of propositions and his theory of truth. As we saw in Chapter 9, a proposition is "[t]he *joining* or *separating* of signs" (E IV.v.2: 574), where joining is the mental operation of affirming and separating is the mental operation of denying (E IV.v.5: 576). But given that "there are two sorts of Signs commonly made use of, *viz. Ideas* and *Words*," it follows that there are two kinds of propositions: mental propositions (in which *ideas* are joined or separated) and verbal propositions (in which *words* are joined or separated) (E II.xxxii.19: 391; E IV.v.2: 574; E IV.v.5: 575–576). Mental propositions, therefore, are similar in content and structure to the propositions that are discussed by Fregean philosophers of language nowadays, whereas verbal propositions are sentences. Now truth in general, for Locke, is *"the joining or separating of Signs, as the Things signified by them, do agree or disagree one with another"* (E IV.v.2: 574; also E II.xxxii.19: 391; E IV.v.5: 576). Given that there are two kinds of signs – ideas and words – it follows that there are two kinds of truth – mental truth and verbal truth (E IV.v.6: 576). Mental truth is the joining or separating of *ideas* (in mental propositions), as the things signified by them (i.e., substances, modes, and relations, but sometimes ideas themselves) agree or disagree one with another; verbal truth is the joining or separating of *words* (in verbal propositions), as the things signified by them (i.e., ideas) agree or disagree one with another.[3] The *mental* proposition that gold is fixed, which consists in the affirmation of the idea of fixedness of the idea of gold, is true when the significatum of the idea of fixedness (i.e., the quality of fixedness) agrees with the significatum of the idea of gold (i.e., gold). The *verbal* proposition, "Gold is fixed," which consists in the joining of the word "fixed" with the word "gold" by way of affirmation, is true when the significatum of the word "fixed" (i.e., the idea of fixedness) agrees with the significatum of the word "gold" (i.e., the idea of gold). This theory of propositions and truth is what allows Locke to say, consistently with his official definition of knowledge, that knowledge is the perception of the truth of an affirmative or negative proposition. For truth consists in the agreement between the significata of an affirmative proposition's constituent signs, or in the disagreement between the significata of a negative proposition's constituent signs.

10.2 The Degrees of Knowledge

Locke tells us that knowledge comes in degrees, though it is important to note that he does not mean by this that knowledge is the sort of thing that admits of more or less (in the way that, say, anger or happiness admits of more or less), for it is not possible for someone to perceive an ideational (dis)agreement *more* than she perceives some other ideational (dis)agreement, or *more* than someone else perceives the same (or a different) ideational (dis)agreement. Officially, Locke tells us that there are *"three degrees of Knowledge, viz. Intuitive, Demonstrative, and Sensitive*: in each of which, there are different degrees and ways of Evidence and Certainty"* (E IV.ii.14: 538). But it is difficult to see how Locke can make room for "sensitive knowledge" as a third degree of genuine knowledge, given his official account of knowledge as the perception of ideational (dis)agreement.

To see this, consider Locke's distinction between intuitive and demonstrative knowledge. Intuitive knowledge occurs when "the Mind perceives the Agreement or Disagreement of two *Ideas* immediately by themselves, without the intervention of any other" (E IV.ii.1: 530–531); by contrast, demonstrative knowledge occurs when "the Mind perceives the Agreement or Disagreement of any *Ideas*, but not immediately" (E IV.ii.2: 531). Intuitive knowledge, then, is the *immediate* perception of ideational (dis)agreement, while demonstrative knowledge is the *mediate* perception of the same sort of (dis)agreement. A mind perceives the (dis)agreement between two ideas immediately, when the perception of this (dis)agreement does not presuppose or require the perception of any other ideational (dis)agreements; but it perceives the (dis)agreement between two ideas mediately, when the perception of this (dis)agreement *does* presuppose or require the perception of some other (mediating) ideational (dis)agreements. Examples of intuitive knowledge include the perception of disagreement between the idea of white and the idea of black, and between the idea of a circle and the idea of a triangle; and they include the perception of agreement between the idea of three and the idea of being greater than two (E IV.ii.1: 531), and, as we have seen, between the idea of oneself and the idea of existence (E IV.iii.21: 552–553; E IV.ix.2: 618; E IV.xi.1: 630). Examples of demonstrative knowledge include the perception of the agreement between the idea of the three angles of a triangle and the idea of two right angles (as well as the ideational agreements and disagreements captured in mathematical theorems) (E IV.ii.2: 532; E IV.iii.18: 549), and between the idea of justice and the idea of property (and between other moral ideas) (E IV.iii.18: 549).

In respect of the epistemic status of "sensitive knowledge," the key feature of Locke's distinction between intuitive and demonstrative knowledge is that it is not merely *exclusive*, but also *exhaustive*: every perception of ideational (dis)agreement must be *either* immediate (not by virtue of perceiving some other ideational (dis)agreements) or mediate (by virtue of perceiving some other ideational (dis)agreements). There is no third option here: all knowledge must be either intuitive or demonstrative. If Locke's epistemology is to remain internally consistent, then, his claim that "sensitive knowledge" is a third degree of knowledge (or some other claim that is part of his epistemological theory, such as his official account of knowledge) must be either discounted or reinterpreted.

Locke himself perhaps half-heartedly suggests that consistency might be purchased at the cost of restricting the general claim that *all* perception of truth must be either intuitive or demonstrative. When he introduces the concept of sensitive knowledge, Locke writes: "These two, (*viz.*) Intuition and Demonstration, are the degrees of our Knowledge; whatever comes short of one of these, with what assurance soever embraced, is but Faith, or Opinion, but not Knowledge" (E IV.ii.14: 536). By itself, this suggests that there is no third degree of knowledge: everything that falls short of intuition or demonstration is not knowledge, but judgment. But he then adds, perhaps as an afterthought designed to make room for the possibility of a third kind of knowledge: "at least in all general Truths." Locke seems to be saying that perception of the truth of *general* propositions must be either intuitive or demonstrative, while perception of the truth of *particular* propositions can be both non-intuitive and non-demonstrative. On this view, perception of the truth of the proposition that all gold is yellow must be either immediate or mediate; but perception of the truth of the proposition that the particular piece of gold in front of me is yellow might be other than immediate or mediate. But a moment's thought should have been sufficient to convince Locke that this view makes no sense. Whether the proposition whose truth I am perceiving is general or particular, I can do no other than perceive its truth immediately or mediately.

What, then, is (or should be) Locke's considered view about the epistemic status of "sensitive knowledge"? The answer, suggested by what Locke says in the chapter devoted to "sensitive knowledge" (E IV.xi), is that "sensitive knowledge" is not genuine knowledge at all, but rather a kind of belief (or judgment). To understand why this is so, we need a more complete understanding of Locke's theory of belief. As we saw above, belief is distinguished from knowledge by being the presumption, rather than the perception, of ideational (dis)agreement. Locke adds that belief (or, in the case of verbal propositions, assent) is grounded not in intuition or demonstration, but in probability or "likeliness to be true" (E IV.xv.3: 655). For example, the acceptance of a mathematical theorem on the basis of "hearing a Mathematician, a Man of credit, affirm [it]" counts as a form of belief, based on the probability of the theorem's being true given the mathematician's credibility and expertise (E IV.xv.1: 654). Locke notes further that belief comes in degrees, depending entirely on the degree of probability that grounds it. The highest degree of probability, which Locke calls "assurance," is "when the general consent of all Men, in all Ages, as far as it can be known, concurs with a Man's constant and never-failing Experience in like cases, to confirm the Truth of any particular matter of fact attested by fair Witnesses" (E IV.xvi.6: 661). The next degree, which Locke calls "confidence," is "when I find by my own Experience, and the Agreement of all others that mention it, a thing to be, for the most part, so; and that the particular instance of it is attested by many and undoubted Witnesses" (E IV.xvi.7: 662). Then, depending on the extent to which the "two foundations of Credibility, *viz.* Common Observation in like cases, and particular Testimonies in that particular instance, favour or contradict" a proposition, the degree of belief moves downwards through the attitudes of "*Belief, Conjecture, Guess, Doubt, Wavering, Distrust, Disbelief*, etc." (E IV.xvi.9: 663).

In E IV.xi, Locke writes:

> The notice we have by our Senses, of the existing of Things without us, though it be not altogether so certain, as our intuitive Knowledge, or the Deductions of our Reason, employ'd about the clear abstract *Ideas* of our own Minds; yet it is an assurance that *deserves the name of Knowledge*. If we persuade our selves, that our Faculties act and inform us right, concerning the existence of those Objects that affect them, it cannot pass for an ill-grounded confidence. (E IV.xi.3: 631)

Here Locke suggests that "sensitive knowledge" is really a kind of assurance that deserves to be called "knowledge" and is superior to "ill-grounded confidence." Although Locke sometimes (though rarely) uses "assurance" in a broader sense than the sense defined at E IV.xvi.6, the contrast here between assurance and confidence (which is the next degree of knowledge defined at E IV.xvi.7) and the replacement of the claim that "sensitive knowledge" *is* knowledge with the claim that "sensitive knowledge" *merits the name of* "knowledge," strongly suggest that Locke takes "sensitive knowledge" to be a kind of assurance (i.e., belief based on the highest degree of probability) that deserves to be called "knowledge" even if it is not knowledge *in the strict sense* (i.e., perception of ideational (dis)agreement).

Why would Locke say that "sensitive knowledge" deserves the name of knowledge if it is not knowledge *strictly understood*? The answer is simple. Locke tells us that the probabilities characteristic of assurance "rise so near to *Certainty*, that they govern our Thoughts as absolutely, and influence all our Actions as fully, as the most evident demonstration: and in what concerns us, we make little or no difference between them and certain Knowledge" (E IV.xvi.6: 662). The suggestion here is that the difference between knowledge and assurance is not significant *for practical purposes*. When it comes to our thoughts, the probabilities that ground assurance put us "past doubt" (E IV.xvi.6: 662) and leave us "as little liberty to believe, or disbelieve, as a Demonstration does" (E IV.xvi.9: 663). And with respect to our actions, our faculties, Locke says, are "suited not . . . to a perfect, clear, comprehensive Knowledge of things . . ., but to the preservation of us, in whom they are; and accommodated to the use of Life: they serve to our purpose well enough, if they will but give us certain notice of those Things, which are convenient or inconvenient to us" (E IV.xi.8: 634; see also E I.i.5: 45). So if we are assured, and hence cannot doubt, of this or that action that it will lead to pleasure (or pain), then we have a kind of belief that "is not only *as great* as our frame can attain to, but *as our Condition needs*" (E IV.xi.8: 634). It is therefore the *practical* indistinguishability of assurance from knowledge, despite their distinguishability in principle, that leads Locke to say that the former "deserves the name of" the latter.

10.3 Anti-Dogmatism and Anti-Skepticism

Having clarified what knowledge is and the nature of its degrees, Locke moves on to discuss what it is that our faculties make it possible for us to know. His position, as described in the Introduction to the *Essay*, is twofold. On the one hand, the nature of knowledge entails that some matters (particularly empirical matters) are "beyond the reach of our Capacities." About these matters we should not be dogmatic – that is, we should not, as the Scholastics, Cartesians, and Epicureans do, assume that we do or can have knowledge of them. Instead, we should "sit down in a quiet ignorance of those Things" and not "perplex our selves and others with Disputes about Things, to which our Understandings are not suited" (E I.i.4: 45). On the other hand, there is much that we can know (or be assured of), certainly enough to secure "our great Concernments": God, our duties, and the attainment of pleasure and the avoidance of pain (E I.i.5: 45).

Knowledge consists of the immediate or mediate perception of (dis)agreement (or necessary (dis)connection) between ideas. When the perception is immediate, knowledge is intuitive; when mediate, it is demonstrative. Locke claims that one can have intuitive knowledge of (i) trifling matters, such as that "*a man is a man*, or *whatsoever is white is white*" (E IV.vii.4: 592), (ii) mathematical propositions, such as the general axioms of arithmetic and Euclidean geometry and particular truths such as that three is more than two, (iii) basic moral truths, such as that injustice is "the Invasion or Violation of [a] right" (E IV.iii.18: 549), (iv) necessary connections between primary qualities, such as that "Figure necessarily supposes Extension" and "receiving or communicating Motion by impulse, supposes Solidity" (E IV.iii.14: 546), and (v) one's own existence (E IV.iii.21: 552–553; E IV.ix.2: 618). Beyond this, there is not much more in the way of intuitive knowledge to be acquired, given that such knowledge consists in the perception of a necessary connection between two ideas without the mediation of any other idea. Demonstrative knowledge, being the mediate perception of such a necessary connection, simply encompasses the necessary consequences of all the propositions that are intuitively known, including mathematical theorems (e.g., that the three angles of a triangle add up to two right angles – E IV.ii.2: 532), moral theorems (e.g., that where there is no property, there is no injustice – E IV.iii.18: 549), and, as Locke believes, the existence of God (E IV.iii.21: 553; E IV.x.1: 619). And "sensitive knowledge," which is not genuine knowledge but rather assurance of the existence of things outside our minds, is, even so, limited to what, at the very place and time it is acquired, is being perceived by means of the senses. Beyond these matters, there is and can be no knowledge *per se*: the most that can be acquired is (some degree of) belief, based on higher or lower probability.

Locke spends a significant portion of Book IV emphasizing just how many kinds of propositions about the world our faculties do not permit us to genuinely know. Even in mathematics, our faculties might not be equal to the task of working out all the necessary connections between ideas that there are, and thus, for example, "perhaps, [we] shall never be able to find a Circle equal to a Square, and certainly know that it is so" (E IV.iii.6: 540). As for empirical matters, we might never discover, among other things, "whether Omnipotency has not given to some Systems of Matter fitly disposed, a power to perceive and think, or else joined and fixed to Matter so disposed, a thinking immaterial Substance" (E IV.iii.6: 540–541); what accounts for "the coherence and continuity of the parts of Matter" (E IV.iii.29: 559); which qualities other than those we take to be definitional of a particular sort of substance necessarily co-exist with the definitional qualities (E IV.iii.11: 544–545); how the primary qualities of the insensible parts of bodies ground the secondary qualities of those bodies, if they do (E IV.iii.13: 545); whether there are spirits more powerful than ours but less powerful than God (E IV.iii.27: 557–558); which powers finite spirits possess (E IV.iii.17: 548); whether the dead will be resurrected and what the "state of this Globe of Earth" will be in the future (E IV.iii.29: 560). Locke attributes our ignorance of these matters to three main causes: (i) "Want of *Ideas*" (our simple ideas being limited to what we receive through sensation and reflection), (ii) "Want of a discoverable Connexion between the *Ideas* we have," and (iii) "Want of tracing, and examining our *Ideas*" (E IV.iii.22: 553). In particular, Locke claims that our faculties are such that we will (or may) always remain ignorant of true propositions about things that are either "*too remote*" or "*too minute*" (E IV.iii.24: 555). And thus, although Locke is optimistic about what can be learned by means of "experimental" philosophy (which concerns facts about particular experiments involving particular substances and their interactions under particular circumstances), he is singularly pessimistic about the possibility of acquiring "scientific" knowledge of the world of bodies and spirits, given its complexity and lack of transparency to our senses (E IV.iii.26: 556–557). Indeed, "as to a perfect *Science* of natural Bodies, (not to mention spiritual Beings,)," Locke writes, "we are, I think, so far from being capable of any such thing, that I conclude it lost labour to seek after it" (E IV.iii.29: 560). This pessimism sets Locke apart from his far more optimistic Scholastic, Cartesian, and Epicurean predecessors and contemporaries.

At a general level, then, Locke's theory of what can and cannot be known by the human mind is fairly straightforward. But there are problems with the details. One problem concerns Locke's claim that we have intuitive knowledge of our own existence. How is this possible? Knowledge is perception of a necessary connection between two ideas. In the case of self-knowledge, Locke does not tell us what the two ideas are, but it is reasonable to suppose that he is thinking of the idea of oneself and the (abstract) idea of existence. After all, what other ideas could constitute the mental proposition expressed by the verbal proposition, "I exist"? The problem here, though, is that there appears to be no necessary connection between these two ideas: it is true that I exist, but it is not *necessary* that I exist, for if my parents had never met, I would never have been born. Locke is hampered here by the fact that he has not developed the conceptual resources (later developed by Immanuel Kant, and brought to fruition by Saul Kripke) to distinguish between *a priori* knowledge (of which knowledge of one's own existence is a good example) and knowledge of necessary truths.

Another problem concerns Locke's proof of God's existence, which is glaringly fallacious.[4] Locke begins the proof by pointing to the intuitive knowledge that one exists (and hence that "there is some real Being") and that "Nonentity cannot produce any real Being" (though here too it is difficult to see why it is that the absence of something, which is what the word "non-entity" immediately signifies (E III.i.4: 403), disagrees with the idea of producing anything real). These two propositions are then supposed to provide us with "an evident demonstration, that from Eternity there has been something" (E IV.x.3: 620), indeed something that Locke calls an "eternal Source . . . of all being"

(E IV.x.4: 620). But the claim that "from Eternity there has been something" is ambiguous. The sentence could mean *either* (ES) that at *every* time there has been *something* in existence at that time *or* (SE) that there is *something* that has existed at *every* time. All that follows from the premises of Locke's argument is (ES), as long as it is supposed in the background that every cause precedes its effect in time and that no period during which nothing exists can come between the exertion of a cause and the production of its effect. But Locke thinks that his argument establishes (SE), even though (ES) does not entail (SE). The problem is that it is compatible with Locke's premises for there to be an infinite series of different entities existing at consecutive moments, with each entity being the cause of its immediate successor. And from this it does not follow that there is some one thing that has existed for all time. So Locke commits the fallacy of equivocation because he fails to distinguish between (ES) and (SE).[5] In the end, it seems that Locke's own theory of knowledge does not provide him with sufficient resources to establish his own existence or the existence of God. From his vantage point, this would be epistemic pessimism gone wild, but logically there appears to be no alternative.

Having emphasized that there is much that human minds do not and cannot know, Locke is equally emphatic that skepticism, at least about the things that matter most, is just as unwarranted as dogmatism. Locke discusses skepticism in several places, and each time engages in raillery. The question Locke considers is whether the possibility that one might be dreaming is sufficient reason to withhold judgment about what one is perceiving by means of the senses. (This was one of the means of inducing rational doubt about sense perception that Descartes, and many skeptics before him, had raised.) Here is his answer:

> If any one say, a Dream may do the same thing, and all these *Ideas* may be produced in us, without any external Objects, he may please to dream that I make him this Answer, 1. That 'tis no great matter, whether I remove his Scruple, or no: Where all is but Dream, Reasoning and Arguments are of no use, Truth and Knowledge nothing. 2. That I believe he will allow a very manifest difference between dreaming of being in the Fire, and being actually in it. But yet if he be resolved to appear so sceptical, as to maintain, that what I call being actually in the Fire, is nothing but a Dream; and that we cannot thereby certainly know, that any such thing as Fire actually exists without us: I answer, That we certainly finding, that Pleasure or Pain follows upon the application of certain Objects to us, whose Existence we perceive, or dream that we perceive, by our Senses, this certainty is as great as our Happiness, or Misery, beyond which, we have no concernment to know, or to be. (E IV.ii.14: 537; see also E IV.xi.8: 634)

Apart from the point that it is pointless to dispute with a serious skeptic (who thinks he has sufficient reason to doubt whether there is anyone really disputing with him), Locke's more serious reply to the skeptic's dream argument is ultimately that the absence of genuine knowledge of the existence of an external world *does not matter*. All that matters is that we have assurance, and hence be free of doubt, about the things that concern us most, particularly how to acquire pleasure and avoid pain. And the reason for Locke's raillery, the reason why he finds it so difficult to take the skeptic's dream hypothesis seriously, is that he thinks, not unreasonably, that no skeptic is so committed to withholding judgment about external matters that he is indifferent about whether to put (what appears to be) his hand in (what appears to be) the fire.

It is important to recognize here that Locke's overt hostility to what he thinks of as external world skepticism is fully compatible with his commitment to the thesis that we cannot really *know* whether there is an external world. For Locke does not think of skepticism as the thesis that we do not (or cannot) *know* that an external world exists, but rather as the thesis that there is sufficient reason to *doubt* (and hence withhold judgment) that an external world exists. If there is anything on which Locke focuses in his discussions of external world skepticism, it is the fact that the existence of a world outside our minds is beyond doubt. Here is a representative passage:

> I think no body can, in earnest, be so sceptical, as to be uncertain of the Existence of those Things which he sees and feels. At least, he that can doubt so far, (whatever he may have with his own Thoughts) will never have any Controversie with me; since he can never be sure I say any thing contrary to his Opinion. (E IV.xi.3: 631)

Locke's point here is that a skeptical attitude is an attitude of doubt, and it is *this attitude* that he thinks the skeptic cannot (or cannot consistently) maintain. Someone who sees a candle burning and has had the painful experience of putting his finger in the flame "will little doubt, that this is something existing without him" (E IV.xi.8: 634); "we cannot so far distrust [the testimony of our senses], as to doubt, that such Collections of simple *Ideas*, as we have observed by our Senses to be united together, do really exist together" (E IV.xi.9: 635); although it is only highly probable, and we do not *know*, that millions of men exist, "the great likelihood of it puts me past doubt, and it [is] reasonable for me to do several things upon the confidence, that there are Men . . . now in the World" (E IV.xi.10: 635–636); and whatever our memory assures of is "past all doubt, so long as we remember well" (E IV.xi.11: 636). The refrain is clear: the skepticism to which Locke is hostile is not the view that we do not (or cannot) *know* that an external world exists, but rather the view that we have sufficient reason to *doubt* the existence of an external world. This is important because, strictly speaking, Locke's view is that we do not *know* that an external world exists; the most we have is *assurance* of its existence.

10.4 Faith and Religious Enthusiasm

Locke's theory of knowledge has application not just to science, mathematics, morals, and the existence of God, but also to religious epistemology more generally. Locke was living at a time of serious religious conflict deepened by the existence of an established Anglican Church and an increasing number of religious dissenters. Part of the Protestant Reformation was that Christians should return to the authority of the Bible rather than submit to the authority of the Pope (and the Catholic Church more generally). But some Protestants (e.g., Quakers) took this one step further, claiming that they were capable of direct communication with God. Locke was well aware of the potentially explosive nature of such claims, given the universal acceptance among Christians of God's infallibility. One sect's claim that God had communicated a particular proposition would contradict another sect's claim that God had communicated the negation of that proposition. Because of the centrality of religious belief to the perceived meaning of life, the multiplication of contradictory claims of this sort would threaten the stability of civil society and lead to more extensive religious and political conflict.

At the end of the *Essay*, Locke therefore turns his attention to what can be known or reasonably believed in matters of religion, and in particular to the proper relationship between faith and reason, as well as the threat of religious enthusiasm. As Locke sees it, reason is "the discovery of the Certainty or Probability of such Propositions or Truths, which the Mind arrives at by Deductions made from such *Ideas*, which it has got by the use of its natural Faculties, *viz.* by Sensation or Reflection." By contrast, faith is "the Assent to any Proposition, not thus made out by the Deductions of Reason; but upon the Credit of the Proposer, as coming from GOD, in some extraordinary way of Communication," namely revelation (E IV.xviii.2: 689).

This initial representation of the distinction between faith and reason suggests that faith concerns assent to propositions that outrun the evidence available to us, and are therefore beyond reason in that sense. Some of what Locke says in other places encourages this way of looking at things. For example, he writes that "*the proper Matter of Faith*" is all those propositions of which "we can have no Knowledge at all . . . as beyond the Discovery of our natural Faculties, and above *Reason*" (E IV.xviii.7: 694). But in the end this way of representing the relation between faith and reason is misleading, even by Locke's own lights. For whether something is to be believed as a matter of faith (as coming from revelation) depends on whether it is rational to do so: "But yet, it still belongs to *Reason*, to judge of the Truth of [something's] being a Revelation, and of the signification of the Words, wherein it is delivered" (E IV.xviii.8: 694).

As Locke sees it, it is possible for God to reveal truths (e.g., the axioms and theorems of geometry) that can be discovered by unaided human reason; but there is "little need or use" of divine revelation under these circumstances (E

IV.xviii.4: 690). This means that God is far more likely to reveal truths that unaided human reason is incapable of discovering. In this sense, propositions that are above unaided human reason are the proper matter of faith. But, as Locke puts it in a chapter added to the fourth edition of the *Essay*, "*Reason must be our last Judge and Guide in every Thing*" (E IV.xix.14: 704). So whether a proposition P that appears to have been revealed by God is to be believed depends on whether reason judges it more probable than not (a) that the words communicated to the recipient of the apparent revelation actually express P (as opposed to some other proposition), (b) that there is exactly one individual communicating those words, and (c) that that single individual is God (and not someone else). In this sense, whether an apparent revelation is to be believed is something that falls squarely within reason's purview. Indeed, the epistemology of revelation, for Locke, is no different from the epistemology of testimony generally. If a handwritten note saying "Find the King of S." were left on my desk, I should take this to be a communication from my mother to find the King of Sweden if, say, the handwriting is recognizably my mother's unique script, my mother (and no one else) had recently told me in person that she wanted to talk to the King of Sweden, and she did not tell me, for example, that she had recently lost the King of Spades in her favorite deck of playing cards. Under very different circumstances, reason might tell me on grounds of insufficient evidence to withhold judgment about how best to interpret the note.

Indeed, it is for this reason that Locke faults enthusiasts. As Locke understands it, enthusiasm is a disposition to believe on evidentially insufficient grounds that a strong opinion that one "cannot account for by the ordinary Methods of Knowledge, and Principles of Reason" is "an Illumination from the Spirit of GOD, and presently of divine Authority" (E IV.xix.5–6: 699). Ever psychologically astute, Locke explains enthusiasm as the product of either "Melancholy . . . mixed with Devotion" or self-conceit (E IV.xix.5: 699). According to his definition, the mistake of enthusiasts is not that they do not have faith, but that they do not allow their faith to be governed by the rational dictate that one should proportion one's belief on the basis of testimony to the degree of the testifier's credibility.

What, then, does Locke think is sufficient evidence of divine revelation? The answer is, "some Marks which Reason cannot be mistaken in" (E IV. xix.14: 704). When the relevant proposition is something that unaided human reason cannot discover, there are two such marks: "the Word of GOD, which is attested Revelation," or "outward signs to convince [one] of the Author of [the revelation]" (E IV.xix.15: 704–705). The outward signs of which Locke is thinking here are, of course, miracles. Thus,

> *Moses* saw the Bush burn without being consumed, and heard a Voice out of it. This was something besides finding an impulse upon his Mind to go to *Pharaoh*, that he might bring his Brethren out of *Egypt*: and yet he thought not this enough to authorise him to go with that Message, till GOD by

another Miracle, of his Rod turned into a Serpent, had assured him of a Power to testify his Mission by the same Miracle repeated before them, whom he was sent to. (E IV.xix.15: 705)

Locke's idea that miracles produced by someone who claims to have heard directly from God constitute evidence of the testifier's credibility is not unreasonable. God, unlike mere finite beings, is omnipotent, and hence is capable of acting in a way opposite to the regular course of nature. If God wants to provide Moses with evidence that the voice he is hearing is God's voice (and not, say, a mere hallucination or trick), it is reasonable for God to give Moses a sign that only a being powerful enough to act contrary to natural law could give.

But there is a serious problem with Locke's claim that miracles are sufficiently probative of divine revelation. Locke believes that, given that "in all the visible corporeal World, we see no Chasms, or Gaps," it is more probable than not that "there are far more *Species* of Creatures above us, than there are beneath" (E III.vi.12: 446; see also E IV.iii.27: 558). Reason therefore suggests that there are extremely powerful and clever spirits other than God with the ability, and quite possibly the motive and opportunity, to change the course of nature for benign or nefarious ends. This means, therefore, that there is no way for reason to tell whether any apparently divine communication that is accompanied by a miracle is the work of God rather than the work of a very powerful angel.

And there is also a problem with Locke's claim that the Bible is "attested" (i.e., certified) revelation. What evidence is there that the Bible is really the word of God? Locke writes as if it is clearly more probable than not that God communicated the contents of the Bible to its human authors, or that the authors of the Bible wrote down what they had heard (e.g., about Moses) from strings of credible sources. But why accept this? Surely what the Bible itself *says* cannot testify to its divine origin. If this were so, then the Quran (or the Book of Mormon) would also testify to *its* divine origin. Reason can speak in favor of the Bible's divine origin only if there is an "outward sign" of its authors' credibility and of the credibility of their sources. But there is no such sign. As far as we can tell, there is no more reason to think that the Bible was divinely inspired than there is to think that the scribblings of an enthusiast were communicated to him by God. This is a puzzle for which Locke's religious epistemology has no solution.

notes

1 I am indebted to Nathan Rockwood for helping me to this conclusion in conversation.
2 Locke appears to treat agreement in respect of real existence as including agreement between the idea of an object obtained through sensation and the idea of existence (E IV.iii.21: 553). But this, as I argue below in the discussion of sensi-

tive knowledge, is not the view that makes the best sense of Locke's writing as a whole.

3 Some ideas (i.e., ideas of modes and relations) signify themselves, while other ideas (i.e., simple ideas and ideas of substances) signify worldly things (i.e., qualities and substances). The fact that some ideas signify themselves while other ideas signify other things explains why Locke says that mental truth occurs "[w]hen *Ideas* are so put together, or separated in the Mind, as they, or the Things they stand for do agree, or not" (E IV.v.6: 576).

4 Were there not independent and highly probative evidence (from his letters and writings) of Locke's theism, one might almost suppose that the major fallacy in the proof was meant to signal a hidden atheism. The lesson, I believe, is that even the most gifted philosophers are potential victims of the irrational influence of wishful thinking on their powers of ratiocination.

5 The rest of Locke's argument is not persuasive either. Assuming the truth of (SE), Locke claims that the source of all power is "*most powerful*" (E IV.x.4: 620). He then points to the fact that one has intuitive knowledge of one's own ability to perceive and know (i.e., that one is a cogitative being) (E IV.x.5: 620). Assuming, then, that something incogitative cannot produce something cogitative (E IV.x.5: 620 – itself a dubious premise, though perhaps not one that Locke is in a position to recognize as dubious, given his ignorance of evolutionary theory), it follows that the eternal source of all being must be cogitative. Locke concludes from all of this that "*there is an eternal, most powerful, and most knowing Being*" (E IV.x.6: 621). But the argument, such as it is, does not prove that the eternal source of all being (call it "G") is *omnipotent* or *omniscient*. And yet this is what Locke needs for his purposes, because the mere fact that G is cogitative and powerful enough to produce everything that exists is compatible with G's powers being limited instead of infinite. (It may be that Locke is misled by the fact that "most powerful" is ambiguous, as between "more powerful than everything else" and "omnipotent," in which case he would be guilty of another fallacy of equivocation.) Moreover, Locke thinks that once G's omniscience and omnipotence have been established, "all his other Attributes necessarily follow" (E IV.x.12: 625). But it is far from self-evident that omnipotence and omniscience, separately or together, entail omnibenevolence.

further reading

Allen, Keith, "Locke and Sensitive Knowledge," *Journal of the History of Philosophy* 51 (2013): 249–266.

Anstey, Peter R., *John Locke and Natural Philosophy*. Oxford: Oxford University Press, 2011.

Jolley, Nicholas, "Locke on Faith and Reason," in *The Cambridge Companion to Locke's "Essay Concerning Human Understanding"*, edited by Lex Newman. Cambridge: Cambridge University Press, 2007, pp. 436–455.

Mattern, Ruth, "Locke: 'Our Knowledge, Which All Consists in Propositions,'" *Canadian Journal of Philosophy* 8 (1978): 677–695. Reprinted in *Locke*, edited by Vere Chappell, Oxford: Oxford University Press, 1998, pp. 226–241.

Nagel, Jennifer, "Sensitive Knowledge: Locke on Skepticism and Sensation," in *A Companion to Locke*, edited by Matthew Stuart. Oxford: Wiley Blackwell, forthcoming.

Newman, Lex, "Locke on Knowledge," in *The Cambridge Companion to Locke's "Essay Concerning Human Understanding"*, edited by Lex Newman. Cambridge: Cambridge University Press, 2007, pp. 313–351.

Owen, David, "Locke on Judgment," in *The Cambridge Companion to Locke's "Essay Concerning Human Understanding"*, edited by Lex Newman. Cambridge: Cambridge University Press, 2007, pp. 406–435.

Rickless, Samuel C., "Is Locke's Theory of Knowledge Inconsistent?," *Philosophy and Phenomenological Research* 77 (2008): 83–104.

Wolterstorff, Nicholas, *John Locke and the Ethics of Belief*. Cambridge: Cambridge University Press, 1996.

moral philosophy

I t is an understatement to say that Locke's moral and political philosophy has been one of the most influential sets of ideas in the history of Western culture. The following ideas, namely that all persons are naturally free and equal, that there are moral rights antecedent to government, that society and government exist in large part (perhaps entirely) to protect those rights, that the legitimacy of government is based on the consent of the governed (and hence that conquest, usurpation, and rebellion are illegitimate ways of changing governments), and that wise government requires a separation of powers, are deeply ingrained in the political culture of modern liberal democracies, thanks in part to the legacy of the French and American revolutions of the late eighteenth century. But we have Locke to thank, not so much for having introduced these ideas into Western culture, but for having put these ideas together in a clear, tightly argued, compelling intellectual package.

The aim of this chapter is to articulate the main features of Locke's moral philosophy. The next chapter is devoted to Locke's political philosophy, which builds directly on his system of morals.

11.1 Morality and God's Will

Locke is a realist and a rationalist about moral rules. What it is that rational creatures are morally required (permitted, forbidden) to do is an objective matter, fixed independently of the wishes or desires of any of them, and is discoverable (at least in principle) by reason, through the discovery of ideational agreements and disagreements. Human beings, though incapable of knowledge of the real essences of substances and thus incapable of scientific knowledge (and even of sensitive knowledge, strictly understood), "have Light enough to lead them to the Knowledge of their Maker, and the sight of their own Duties" (E I.i.5: 45). The reason for this is that the vast majority of

Locke, First Edition. Samuel C. Rickless.
© 2014 Samuel C. Rickless. Published 2014 by John Wiley & Sons, Ltd.

moral words (i.e., "justice," "charity," "virtue," "right," "wrong," "morally good," "morally bad," etc.) signify ideas of mixed modes (E III.v.12: 436), and since the nominal essence of any mixed mode is identical to its real essence (E III.v.14: 436–437) and can be known by anyone who understands the word that signifies the relevant nominal essence, it follows that moral truths can be known (at least in principle) merely by unpacking moral ideas and comparing them with each other to discover whether they agree or disagree. Thus, Locke is "bold to think, that *Morality is capable of Demonstration*, as well as Mathematicks: Since the precise real Essence of the Things moral Words stand for, may be perfectly known; and so the Congruity, or Incongruity of the Things themselves, be certainly discovered, in which consists perfect Knowledge" (E III.xi.16: 516).[1]

The ideas that Locke takes to be foundational for the purposes of moral demonstration are "[t]he Idea of a Supreme Being, infinite in Power, Goodness, and Wisdom, whose Workmanship we are, and on whom we depend; and the *Idea* of our selves, as understanding, rational Beings" (E IV.iii.18: 549). In the *Essay*, Locke does not explain *how* comparison of these ideas is supposed to yield knowledge of moral rules and duties. But in the *Essays on the Law of Nature*, composed in the 1660s and shared with some of his friends during the time that he was writing the *Essay*, Locke fills out the picture slightly. Locke argues on standard cosmological grounds that the universe must have been created by a being of the utmost wisdom and power, and then infers from God's wisdom "that [he] has not created this world for nothing and without purpose." Locke then infers that the rationality of our minds and the versatility of our bodies must have been given to us for a reason, and hence that "God wills that we do something" (rather than willing that we be "splendidly idle and sluggish"). Moreover, "what it is that is to be done by us can be partly gathered from the end in view for all things," namely God's glory, and partly from "[our] own constitution and the faculties with which [we are] equipped," namely sense-experience and reason (which dispose us to contemplate God's works, and as a result honor and praise him), as well as the propensity to preserve ourselves, in part by entering into society with others and maintaining that society "through the intercourse of language" (ELN 4: 157).[2] Locke's strategy, therefore, is to infer "all that men owe to God, their neighbor, and themselves" from what (as he assumes) can be proved to be God's intentions in creating rational human beings possessing a strong propensity to preserve themselves, procreate, and enter into society with others (ELN 4: 158). As we will see shortly, Locke's argumentation in the *Second Treatise*, which focuses on the nature and source of legitimate government, fits this strategy to a tee.

It follows from Locke's approach that the content of morality is determined at least in part by what God wills. It is God's will that we not be idle, from which it follows that we should work; it is God's will that we preserve humanity, and thus we should preserve ourselves and others (as much as possible, at least within the rest of the constraints established by God's will); it is God's will that we discover his existence and as a result honor and praise him, and thus worshipping him is something we should all do. Grounding this approach is the axiom that all inferior creatures should follow the will of their superior creator. But what makes this axiom true, if anything, is not the fact that God wills it. For it is circular to claim *both* that inferiors should follow the will of their superior because God wills that it be so *and* that we should follow God's will because inferiors should follow the will of their superior. So, for Locke, even though a large part of the content of morality is determined by what God wills, it is not the fact of being willed by God that makes moral principles true: God's will fixes (part of) the content, but not the truth, of morality. In this sense, Locke does not accept a divine command theory of morals: he is an intellectualist, rather than a voluntarist, about morality.[3]

However, the fact that moral principles are not made true by God's will does not entail that something other than God's will makes these principles *obligatory*.[4] Indeed, Locke distinguishes between the ground of moral truth and the ground of moral obligation. "The formal cause of obligation," Locke writes, is "the will of a superior," for "we are bound to something for the very reason that he, under whose rule we are, wills it" (ELN 6: 185). Since we are created by God, it follows that "all obligation leads back to God," and "the force of this obligation seems to be grounded in [his] authority" (ELN 6: 183). It is in this sense, then, and not in the divine command theory sense, that "the true ground of Morality . . . can only be the Will and Law of a God" (E I.iii.6: 69). Locke's picture seems to be that God sees and knows moral truths (by perceiving the agreement and disagreement of moral ideas), including propositions about his will, and, because of his infinite goodness, places us under an obligation to act in conformity with them for our own benefit.

Thus far, we have been looking at Locke's views about the content of morality and the ground of moral obligation. But what of moral motivation? Locke's answer is that God provides us with motivation to comply with moral rules in the form of rewards or punishments in an afterlife. That such rewards and punishments must exist follows directly from the fact that making rules obligatory would be pointless in their absence (E II.xxviii.6: 351). The reason is that most of the principles that are "lodged in Men's Appetites [if] left to their full swing . . . would carry Men to the over-turning of all Morality" (E I.iii.13: 75). As Locke well understands, human beings are "biassed by their Interest, as well as ignorant for want of study of [the law of nature]" as well as "partial to themselves," passionate, vengeful, negligent, and insufficiently concerned about others (T2: 124–125). Many, then, do not know what they should do in any given situation, and even when they do, self-interest and passions routinely overcome whatever desire they may have to do the right thing. Under these circumstances, God's promulgation of moral rules to humanity would be completely useless if he did not at the same time promise to reward the righteous and punish the wicked (and the weak-willed). And given that the righteous are most often not rewarded and the wicked not punished in *this* life, it follows that God's judgment will take place, and its consequences experienced, in a "Life after this" (E.iii.12: 74).[5]

11.2 Natural Law

The objective moral rules that Locke thinks we can discover by the use of reason are, taken collectively, known as natural law. And the fundamental law of nature, from which all (or, at least, many) other natural laws may be derived, is that "*Man [is] to be preserved*, as much as possible" (T2: 16) or "as much as may be" (T2: 159, 183). But what does this law mean, and how does Locke arrive at it?

It is clear that Locke thinks it a basic rule of morality that the whole of humankind should be preserved. But it is also clear that it is not always possible to follow this rule, for there are (possible and actual) circumstances in which it is simply not possible to preserve all human beings. It can happen that human beings threaten to kill other human beings. In such situations, if one does nothing some human beings will be killed, and yet the only way of preventing such atrocity is to kill the aggressors themselves. It can also happen that some human beings are facing the prospect of death (though not at the hands of other humans) if one does not sacrifice oneself in order to save them. In such a situation, either one dies or others die. Aware of these sorts of circumstances, Locke qualifies the fundamental law of nature by saying that it prescribes the preservation of humans "as much as may be." Elsewhere, he adds that every person in society should be preserved "as far as will consist with the publick good" (T2: 134), and that one ought to preserve the rest of mankind "when [one's] own Preservation comes not in competition" (T2: 6). Admittedly, these qualifications are not obviously mutually consistent. Locke tells us (about which more below) that culpable aggressors forfeit their right to life and may therefore be killed in order to preserve one's own life or the lives of others. It is in this sense that killing another human being can "consist with the publick good." But Locke does not explain how it can "consist with the publick good" for one not to be required to sacrifice one's own life in order to save a greater number of lives when all are innocent.

Leaving this problem aside, how does Locke arrive at the fundamental law of nature? In the *Second Treatise*, Locke's argument for this law follows directly upon his argument for a duty of self-preservation:

> For Men being all the Workmanship of one Omnipotent, and infinitely wise Maker; All the Servants of one Sovereign Master, sent into the World by his order and about his business, they are his Property, whose Workmanship they are, made to last during his, not one anothers Pleasure. And being furnished with like Faculties, sharing all in one Community of Nature, there cannot be supposed any such *Subordination* among us, that may Authorize us to destroy one another, as if we were made for one anothers uses, as the inferior ranks of Creatures are for ours. Every one as he is *bound to preserve himself*, and not to quit his Station willfully; so by the like reason when his own Preservation comes not in competition, ought he, as much as he can, *to preserve the rest of Mankind*. (T2: 6)

Locke is here either taking for granted or explicitly stating several assumptions, from which the law of self-preservation and the fundamental law of nature are supposed to follow. The first assumption is that God exists and created the universe. This much Locke already takes himself to have established in the *Essay* (E IV.x: 619–630). From this it follows directly that all human beings are created by God.[6] The second assumption is that creation is sufficient for ownership: if X creates Y, then X owns Y.[7] So from the fact that "God [is] the Maker of Heaven and Earth," it follows that "[God] is sole Lord and Proprietor of the whole World" (T1: 39), including of course all the human beings in it. The third assumption is that, unless X has waived, forfeited, or alienated X's property right in Y to Z, Z is not morally permitted to destroy Y. (To waive a right in Y to Z is to give Z permission to do something to Y; to forfeit a right in Y to Z is to wrong Z in a way that results in Z's acquiring a right in Y; and to alienate a right in Y to Z is to transfer the right in Y *in toto* to Z.) It follows that no human being is morally permitted to destroy any human being (including herself), unless God has in some way waived, forfeited, or alienated his property right in the latter to the former. But given that God is good and therefore cannot wrong anyone, it follows that God cannot forfeit any of his property rights; and given that God has not explicitly given or donated any human being to that human being or to any other human being, it follows that God has not alienated any of his property rights in human beings. Whether human beings are permitted to destroy themselves or other human beings therefore depends on whether God has granted them permission to do so (by waiving the relevant property rights).

Interestingly, Locke thinks that God waives his property right in plants and inferior creatures (non-human animals) to human beings, thereby giving humans permission to use plants and non-human animals for certain purposes. *Which* purposes? Locke writes that "a Man [has the right] to use any of the Inferior Creatures, for the Subsistence and Comfort of his Life, [and thus] may even destroy the thing . . . where need requires" (T1: 92). The argument for this claim runs through assumptions about God's *purposes* in creating human beings and other living things (including animals and plants). Locke notes that human beings have "a strong desire of Self-preservation," that this desire (like all basic desires and faculties with which humans are born) was created by God, and that God, being wise, does everything for a reason. So God must have meant for humans to act on their desire for self-preservation, and hence must have meant humans to "live and abide for some time upon the Face of the Earth." But if God intended that humans survive, then he must also have intended that they "use . . . those things, which were serviceable for [their] Subsistence" (T1: 86). And given that the plants and inferior ranks of animals are serviceable for the subsistence of humans (in the way of food), God must have intended that humans use (and hence destroy) those creatures for food, as a means to self-preservation. As Locke sees it, God's intentions here, being evident to humans, serve as a waiver of his property right in animals and plants to human beings.

But why not also suppose, given that human beings too can be used for food by other humans (Locke was well acquainted with stories of cannibalism – see E I.iii.9: 71), that God has waived his property right in humans to other humans (or even to themselves)? Locke's answer depends on another axiom of his moral theory, which is that "Creatures of the same species and rank promiscuously born to all the same advantages of Nature, and the use of the same faculties, [are] equal one amongst another without Subordination or Subjection [unless their creator expressly indicates that some should have dominion over others]" (T2: 4). All human beings are naturally equal, with none naturally inferior to any other. From God's wisdom (and beneficence), we can infer from the evident irrationality, and hence natural inferiority, of non-human animals, that he must have intended them to be available to humans as food. But we cannot infer that humans, no matter how deficient they may be in respect of ability, knowledge, merit, or birth, should be a source of food for other humans; for their rationality puts them all on the same moral plane. Given the natural equality of human beings, it follows that God has not given humans permission to use other humans (or themselves) as a means of self- (or other-)preservation.

We can therefore be sure that God has not forfeited, alienated, or waived his property right in human beings. It then follows directly from the rest of Locke's reasoning that no human being is morally permitted to destroy herself or any other human being (unless, perhaps, the latter human has forfeited or waived his right to life). This is Locke's argument for the immorality of suicide and murder. Still, the duty not to destroy does not entail the duty to preserve. The latter duty follows from the very same premises Locke uses to prove that humans have the right to use non-human animals for food. Given that God created humans with a strong desire for self-preservation, he must have meant them to live for some time. And since it is every human's duty to follow God's will, it follows that every human ought to preserve herself and every other human as much as possible. This is Locke's argument for a duty of self- and other-preservation, and hence a duty to preserve all of humankind as much as possible.

As we have just seen, the proposition that human beings are naturally equal plays a crucial role in Locke's moral philosophy. But the meaning of this claim requires further clarification and its significance needs to be emphasized. Locke well understands that there are different *kinds* of equality. It is possible for humans to be equal in one respect, but not in another. Indeed, it may even be that one human being is deficient in *numerous* respects relative to another. Among these respects, Locke counts age, virtue, excellency of parts and merit, birth, alliance, and benefits (T2: 54). And yet, Locke insists, even when humans are unequal in *these* respects, they remain equal in the one respect that matters most for Locke's purposes, namely "in respect of Jurisdiction or Dominion one over another." What Locke takes to follow from the fact that all humans are rational is that each has an *equal Right . . . to his Natural Freedom*, without being subjected to the Will or Authority of any other Man"

(T2: 54). By this Locke means that every human being has a natural "*Liberty* to dispose, and order, as he lists, his Person, Actions, Possessions, and his whole Property, within the Allowance of those Laws under which he is [including the law of nature]" (T2: 57; see also T2: 6, 22, and 128). It is worth emphasizing that the claim that every human being is naturally free to arrange her life as she sees fit without being interfered with or coerced by others is a truly revolutionary proposition. Under the influence of Aristotle, many moral philosophers were drawn to the view that some human beings are *naturally* inferior to, and hence may be enslaved or coerced by, other human beings (notably, white men).[8] It is Locke's implacable opposition to this reactionary Aristotelian thesis, perhaps more than anything else, that deserves our undying admiration (even if Locke goes on to provide, as we will see, what turns out to be an exceedingly weak justification for the slave-holding of his own day).

The thesis that the common nature of human beings (i.e., their rationality) guarantees their moral equality is one of Locke's fundamental assumptions. But the thesis that the right to freedom is what humans naturally possess in equal measure is something for which Locke argues. And like most of the natural rights with which Locke takes humans to be endowed, the right (or liberty) to live one's life as one chooses (within the bounds of the law of nature) derives from one's duty to preserve oneself. For the duty of self-preservation entails the right to self-preservation. And the right to preserve oneself entails the right to use all means necessary to self-preservation that do not contravene the law of nature (see T2: 128). Because the freedom to live one's life free of the arbitrary will of another is necessary to self-preservation, the fundamental law of nature entails that every human being has the right to act as she pleases as long as she does not thereby violate natural law.

What follows from possession of the right to freedom (within the bounds of natural law) is that no one is permitted to interfere with another person's freedom unless it be to prevent (or respond appropriately to) a violation of natural law. Locke infers this duty from the duty to preserve humanity in general. But this is not the only duty that he infers from the fundamental law of nature. Above, I quoted a passage from Section 6 of the *Second Treatise*. The passage continues:

> [Everyone] may not unless it be to do Justice on an Offender, take away, or impair the life, or what tends to the Preservation of the Life, the Liberty, Health, Limb or Goods of another. (T2: 6)

This is a difficult sentence. Is Locke saying that no one may take away or impair the life or what tends to preserve five things, namely the life, liberty, health, limb, and goods of another? Or is he saying that no one may take away or impair the life of another or what tends to preserve the life of another, namely his liberty, health, limbs, or goods? Because it does not make much sense to suppose that Locke means to prohibit the taking of what tends to preserve another's goods, the latter reading is to be preferred. Locke's point is that there are things that tend to the preservation of someone's life, namely his liberty, health, limbs, and goods, and that, for the same reason that we are not permitted to take away someone's life, we are not permitted to take away or impair his liberty, health, limbs, or goods. If we deprive someone of his liberty, health, or limbs, he may not be able to find the food and drink he needs to survive; if we deprive him of his goods, including his food and drink, he will surely die. As Locke sees it, then, the same reasons that back the prohibition against killing and the duty of charity also back the prohibition against enslaving, harming (e.g., by poisoning), maiming, and stealing from others.

In addition to the right not to be killed and the right to be helped when in dire need, then, humans have the right that other humans not interfere with their liberty, health, limbs, or goods. But Locke makes it clear that there is one situation in which such interference may be called for, namely when the rights that would otherwise stand in the way of such interference are forfeited. This brings us to Locke's views on punishment.

11.3   Punishment and Slavery

"[W]hat Duty is, cannot be understood without a Law; nor a Law be known, or supposed without a Law-maker, or without Reward and Punishment" (E I.iii.12: 74). According to Locke, the laws of nature are promulgated by God in order to achieve his purposes, which include the preservation of those of his works that are made in his image (i.e., rational corporeal beings). But the promulgation of any law would "be in vain, if there were nobody . . . had a *Power to Execute* that Law, and thereby preserve the innocent and restrain offenders" (T2: 7). Given that God's wisdom entails that he does nothing in vain, it follows that *someone* must have the power (i.e., the right) to enforce the law of nature, even in the absence of political society and government – that is, in the state of nature.

But *who* exactly has the right to enforce the laws of nature in the state of nature? The obvious answer would be God himself. This is in fact the natural conclusion to draw from the clearest piece of reasoning on the topic to be found in Locke's *Essay*:

> It would be in vain for one intelligent Being, to set a Rule to the Actions of another, if he had it not in his Power, to reward the compliance with, and punish deviation from his Rule, by some Good and Evil, that is not a natural product and consequence of the Action it self. For that being a natural Convenience, or Inconvenience, would operate of it self without a Law. (E II. xxviii.6: 351–352)

And in the case of natural law in particular, Locke says that God "has Power to enforce it by Rewards and Punishments, of infinite weight and duration, in another Life" (E II.xxviii.8: 352).

It is therefore interesting that in the *Second Treatise* Locke emphasizes that not only God but also human beings have the right to enforce the law of nature in the state of nature. For what would be "in vain" is "if there were no body that in the State of Nature, had a *Power to Execute*" the law of nature (T2: 7 – underlining added). Why does Locke think this? The answer is that God's offer of rewards and threat to punish in the life to come are not sufficient to induce general conformity to natural law. Ever alive to the ignorance and weak wills of human beings, Locke acknowledges, first, that there are "whole [uncivilized] Nations . . . amongst whom there [is] to be found no Notion of a God" and that even "many, in more civilized Countries, have no very strong, and clear Impressions of a Deity upon their Minds" (E I.iv.8: 87–88); and, second, that "[t]he Penalties that attend the breach of God's Laws, some, nay, perhaps, most Men seldom seriously reflect on: and amongst those that do, many, whilst they break the Law, entertain Thoughts of future reconciliation, and making their Peace for such Breaches" (E II.xxviii.12: 357). In the state of nature, then, most human beings either do not realize that they are required to follow the law of nature or, when they do, successfully rationalize making an exception to the law in their own case. The result is that effective enforcement of the law of nature in the state of nature requires more than God's own incentives and threats. Hence, God's promulgation of natural law would indeed serve no purpose if no one *in the state of nature* had the right to enforce it.

Humans, then, have the right to reward compliance with, and punish breaches of, the law of nature in the state of nature. But *which* humans? Locke's answer is: *all* humans (or, more precisely, all humans who have not waived, alienated, or forfeited this right). His argument for this is brief but straightforward: "[I]f any one in the State of Nature may punish another, for any evil he has done, every one may do so. For in that *State of perfect Equality*, where naturally there is no superiority or jurisdiction of one, over another, what any may do in Prosecution of that Law, every one must needs have a Right to do" (T2: 7). Locke's idea is that if anyone has the right to punish, then all (save the ones who have in some way lost or waived the right) do. The reason for this is that the state of nature is a state in which all (at least initially) have an equal right to freedom. This makes sense, as long as God has not given any sign that he has deputized some subset of human beings to enforce natural law.

If humans are permitted to punish those who violate the law of nature, then it must be the case that offenders lose their right not to be subject to the will of another. The loss of a right that is the direct result of wrongdoing Locke calls the "forfeiture" of that right. Locke does not use the doctrine of forfeiture to argue for the right to punish. Rather, Locke argues from God's intention to promulgate an effective law (to preserve the human species he has created) to God's intention to dissuade lawbreaking via human enforcement, and it is a direct result of the permissibility of human enforcement of the law of nature that those who break the law are no longer protected by it.

Contemporary justifications of punishment usually take one of two forms: retribution or deterrence. Retributivism is the view that punishment is appropriate inasmuch as it is what the criminal deserves for his crime. Those who favor a deterrence-based justification say that punishment is appropriate inasmuch as it functions to deter the lawbreaker and others from committing crimes. Some of what Locke says about punishment suggests that he is a retributivist. He suggests, for example, that *"Murther deserves Death"* (E IV.iv.8: 566; see also T2: 23, 87), and claims that the right to punish a lawbreaker is the right "only to retribute to him, so far as calm reason and conscience dictates, what is proportionate to his Transgression" (T2:8). But Locke's retributivism, such as it is, is completely parasitic on a deterrence-based justification for punishment. The right to punish, which follows from the right "to preserve Mankind in general," is the right to "bring such evil on any one, who hath transgressed [the law of nature], as may make him repent the doing of it, and thereby deter him, and by his Example others, from doing the like mischief" (T2: 8). To retribute, for Locke, *is* to deter. And which punishment fits (or is "proportionate to") which crime is determined solely by what "may serve for *Reparation* and *Restraint*" (T2: 8): thus, "[e]ach Transgression may be *punished* to that *degree*, and with so much *Severity* as will suffice to make it an ill bargain to the Offender, give him cause to repent, and terrifie others from doing the like" (T2: 12). So, for example, if the threat of a beating were sufficient to deter theft, then Locke would count the maiming of a thief (e.g., by cutting off one of his hands) impermissible even if it were justified by the most plausible non-deterrence-based retributivist theory. Indeed, Locke insists that "even the guilty are to be spared, where it can prove no prejudice to the innocent" (T2: 159), something that is anathema to any non-deterrence-based retributivist. For if a guilty person deserves punishment, then, according to such a form of retributivism, one ought to punish that person.[9] Locke's theory of punishment, like much else in his moral system, derives from the fundamental law of nature, which is that humanity should be preserved as much as possible. So if punishing a lawbreaker would not prevent any other crimes, then, even if he has forfeited his right to life, his life should be preserved.[10]

As Locke says, reparation and restraint are the purposes appropriately served by punishment. Reparation (or compensation) is what a lawbreaker owes to anyone who has suffered loss or damage as a direct result of the offense; restraint is simply deterrence. Thus far, we have been looking at the restraining function of punishment. As Locke argues, everyone in the state of nature has the right to punish breaches of natural law for the purpose of restraint. But, as he also argues, *not* everyone in the state of nature has the right to punish breaches of natural law for the purpose of *reparation*. The reason for this is that, unlike the right to deter through punishment, which is grounded in *"the Right . . . of Preserving all Mankind,"* the right of reparation, which takes the form of "appropriating to [oneself], the Goods or Service of the Offender," is grounded in the *"Right of Self-preservation"* (T2: 11).

It might be asked whether slavery can be justified in the state of nature. Locke's answer to this is that it can. To be a slave is to be "under the Absolute, Arbitrary Power of another" (T2: 23). By "power" here, as in most other places in the *Treatises*, Locke means "right." And the absolute right possessed by a master over a slave, Locke says, is (or goes so far as to include) the right of the former to "take away [the] Life [of the latter], when he pleases" (T2: 23). A lawful master, on this view, therefore has the right to compel any one of his lawful slaves to do his bidding under threat of death. Locke emphasizes that no human being has the right to enslave himself to anyone "by Compact, or his own Consent," whether in exchange for money or for any other purpose. For, not having the right to take his own life (as has already been shown), and not being able to "give more Power than he has himself," a human being cannot transfer or alienate to another the right to threaten or end his life. Justified slavery, then, cannot arise via alienation or waiver.[11] This leaves forfeiture of the right not to be killed as the only means whereby justified slavery can arise.

Locke's views about the relation between forfeiture and slavery are clear, but also difficult to square with his claim that the right to enforce the law of nature in the state of nature belongs to all law-abiding persons. Locke's account of how one person may lawfully come to enslave another is this:

> [A man] having, by his fault, forfeited his own Life, by some Act that deserves Death; he, to whom he has forfeited it, may (when he has him in his Power) delay to take it, and make use of him to his own Service, and he does him no injury by it. (T2: 23; see also T2: 85)

The central claim here is that, in the state of nature, if X threatens to commit an act against Y sufficient to justify X's being killed by Y as a means of self-preservation, then X forfeits his right not to be killed *by* Y and, further, Y is also permitted to kill X. Given that Y is permitted to kill X, Y is also permitted to force X to work for Y under threat of death. This is all coherent. But recall that Locke holds that *every* law-abiding person in the state of nature has the natural right to execute or enforce the law of nature. So when X threatens to commit an act against Y sufficient to justify X's being killed *by* Y, X forfeits the right not to be killed not only with respect to Y but with respect to *any other law-abiding person*. It follows that *any* law-abiding person is permitted to enslave someone who threatens to commit a sufficiently heinous crime against any *other* law-abiding person. This result goes beyond what Locke explicitly allows in T2: 23, for there Locke suggests that the only person who can become a lawful master over a slave is "he, to whom [the slave] has forfeited [the right not to be killed]," namely the slave's intended victim.

Locke's justification for holding slaves derives from the right of self-preservation, which is entailed by the right to preserve human beings in general. If X threatens to kill Y, then Y may kill X in self-defense; and if Y may kill X, then Y may threaten to kill X; and if Y may threaten to kill X, then Y may enslave X rather than killing X. The potential difficulty here is that, on Locke's view, serious crime in the state of nature is tantamount to the renunciation of one's status as a rational being: in "violating the Law . . . a Man so far becomes degenerate, and declares himself . . . to be a noxious Creature" (T2: 10), and "a Criminal, . . . having renounced Reason . . . hath by the unjust Violence and Slaughter he hath committed . . . declared War against all Mankind, and therefore may be destroyed as a *Lyon* or a *Tyger*, one of those wild Savage Beasts, with whom Men can have no Society or Security" (T2: 11; see also T2: 16, 172, 181). And if X has renounced his own rationality and thereby joined the ranks of "wild Savage Beasts," then *any* law-abiding person may kill X (in defense of herself or others), and hence threaten to kill X, and hence enslave X. It may be that Locke is committed to this result, even though there is reason to question it. If X makes war *against* Y, then it is arguable that Y may enslave X (at least in the state of nature); but if X does not make war *against* Z, then it stands to reason that Z may not enslave X (even in the state of nature).

Be that as it may, the right to enslave, on Locke's view, derives from the right to enforce the right of self-preservation in the state of nature. This is a relatively enlightened view of slavery (if one prescinds from the main case for abolitionism, predicated on the Kantian conception of the dignity of even the most depraved human being), one that, as we have seen, is not based on claims of natural inferiority. Locke goes on to say that the forfeiture of one's right not to be killed (and the consequent legitimacy of enslavement) does not entail the forfeiture of *other* rights, particularly the right to property: "For though I may kill a Thief that sets on me in the Highway, yet I may not . . . take away his Money and let him go; this would be Robbery on my side. His force . . . made him forfeit his Life, but gave me no Title to his Goods" (T2: 182).[12] But it is also true that Locke, some 15 to 20 years before publishing the *Two Treatises*, did not object to the slave-raids or to the transporting of slaves from Africa to the West Indies engaged in by the Royal African Company (in which Locke invested from 1672 to 1675). As one of Locke's biographers points out, even if slaves are "Captives taken in a just War" (T2: 85), "Locke can hardly have thought that slave raids were just wars; and he explicitly denied that such aggressors forfeited the lives of their children . . ., and so could not even begin to justify hereditary slavery."[13] It may be that the sale of his investments in the Royal African Company in 1675 indicated the beginning of a change of heart about the legitimacy of African slavery, but there is no indication of any explicit renunciation of his earlier views in any of his later works.

11.4 Property

Locke uses the word "property" both in a general sense and in a more particular sense. In the *Essay*, Locke writes that "the *Idea* of *Property* [is] a right to any thing" (E IV.iii.18: 549). This account of the general idea of property is a little underspecified. In the general sense, to have property in something is to have a right to use it as one sees fit (within the bounds of the law of nature) and to exclude others from using it. This is why Locke says that he applies "the general name, *Property*" to the "Lives, Liberties and Estates" of persons (T2: 123; see also T2: 87), and that "[w]hat other Property Man can have in [non-human animals], but the *Liberty of using them*, is hard to be understood" (T1: 39; see also T1: 86–87). Whatever property one has, in the general sense, one has as a direct result of the fundamental law of nature, which is that humankind is to be preserved as much as possible. The use of one's own body and self, the use of one's liberty, and the use of one's goods all being necessary to one's self-preservation, it follows that one has an exclusive right to all of these things. In the more particular sense, property in something is "Property in Possession" (T1: 39) – that is, an exclusive right to use particular moveable and immoveable external goods (e.g., apples, water, gold, air, and land) for one's own purposes.

What rights does Locke take to be included in, or to follow from, having property in possession? Like any other right, property in possession can be waived, alienated, or forfeited. I waive my property right to my hairbrush when I give you permission to use it; I alienate (i.e., transfer) my property right via gift, barter, sale (T2: 46) or bequest (T2: 72); and I forfeit my property right to someone when I unjustifiably harm her or damage her property, and owe her something in reparation for the harm or damage (T2: 11). In addition, as we will see, property in possession endows one with a right to destroy what one owns, but only for certain reasonable purposes (T1: 39, 92).

In Chapter 5 of the *Second Treatise*, Locke defends a particular account of how human beings in the state of nature can acquire property in an external good that is not yet owned by anyone in particular.[14] It is important that, for Locke, there is no such thing as fully exclusive property in possession (any more than there is fully exclusive property in one's self). As we have seen, one does not have the right to destroy oneself, because one is God's property. Rather, just as God has given us a license to use our selves for certain purposes (particularly, self-preservation and the preservation of humanity in general), he has given us a license to use external goods for certain purposes, and hence acquire property in them in this restricted sense. On Locke's picture, it is much as if every human being is the trustee of a trust established by God for the benefit of humanity as a whole, with each trustee holding her own body, labor, and goods in trust, subject to the conditions of the trust.[15] As we will see, the fact that humans hold all of their property in trust entails that the uses to which they can permissibly put their property are limited.

How, according to Locke, does any human being in the state of nature acquire "first property," – that is, property in (i.e., the right to use, and to exclude other human beings from using) external goods not previously owned by any particular individual? The first thing to notice is that Locke takes it to be evident (not merely on the basis of revelation, but also on the basis of reason) that God "*has given the Earth to the Children of Men*, given it to Mankind in common" (T2: 25), and has done this "for the Support and Comfort of their being" (T2: 26). We know this (without revelation) because we know that God created human beings, as well as the Earth on which they live, that human beings need food and drink, and that the only source of food and drink available to them is the Earth (and the plants and non-human animals living on it). So God must have intended that humans use the Earth and its irrational denizens to survive (T2: 35). Thus, we can think of the Earth as having been "given" to humankind. And in the absence of any sign that any particular human being or group of human beings has more right to the Earth (or to parts of the Earth) than any other, it follows that God's gift is to *all* of humankind (including future human beings), rather than to any particular human being or group of human beings.[16] The gift here, of course, comes with strings attached, the most important one being the fundamental law of nature, that humanity be preserved as much as possible.

Some natural law theorists (including Locke's illustrious predecessor, Hugo Grotius, and his contemporary, Samuel Pufendorf) had previously argued that common ownership of the Earth entails that one human being's legitimate appropriation of any part of the Earth requires the consent of all human beings.[17] Locke disagrees, and takes it as his charge to "shew, how Men might come to have a *property* in several parts of that which God gave to Mankind in common, and that without any express Compact of all the Commoners" (T2: 25). Locke's argument that God could not have intended individual property in parts of the commons to come about through the consent of all is that "[i]f such a consent as that was necessary, Man had starved, notwithstanding the Plenty God had given him" (T2: 28). The reason is that, human nature being what it is, *universal* agreement about the proper division of goods is practically impossible, and hence, on the Grotius-Pufendorf theory, no individual appropriation could ever be justified. And yet God must have intended justified individual appropriation to be possible, because he intended the preservation of humankind.

Locke's central claim is that it is by mixing their labor with external things (land, water, plants, and non-human animals) initially owned by humankind in common that individual human beings come to own them (i.e., come to have the right to use them for their own purposes under the conditions fixed by natural law):

> Though the Earth, and all inferior Creatures be in common to all Men, yet every Man has a *Property* in his own *Person*. This no Body has any Right to but himself. The *Labour* of his Body, and the *Work* of his Hands, we may say, are properly his. Whatsoever then he removes out of the State that Nature hath provided, and left it in, he hath mixed his *Labour* with, and joyned to it something that is his own, and thereby makes it his *Property*. (T2: 27)

Locke appears to be arguing as follows. If I own X, then I own everything with which X is mixed; but I own my labor; therefore, I own everything with which my labor is mixed. This argument, as it stands, is not persuasive. As Robert Nozick famously objects: "But why isn't mixing what I own with what I don't a way of losing what I own rather than a way of gaining what I don't? If I own a can of tomato juice and spill it in the sea so that its molecules . . . mingle evenly throughout the sea, do I thereby come to own the sea, or have I foolishly dissipated my tomato juice?"[18] Matters are not helped by adding that dissipation of one's tomato juice yields ownership of that with which it is mixed as long as one intends to use the resulting mixture. Nor are matters helped by adding something that Locke later says about labor, which is that it *"puts the difference of value* on every thing" (T2: 40) and that it *"makes the far greater part of the value* of things, we enjoy in this World" (T2: 42). For if I turn a small piece of gold into a sculpture, and if labor adds value to the shaped gold, why isn't what I own as the result of my labor no more than the value added by my labor, rather than the total value of the sculpture itself inclusive of the value of the unshaped piece of gold?

Locke uses many different expressions to speak of the ways in which one can legitimately arrive at first possession of X: by mixing or joining one's labor with X (T2: 27), by adding (T2: 28) or annexing (T2: 27, 32) one's labor to X, by placing one's labor on X (T2: 37), or by affecting X with one's labor (T2: 46). This suggests that it is *mixing one's labor in particular*, rather than mixing anything that one happens to own, with something that creates first property in the state of nature. Admittedly, though, if there is some special property of labor that explains its power to generate first property, Locke does not do enough to explain what that property is.

It might be thought that the special property possessed by labor is the power of creation. Just as God owns the universe as a result of having created it, so human beings come to possess external things initially held in common by laboring on them to create something new. It might be thought that by planting a seed, I create a new plant (see T2: 32); by molding a piece of bronze, I create a new statue; and so on. But the vast majority of Locke's examples of first property do not conform to this 'workmanship' model of appropriation. Locke writes of picking up acorns, gathering apples from trees, his horse biting grass, his servant cutting turfs, digging up ore (T2: 28), drawing water from a fountain (T2: 29), killing a deer, catching fish in the ocean, taking up ambergris (from a sperm whale), and pursuing a hare (T2: 30). In none of these cases, does the agent *create* anything new.

But there *is* something that all of these examples of appropriation have in common, and that is *effort*. Locke writes that if a human being "employed his Pains about any of the spontaneous Products of Nature, as any way to alter them, from the state which Nature put them in," then he would "acquire a Propriety in them" (T2: 37 – underlining added).[19] It requires effort to pick something up off the ground, dig for ore, cut turf, draw water, catch a fish, or pursue a hare. Sometimes the effort is fairly minimal (as in the case of picking up an acorn or cupping one's hands to remove water from a stream), but it is always there in some form. The other characteristic that these examples share is that the relevant expenditure of effort results in the transformation of something that is not in a state that renders it usable for human survival into something that is. When it is on the ground, an acorn is not usable; it cannot be ground to make flour, an essential ingredient of bread. But if the acorn is picked up and placed in a mortar, then it is fit to be ground with a pestle. Similarly, when a fish is swimming in a stream, it is not usable for food; but if it is caught, then it can be cooked and eaten. Perhaps Locke's view is that it is only fair that those who expend effort to transform unusable external things into usable goods should benefit from what results from the effort. Alternatively, there is a sense in which someone who, without my permission, takes possession of the acorn I have gathered or the fish I have caught is taking wrongful possession of the fruits of my labor, and thus in some sense taking wrongful possession of the added value produced by my labor. If anyone should have the right to use the transformed thing, it is the one who transformed it: "He that had as good left for his Improvement, as was already taken up, needed not complain, ought not to meddle with what was already improved by another's Labour: If he did, 'tis plain he desired the benefit of another's Pains, which he had no right to" (T2: 34).

One of the more pressing questions about first property that it is sometimes alleged Locke finds it difficult to answer concerns the proper boundaries of what human beings can legitimately appropriate through their labor in the state of nature. If I draw a line in the ground around 10 square miles of land, do I come to own the narrow strip of land on which I have drawn, the 10 square miles of topsoil enclosed by my square, or those 10 square miles of topsoil plus every atom of rock and dirt that can be removed from the Earth under the layer of topsoil? Alternatively, do I come to own all the land (topsoil? more?) on Earth apart from the 10 square miles of land defined by the line I have drawn? The answer to this question is that, merely by drawing a line in the earth, I come to own none of these parcels of land. Although it is true that drawing a line requires effort, more than mere effort is required for legitimate appropriation. In order to be in a position to appropriate, one must also transform the object of one's labor into something usable. Thus, it is only by, say, *tilling* 10 square miles of land that one comes to own it. And the tilling is sufficient to endow me with a property right to the 10 square miles of topsoil (as long as it is used for agriculture), but not to any part of the Earth on which I have not labored, including the vast layers of rock (and, say, oil and gas) that may be found beneath the topsoil.

In addition to the thesis that first possession results from laboring on an external (non-rational) object, Locke insists on two famous limits on individual appropriation from the commons: the sufficiency proviso (sometimes called simply "the Lockean proviso") and the spoilage proviso. What are these limitations and how does Locke justify them?

Begin with the sufficiency proviso. Locke writes:

> For this *Labour* being the unquestionable Property of the Labourer, no Man but he can have a right to what that is once joyned to, at least where there is enough, and as good left in common for others. (T2: 27; see also T2: 33–36)

The "enough, and as good" proviso is a fairness condition on appropriation that derives from what we can and should infer from the goodness of God's intentions. In giving the Earth to humankind in common, God permits each human being to use no more than her fair share of it. Were God to permit more than this, he would be favoring one human being (or group of human beings) over another with no good reason to do so, which would be contrary to his goodness. Notice that the sufficiency proviso has two parts, one quantitative and the other qualitative. If I drink from the only stream on an island and I leave *enough* water to quench the thirst of all others, then I satisfy the "mere sufficiency" condition. But it is possible to satisfy this condition without satisfying the qualitative "as good" condition. For example, if my act of drinking from the stream stirs up sediment that would take years to settle back on the stream bed, then the water that I leave for others, though sufficient to quench their thirst, would not be "as good" as the water I myself have removed. Locke's quantitative condition is a simple consequence of the fundamental law of nature, but the qualitative condition is not. The qualitative condition is a matter of fairness, not a matter of preservation.

Here, now, is how Locke presents the spoilage proviso:

> As much as any one can make use of to any advantage of life before it spoils; so much he may by his labour fix a Property in. Whatever is beyond this, is more than his share, and belongs to others. Nothing was made by God for Man to spoil or destroy.[20] (T2: 31; see also T2: 37–38, 46)

Locke's reference here to not taking more than one's share might suggest that the spoilage proviso could be reduced to the sufficiency proviso. But not so. It is possible to take more from the commons than one can use before it spoils, even while leaving enough and as good for others. So Locke must mean to distinguish between the two provisos. And yet it seems right to say that both provisos *could* be similarly *justified*. Just as it would be unfair to leave the rest of humanity with a smaller or worse share of the commons than one has taken possession of, so it would be unfair to others to deprive them of the opportunity to appropriate something that could be used instead of spoiling while in one's possession.

It might be thought that the spoilage proviso is really just a restriction on *wasting* (i.e., not using or frivolously destroying) natural resources. Perhaps Locke is more worried about natural resources *standing idle* than he is about them *spoiling* or *perishing* while in someone's possession. But this would be a mistake. Locke insists that any human being "might heap up [through barter or exchange] as much of these durable things [i.e., metals, shells, pebbles, diamonds] as he pleased; the *exceeding of the bounds of his* just *Property* not lying in the largeness of his Possession, but the perishing of any thing uselessly in it" (T2: 46). So what bothers Locke is not the fact that something that one possesses *is* not used; what bothers him is the fact that something one possesses *can no longer* be used (because it has disintegrated or spoiled), though it might have been used by others had one not taken possession of it.

Although Locke writes that one who allows goods to spoil in his possession takes more than his fair share of the commons, there is little doubt that his most basic justification for the spoilage proviso is theological. Imagine an island with only two inhabitants, Annie and Barbara. Annie is industrious and a gourmand; Barbara is lazy but has very simple tastes, easily satisfied. Annie encloses and labors on 50% of the island (leaving enough and as good for Barbara), gathering up stores of fruits and vegetables, from which she selects the ingredients for her complicated culinary concoctions; Barbara encloses and labors on only 5% of the island, and lives very simply off what she gathers there. As it happens, though, some of Annie's stock of fruits and vegetables spoils before it can be used. At the same time, Barbara has no interest in those fruits and vegetables, and would not have used them if they had been made available to her. According to Locke, it is plain that Annie has violated the spoilage proviso, even though she has not acted unfairly toward Barbara. If anything underpins the spoilage proviso, then, it must be that it is an insult to God (by contravening his intentions) not to preserve the natural resources he has given us for our sustenance and comfort.

It has been a matter of some debate whether the justification of Locke's theory of property generally (i.e., his theory of the right to one's person, liberty, and possessions) bottoms out in secular or religious premises. It should be clear now how this debate should be settled. Although a few elements of Locke's theory of property (e.g., the "as good as" aspect of the sufficiency proviso, or the wrongness of appropriating what another has made usable by laboring on it) might be justified on secular grounds, the overall structure and myriad details of Locke's theory would not make much sense if it were not grounded in assumptions about God's wisdom and goodness. Human persons own themselves only inasmuch as God has entrusted them with their minds and bodies for certain purposes and not for others; their freedom is circumscribed by the fundamental law of nature, itself grounded in God's purposes; their right to punish lawbreakers in the state of nature derives from the fact that God would not have established a law without having made some provision for its enforcement; the state of nature's being one in which the Earth belongs (in trust) to all human beings in common derives from God's having intended its myriad resources for human sustenance and comfort; and the "as much" aspect of the sufficiency proviso, as well as the spoilage proviso, are firmly grounded in God's goodness and the fact that we should honor his gifts to humanity. Much of this Locke takes to be revealed to humanity in the Bible.

But he takes *all* of it to be demonstratively knowable on purely rational grounds independent of revelation. So the justification is secular only insofar as the argument for God's existence and nature does not itself depend on religious assumptions. But the nature of the justification itself makes no sense without appeal to God's nature and purposes.

11.5 Family

In his *Patriarcha* (1680), Robert Filmer argues that fathers have absolute power (of life and death) over their children as a result of having begotten them, that the political power of kings is a form of paternal power (handed down to them from Adam through primogeniture), and hence that kings have absolute power over their subjects. Because Filmer's arguments, and other arguments for the divine right of kings floating around while Locke was writing the *Two Treatises*, rely on premises about the nature of paternal power and the nature of the duties that children (subjects) owe to their parents (kings), it is important to Locke to enquire into the nature and extent of the rights and duties of parents and children.

Locke distinguishes between five different kinds of powers: (i) political power (the subject of Chapter 12), (ii) the power "of a *Father* over his Children," (iii) the power of "a *Master* over his Servant," (iv) the power of "a *Husband* over his Wife," and (v) the power of "a *Lord* over his Slave" (T2: 2). Having already discussed (v), Locke turns his attention to (ii)–(iv) in sections 52–86 of the *Second Treatise*.

11.5.1 The rights and duties of parents

As Locke sees it, parents beget, but do not create, their children: only God creates the children that human beings beget (T1: 52–53). Having created vulnerable, defenseless beings that have not yet developed the ability to reason or fend for themselves, and having created them for the purpose of living and abiding "for some time upon the Face of the Earth" (T1: 86), God must intend that rational, adult human beings care for those children until they acquire reason and the ability to support themselves, at which point children acquire all the rights and duties that apply to any rational person. Children, therefore, as Locke puts it, are not "born in," but rather "born to," the state of equal freedom (T2: 55).

By itself, this piece of demonstrative reasoning establishes no more than that *some adult(s)* should have the job of raising children from birth to maturity: in particular, it does not show that this job belongs to the *parents* of newborns, let alone the same persons throughout their childhood. But Locke clearly states that it is a "Law of Nature" that "*Parents* [are] *under an obligation to preserve, nourish, and educate the Children*, they [have] begotten" (T2: 56). The reason for this harks back, yet again, to God's intentions. What puts "the *Authority* into the *Parents* hands to govern the *Minority* of their Children" is that "God hath made it their business to imploy this Care on their Off-spring, and hath placed in them suitable Inclinations of Tenderness and Concern to temper this power, to apply it as his Wisdom designed it, to the Childrens good, as long as they should need to be under it" (T2: 63; see also T1: 89). So God means for parents to care for their children because he has children's best interests at heart and has given their parents (and no other human beings) a special love and concern for them (see T2: 170). Given that parents should do what God intends, it follows that they should be the ones to feed their children and given them the wherewithal (i.e., the education necessary) to survive on their own once they reach the age of reason.

It is an important part of Locke's conception of parental rights that they are limited not only in duration but also in extent or scope.[21] In particular, a father's "Command over his Children is but temporary, and reaches not their Life or Property" (T2: 65; see also T2: 69, 86). So a father is not permitted to threaten to kill or disinherit his children (for any purpose). In addition, Locke emphasizes that the rights and duties in respect of children are shared by *both* parents: the phrase *"Paternal Power"* leads those who use it to suppose, wrongly, that "the Power of Parents over their Children [is placed] wholly in the *Father*, as if the *Mother* had no share in it, whereas if we consult Reason or Revelation, we shall find she hath an equal Title" (T2: 52). Finally, parental rights are all conditional: "[Parental] *power* so little belongs to the *Father* by any peculiar right of Nature, but only as he is Guardian of his Children, that when he quits his Care of them, he loses his power over them" (T2: 65). So conceiving and giving birth are not sufficient by themselves to generate parental rights: one's parental rights extend only to those children for whom one is caring. In sum, the scope and extent of parental rights, which both parents share, is determined entirely by God's purpose in creating children, which is the preservation and continuation of the human race. As we will see in Chapter 12, this result plays an important role in Locke's argument for distinguishing between political power and parental power.

11.5.2 The rights and duties of children

Children, then, have a moral right to be supported and educated by their parents until they reach the age of reason. But children also have a stringent duty toward their parents, namely "a perpetual Obligation of *honouring*" them (T2: 66), and thus parents have a corresponding "perpetual right to respect, reverence, support and compliance too" from their children (T2: 67). Children, then, have a duty to adopt certain attitudes towards their parents (respect and reverence), to help their parents when in need (e.g., in their old age), and to comply with their parents' demands until they acquire the ability to take rational control of their own lives.

Locke writes that the duty to honor one's parents exists "by the Law of God and Nature" (T2: 66).[22] But the argument for such a duty from natural law is not grounded on conclusions that may be derived from what one knows to be God's intentions. Rather, the argument is purely secular in nature. The basis for the honor and support that a child owes her parents is "Gratitude . . . for the Benefits received by and from them" (T2: 68). This is therefore a duty of justice or fair play, rather than a direct duty to do what God intends. (Though, of course, the duty to honor one's parents is also indirectly responsive to God's intentions, inasmuch as God intends all human beings to act justly.) Indeed, the extent of what a child owes her parents is wholly determined by how much they gave her in the way of nourishment, support, and education: "Obligations to Parents, and the degrees of what is required of Children, may be varied, by the different care and kindness, trouble and expence, which is often imployed upon one Child, more than another" (T2: 70). The more parents give their children in the way of support, the more children are required to give back to their parents in the way of respect, reverence, and support. And, of course, the more irresponsible and unhelpful the parents, the less their children owe them on the basis of gratitude. Again, as we will see, Locke is concerned to show that the duties of subjects in respect of their monarchs cannot be modeled on the duties of children in respect of their parents (T2: 69).

11.5.3 The rights and duties of spouses, masters, and servants

If a king is compared to the head of a household, then his powers could be analogized to the powers of a husband in respect of his wife and to the powers of a master in respect of his servants. Again, Locke argues that these analogies will give little solace to those, such as Filmer, who think that kings have absolute power by divine dispensation. The main reason for this is that the relation between spouses and the relation between master and servant are both established by mutual consent or agreement. "*Conjugal Society*," Locke writes, "is made by a voluntary Compact between Man and Woman" (T2: 78), and "a Free-man makes himself a Servant to another, by selling him for a certain time, the Service he undertakes to do, in exchange for Wages he is to receive" (T2: 85). But if natural law, as we have seen, does not permit me to sell myself into absolute subjection to the will of another, then no lawful contract can be the source of absolute power in any monarch.

Locke is concerned to show that the contract between master and servant, like the parental power of parents over their children, is limited in duration and extent. The contract signed by a servant "gives the Master but a Temporary Power over him, and no greater, than what is contained in the *Contract* between 'em" (T2: 85). It is only "for a certain time" that any servant agrees to sell his services to a master, and we may reasonably presume that most servants will not agree to sell any more of their freedom than is required to perform the tasks that their masters are hiring them to perform. Thus any constraint that a master would place on a servant (e.g., requiring the butler to serve as a cook, or demanding that the butler provide services on his day off) beyond the bounds of their mutual agreement is automatically morally void.

The same concern manifests itself in Locke's discussion of conjugal society. Locke defines marriage as consisting chiefly in "such a Communion and Right to one anothers Bodies, as is necessary to its chief End, Procreation [and] the continuation of the Species" (T2: 78–79). So when two persons enter into a marriage compact, they necessarily agree to perform all the functions and roles that will enable them to realize the purpose of their union, including the provision of "mutual Support, and Assistance" (T2: 78; see also T2: 83) and "Community of Goods" (T2: 83). It follows from this conception of marriage, enlightened in many ways for its time, that any restriction on a spouse's liberty that is not explicitly licensed by the nature or aim of the conjugal contract is morally impermissible. For example, although it is true that in order to achieve the aim of raising children any marriage must be of "*lasting*" duration (T2: 80), there is "no necessity in the nature of the thing, nor to the ends of it, that it should always be for Life" (T2: 81); and, indeed, "the *Wife* has, in many cases, a Liberty to *separate* from [her husband]; where natural Right, or their Contract allows it" (T2: 82). Locke therefore allows for the possibility of temporary marriage contracts as well as divorce, presumably on grounds of breach of contract. In addition, Locke insists that the rights of a spouse extend only to matters of "common Interest and Property," thus leaving each wife "in the full and free possession of what by Contract is her peculiar Right" (T2: 82). This conception of the economic rights of wives is therefore far more progressive than the prevailing doctrine of coverture, according to which all of a wife's economic rights, including the right to work and the right to own and convey property, were subsumed under the rights of her husband.

Locke's contractual conception of conjugal society is remarkably egalitarian (especially for its day). It is therefore worthy of our admiration, even if it is imperfect as it stands. The main imperfection is that there is nothing in Locke's moral theory to prevent exploitative contracts. If one spouse is weaker or less intelligent or slower than the other, then the latter will be in a better bargaining position with respect to the provisions of the marriage contract than the former. (This problem is exacerbated if, say, boys are educated and girls are not.) To his credit, Locke emphasizes that no human being should take advantage of the penurious state of another in order to get the latter to do his bidding, but he never articulates a general rule against exploitation.

Unfortunately, Locke's account of conjugal rights is also marred by sexism. At one point, Locke considers whose views should have precedence in case of a dispute between spouses. Reasonably, Locke recognizes that, if any marriage is to fulfill its aims, some way of resolving conflict must be found. His answer, though, is that "the last Determination . . . naturally falls to the Man's share, as the abler and the stronger" (T2: 82). This claim is not only shockingly sexist but also surprisingly unmoored from the rest of Locke's strongly held philosophical views. For the very idea that might makes right is itself anathema to

Locke (see T2: 186), and he must have known that many wives are far abler than their husbands. Besides, in the state of nature, surely the most rational way of resolving disputes between equals in any partnership (i.e., a marriage) is to draw straws, and, indeed, to agree to the drawing of straws as a method of dispute resolution as a part of the marriage contract itself.

notes

1   Locke qualifies this "bold" conjecture elsewhere in the *Essay*. For example, he writes of some particular ideas that they "would, I suppose, if duly considered, and pursued, afford such Foundations of our Duty and Rules of Action, as <u>might</u> place *Morality amongst the Sciences capable of Demonstration* . . . [by] any one <u>that will apply himself with the same Indifferency and Attention</u> [to it] as he does to [mathematics]" (E IV.iii.18: 549 – underlining added). For Locke, then, it is clear that *how much* one discovers about morality is a direct function of the degree of assiduousness (in the comparison of ideas) with which one approaches the subject. Moreover, Locke writes that he does not doubt that "if a right method were taken, <u>a great part of Morality</u> might be made out" with the kind of clarity one finds in mathematical proofs (E IV.xii.8: 643–44 – underlining added). So Locke might well accept that, even under the best of circumstances, given that the faculties of rational creatures are limited and finite, it might not be possible for human reason to discover *every* moral truth. And given that "[t]he greatest part of mankind want leisure or capacity for demonstration," Locke argues that "the instruction of the people were best still to be left to the precepts and principles of the Gospel" (W7: 146). All of this, of course, is fully consistent with his initial conjecture that the entirety of morality is demonstrable *in principle* (e.g., by one with unlimited leisure and rational ability).
2   Apart from the fact that Locke's proof of God's existence in the *Essay* does not rest on standard cosmological grounds (but starts, rather, from one's own existence, which, unlike the existence of an external world full of beauty and order, is intuitively knowable), there is no reason to suppose that Locke abandoned this reasoning while composing the *Essay*.
3   Indeed, Locke's views about God would be grossly inconsistent if he were a voluntarist, given his insistence that God himself is subject to natural law: "[T]he Obligations of that Eternal Law . . . are so great, and so strong, in the case of *Promises*, that Omnipotency it self can be tyed by them. *Grants, Promises* and *Oaths* are Bonds that *Hold the Almighty*" (T2: 195). Surely the proposition that God should keep his promises is not made true by divine command. Rather, what makes it true is the very nature of a promise, which is such as to bind promiser to promisee to the performance of some particular action.
4   I am grateful to Donald Rutherford for helping me to see this.
5   Notice that this reasoning establishes that Locke takes himself to have a demonstrative proof of the existence of an afterlife (though not a demonstrative proof of the existence of eternal life or immortality): the proof goes through God's wisdom, goodness, and power, his promulgation of rules for the benefit of all rational creatures, the backing of these rules with rewards and

punishments, and the obvious fact that the latter will not be experienced on Earth.

6   In the *First Treatise*, Locke considers the objection that human children are created not by God but by their parents (or fathers). His answer (which echoes Nicolas Malebranche's theory of causation in *The Search After Truth*) is that in order to create something complex and give it life, one must know the "Structure and Use of [its] many parts" (T1: 52), "that Operation wherein Life consists in the whole" (T1: 52), and "when it is out of order, [how to] mend it, at least tell wherein its defects lie" (T1: 53). But even the most diligent philosophers and anatomists "confess their Ignorance" in these matters. Given, then, that no human being has the requisite knowledge, it follows that no human being (alone or in combination) creates another.

7   This is an important and, for Locke, self-evident principle, connected to the principle – see Section 11.4 below – that *labor* under certain conditions is sufficient for ownership. Indeed, if creation is a form of labor, then the former principle can be seen as just a corollary of the latter.

8   See Aristotle, *Politics*, 1254b16–21, 1255a1–3.

9   Immanuel Kant, the quintessential non-deterrence-based retributivist, famously insists that "even if a civil society were to be dissolved by the consent of all its members (e.g., if a people inhabiting an island decided to separate and disperse throughout the world), the last murderer remaining in prison would first have to be executed, so that each has done to him what his deeds deserve" (Immanuel Kant, *The Metaphysics of Morals*, edited by Mary Gregor. Cambridge: Cambridge University Press, 1996, 6: 333).

10 The consequentialist tenor of Locke's theory of punishment is evident from a portion of his *A Second Letter Concerning Toleration*: "Now all punishment is some evil, some inconvenience, some suffering; by taking away or abridging some good thing, which he who is punished has otherwise a right to. Now to justify the bringing any such evil upon any man, two things are requisite. First, That he who does it has commission and power so to do. Secondly, That it be directly useful for the procuring some greater good. Whatever punishment one man uses to another, without these two conditions, whatever he may pretend, proves an injury and injustice, and so of right ought to have been let alone" (W6: 112).

11 In this, Locke differs from his predecessor, Hugo Grotius, who argued that people may sell not only some of their liberty, but all of their liberty (*On the Law of War and Peace* (1625), 1.3.8.1).

12 At the same time, Locke insists that those who forfeit their lives thereby lose "their Estates," and that those "in the *State of Slavery* [are] not capable of any Property" (T2: 85). For if a slave had property, then he would be permitted to defend his property against his lawful master by force. But no slave has the right to use force against his lawful master. So Locke argues that the property of a person who is rightfully enslaved by another is rightfully inherited by that person's lawful heirs (T2: 183).

13 Roger Woolhouse, *Locke: A Biography*. Cambridge: Cambridge University Press, 2007, 187.

14 Locke differs from theorists, such as Hume, who think that property exists only by convention. For Hume, "[o]ur property is nothing but those goods, whose constant possession is establish'd by the laws of society," these laws

being a "convention enter'd into by all the members of the society to bestow stability on the possession of those external goods, and leave every one in the peaceable enjoyment of what he may acquire by his fortune and industry" (David Hume, *A Treatise of Human Nature*, edited by David Fate Norton and Mary J. Norton. Oxford: Oxford University Press, 2000, 3.2.2.11 and 3.2.2.9).

15 This idea is emphasized in A. John Simmons, *The Lockean Theory of Rights*. Princeton, NJ: Princeton University Press, 1992.

16 For Locke's purposes, the proof that the Earth was given to all human beings in common is important not only because it is the first part of his proof that individual human beings have ways of legitimately acquiring external goods as property in possession but also because it is an essential part of his response to one of Robert Filmer's premises for the argument that kings rule by divine right, namely the premise that the Earth was given to Adam, and thereafter to Adam's descendants by primogeniture – see T1: 21–43 and 81–103.

17 See Grotius 1625, 2.2.2.5, and Pufendorf, *Of the Law of Nature and Nations* (1672), 4.4.4–5.

18 Robert Nozick, *Anarchy, State, and Utopia*. New York: Basic Books, 1974, 174–175.

19 Locke also writes that what "is to be counted into the *Bread* we eat" includes not only "the Plough-man's Pains, the Reaper's and Thresher's Toil, and the Bakers Sweat," but also "the Labour of those who broke the Oxen, who digged and wrought the Iron and Stones, who felled and framed the Timber imployed about the Plough, Mill, Oven, or any other Utensils . . . requisite to this Corn" (T2: 43).

20 Note that Locke here suggests that human beings are not permitted to destroy anything on Earth. But this is clearly an overstatement. Locke recognizes that eating an apple one has picked destroys it, that killing a fish one has caught destroys it, and so on; and yet he counts all of these activities as permissible: "Property . . . is for the benefit and sole Advantage of the Proprietor, so that he may even destroy the thing, that he has Property in by his use of it, where need requires" (T1: 92—see also T1: 39). What Locke must be thinking at T2: 31, then, is that human beings are not permitted to destroy God's gifts, *unless it be to some reasonable purpose* (i.e., self-preservation).

21 Note, though, that because they will never acquire the reason needed to govern their own lives according to the laws of nature, "*Lunaticks* and *Ideots* are never set free from the Government of their Parents" (T2: 60).

22 Locke seems unaware of a potential difficulty for his theory here. For, on his view, the law of nature obligates only *rational* persons: "[N]o Body can be under a Law, which is not promulgated to him; he that is not come to the use of his *Reason*, cannot be said to be *under this Law*" (T2: 57). It follows that young children, not having yet reached the age of reason, have no duties that derive from natural law. Thus, they do not have any natural law duty to comply with the demands of their parents. Locke's claim that children have a duty of compliance cannot be saved by supposing that it applies only to children who have already reached the age of reason. For, once rational, children immediately graduate from the paternalistic rule of their parents, and are no longer required to follow their parents' wishes. On reflection, then, perhaps Locke's theory cannot be used to derive a duty of compliance, much as he would like to be able to find justification for such a duty.

further reading

Colman, John, *Locke's Moral Philosophy*. Edinburgh: Edinburgh University Press, 1983.

Darwall, Stephen, *The British Moralists and the Internal 'Ought': 1640–1740*. Cambridge: Cambridge University Press, 1995, chapter 6.

Grant, Ruth W., *John Locke's Liberalism*. Chicago: University of Chicago Press, 1987, chapter 1.

Nozick, Robert, *Anarchy, State, and Utopia*. New York: Basic Books, 1974.

Ryan, Alan, *Property and Political Theory*. Oxford: Blackwell, 1984.

Schneewind, J.B., "Locke's Moral Philosophy," in *The Cambridge Companion to Locke*, edited by Vere Chappell. Cambridge: Cambridge University Press, 1994, pp. 199–225.

Simmons, A. John, *The Lockean Theory of Rights*. Princeton, NJ: Princeton University Press, 1992.

Tully, James, *A Discourse on Property: John Locke and His Adversaries*. Cambridge: Cambridge University Press, 1980.

Tully, James, *An Approach to Political Philosophy: Locke in Contexts*. Cambridge: Cambridge University Press, 1993.

Waldron, Jeremy, *The Right to Private Property*. Oxford: Oxford University Press, 1988.

Waldron, Jeremy, *God, Locke, and Equality: Christian Foundations in Locke's Political Thought*. Cambridge: Cambridge University Press, 2002.

Roger Woolhouse, *Locke: A Biography*. Cambridge: Cambridge University Press, 2007.

political philosophy

According to Locke's moral theory, every human being is born to the state of equal freedom to choose her own path in life as she sees fit within the bounds of natural law, and acquires this freedom upon reaching the age of reason, which is when she acquires the ability to obtain demonstrative knowledge of the law. Natural law requires that she respect God's property (including her own body and mind, as well as the bodies and minds of other rational beings) by preserving it as much as possible, that she have the right to punish those who transgress natural law (as a way of deterring further transgressions of the law), that she have the right to acquire property in possession by laboring on a part of what God has given human beings in common, that she have the right to alienate her labor and possessions in exchange for the labor or possessions of others, and that she keep her promises and honor her contracts.

Unfortunately, on Locke's view, the state of nature, a state in which the law of nature applies but in which there is no common judge or authoritative enforcement mechanism to which its subjects can appeal, is not a utopia. Human nature being what it is, and the circumstances in which humans live being what they are, the state of nature threatens to devolve into a state of war – that is, "a State of Enmity, Malice, Violence, and Mutual Destruction" (T2: 19). There are five main "Inconveniences" of the state of nature that tend towards mutual enmity and destruction: first, even though the law of nature is discoverable by all rational persons, "yet Men being biased by their Interest, as well as ignorant for want of study of it, are not apt to allow of it as a Law binding to them in the application of it to their particular Cases" (T2: 124); second, when disputes arise (over property, contracts, and other matters human beings care deeply about), "Self-love will make Men partial to themselves and their Friends," and thus, when left as "Judges in their own Cases," they will tend not to rule against their own interests or the interests of the members of their circle (T2: 13; see also T2: 125); third, "negligence, and unconcernedness" will make human beings "too remiss, in other Mens [cases]," and thus they

Locke, First Edition. Samuel C. Rickless.
© 2014 Samuel C. Rickless. Published 2014 by John Wiley & Sons, Ltd.

will not be motivated to punish those who violate natural law to the detriment of strangers (T2: 125); fourth, once a judgment that others have violated natural law has been made, "Ill Nature, Passion and Revenge will carry [human beings] too far in punishing others" (T2: 13; see also T2: 125); and, fifth, enforcement of natural law is uncertain and spotty, for "there often wants *Power* to back and support the Sentence when right, and to *give* it due *Execution*," given that those who have been found guilty but take themselves to be innocent will seldom fail to resist (T2: 126).

It is for these reasons, says Locke, that "notwithstanding all the Priviledges of the state of Nature," human beings "are quickly driven into [political] Society" (T2: 127). What political society is, how it comes to be and how it sometimes ceases to be, why it requires government, and how to distinguish between legitimate and illegitimate government: these are the questions Locke offers to answer in sections 87–243 of the *Second Treatise*. Those answers are the heart of Locke's political philosophy. As we will see, Locke takes his political principles to entail a number of further conclusions about the limitations on legitimate political power, including a principle of religious toleration that has played a crucial role in the development of religious freedom in Europe and North America.

12.1   Political Society

A political society exists when and only when a number of human beings "are united into one Body, and have a common establish'd Law and Judicature to appeal to, with Authority to decide Controversies between them, and punish Offenders" (T2: 87). Locke makes clear that a member of a society is a "perpetual Subject of that Commonwealth" (T2: 122; see also T2: 121): once a member, always a member. The nature of political society is determined by its function, which is to serve as a "Remedy for the Inconveniences of the State of Nature" (T2: 13), by securing the general property (i.e., the life, liberty, and possessions) of each member according to natural law (T2: 88). The main defects of the state of nature, as Locke argues, concern ignorance of natural law, partiality and lack of concern for others in the resolution of disputes according to natural law, and wrongful excesses or deficiencies in the enforcement of natural law. The best (though not perfect) solution to these defects, Locke suggests, is collective action through a unitary living body with a single will (T2: 96, 212), whose function it is to understand natural law and both establish and enforce conflict-settling rules for the preservation of property (T2: 88, 94, 124, 134, 222) within the bounds of that law (see T2: 135) against the unlawful encroachments of both members and non-members (T2: 88, 95, 131). "[T]he Soul that gives Form, Life, and Unity to the Commonwealth," in Locke's metaphor, is its "Legislative," which has "Supream" power (T2: 134–135, 150) and whose function it is to declare the society's unitary will (T2: 214) in the form of "promulgated standing laws" (T2: 136).

Locke distinguishes between society and government (T2: 133). Every society (or group of people who have united in perpetuity to preserve their properties under common standing laws) has a government (i.e., a subset of the society that constitutes the legislative), and the dissolution or destruction of a society entails the dissolution or destruction of its government (T2: 211). But, as Locke argues, it is possible for government to be dissolved without dissolving society as a whole (T2: 212–219, 221–222).

The power (or right) possessed by the legislative in a society is what Locke calls "*Political Power*" (T2: 3). Such power involves the making of "standing Rules, which shall be of perpetual Obligation, by which [citizens] ought to regulate all the Concerns of their Property, and bound their Liberty all the course of their Lives" (T2: 65). With respect to its citizens, the political power of a society's legislative is unlimited in duration ("perpetual") and extensive in its reach (i.e., property in the general sense: life, liberty, and possessions). As such it contrasts with the rights of parents over children, the rights of children over parents, the rights of spouses over each other, and the rights of masters over their servants, all of which are limited in duration and extent. It follows that political power cannot rightfully be modeled on any of these relations, contrary to what some defenders of the divine right of kings, including Robert Filmer, had previously argued.

Interestingly, Locke argues that the very *nature* of political society is incompatible with absolute monarchy. For absolute power is the power to compel and coerce (i.e., enslave) others under threat of death (T1: 9), and political society requires a known authority to decide disputes under standing promulgated laws. Yet in an absolute monarchy, there is no possibility of having a "known Authority, to which every one of that Society may Appeal upon any Injury received, or Controversie that may arise, and which every one of the Society ought to obey" (T2: 90). For there is no such authority to decide disputes between an absolute monarch and any of his (or her) subjects (T2: 91). By contrast, in any political society there *is* a known authority to decide disputes between any of its members and the legislative, namely the legislative itself. This shows that the crucial element of Locke's argument for the incompatibility of absolute monarchy with political society is the fact that absolute monarchs do not have the authority, or right, to rule: absolute monarchy is an illegitimate form of government. To see why this is, however, we need to understand Locke's conception of what is necessary and sufficient to endow any government with moral legitimacy.

12.2 Legitimate Rule

It is a fundamental axiom of Locke's political theory that legitimate rule is grounded in consent. Because all rational human beings are naturally free to run their lives as they see fit within the bounds of natural law, it cannot be rightful to coerce them to join any association, whatever that group's function may be. Freedom to choose involves the right to dissent from any activity that is not already obligatory under natural law. Because joining with others to form a society is not required by the law of nature, it is entirely up to each and every rational being whether to do so or to remain in the state of nature: "Men being . . . by Nature, all free, equal and independent, no one can be put out of this Estate, and subjected to the Political Power of another, without his own *Consent*" (T2: 95).

The freedom to form a society follows from the freedom to associate for any purpose. Just as one is free to consent to a marriage contract or to an agreement to serve a particular master in exchange for wages, so one is free to join with others to establish a common set of rules and a mechanism to enforce them for the purpose of preserving the property of all members. It is important to Locke that the formation of society should not encroach in any way on the moral rights possessed by others in the state of nature, for otherwise the creation of societies would be impermissible according to natural law. And, indeed, Locke insists that free associations of this sort do not violate the natural rights of anyone else: "[Uniting into a community is something] any number of Men may do, because it injures not the Freedom of the rest; they are left as they were in the Liberty of the State of Nature" (T2: 95).[1]

12.2.1   Majority rule

Locke argues that consent to form a political society entails consent to be ruled by a legislative. This much is uncontroversial, given that it is entailed by the very definition of political society. But Locke goes on to argue that consent to be ruled by a legislative also entails consent to majority rule. His argument for this proposition is potentially problematic:

> For that which acts any Community, being only the consent of the individuals of it, and it being necessary to that which is one body to move one way; it is necessary the Body should move that way whither the greater force carries it, which is the *consent of the majority*: or else it is impossible it should act or continue one Body, *one Community*, which the consent of every individual that united into it, agreed that it should; and so every one is bound by that consent to be concluded by the *majority*. (T2: 96)

Here Locke seems caught between the horns of a dilemma. The conception of force with which he is working is either metaphorical, in which case the bearing of the mechanical analogy is unclear (in what sense is the consent of the majority a greater "force"?), or quite literal, in which case the argument makes no sense (the consent of the majority is not *literally* a physical force). What is clear is that in order for the rule-making and enforcement functions of political society to be possible, there must be *some* decision-making procedure the results of which bind all of its members. But what that decision procedure should be is not determined by the very decision to unite together for the purpose of property protection.

It may be that Locke's focus on majority rule is motivated by practical more than by philosophical considerations. One of the points he makes is that any decision procedure that requires unanimous consent of all the members of society is not practically feasible: "But such a consent is next impossible ever to be had, if we consider the Infirmities of Health, and Avocations of Business, which in a number . . . will necessarily keep many away from the publick Assembly. To which [might be added] the variety of Opinions, and contrariety of Interests, which unavoidably happen in all Collections of Men" (T2: 98). This is all very reasonable. But Locke also claims, without argument, that the only *possible* alternative to unanimous consent is majority rule (T2: 98). Perhaps the most reasonable position for Locke to take here is that, given the inevitable disagreements that arise within large groups of people and the fact that the balance of reasons on many important matters will not point very clearly for or against any given proposal, it will often happen that the citizens of a commonwealth are very nearly evenly divided about what to do. Were consent to join a given society not to be understood to include agreement to be bound by the consent of the majority, the inevitable result, given human nature and the circumstances of human life, would be gridlock or worse.

12.2.2 Express consent and tacit consent

One interpretive issue that has caused no end of consternation among Locke scholars is what form of consent he takes to be necessary and sufficient for societal membership. Locke distinguishes between two forms of consent, express and tacit (T2: 119). Unfortunately, he does little to elucidate the distinction, except to say that consent is express when one makes an expression of it (T2: 119). But what exactly counts as an expression of consent? One obvious possibility is that consent is express when it takes the form of a linguistic utterance. Locke sometimes speaks of societies requiring "Oaths of Fealty, or Allegiance, or other publick owning of, or Submission to the Government" (T2: 62; see also T2: 151).[2] Another possibility is that consent is express when it is externalized in some form, not necessarily through speech. For example, Locke might hold that I give express consent to receive offers by mail if I check a box on a form that lies next to the words: "Check here if you consent to receive offers by mail." The thought here is that I make my consent known to others (I externalize it) by means of a publicly scrutinizable action, and this is sufficient to count as express consent. Tacit consent, then, is a form of consent that is not express. Hence, it involves an omission to give expression to one's consent. We may presume that a paradigm of tacit consent takes place in a context in which it is possible for one to dissent and yet everyone believes (and everyone believes that everyone believes, etc.), often or always on the basis of convention, that one's failure to dissent counts as consent. In Amsterdam, many houses are built right up to the street, and their large living-room windows look onto busy thoroughfares. A resident living on the ground floor who does not wish passers-by to see what he is doing in his living room will close the curtain. But when he does not close the curtain, he arguably tacitly consents to passers-by gaining visual access to what is happening in his living room.

Locke states in no uncertain terms that membership in a society requires express consent: "Nothing can make any Man [a subject or member of a commonwealth], but his actually entering into it by positive Engagement, and express Promise and Compact" (T2: 122). And yet many readers of the *Second Treatise* come away thinking that for Locke, under certain conditions, tacit consent in the absence of express consent can be sufficient for societal membership. Are Locke's views inconsistent, or has he simply been misread?

The problem is that, although Locke's views are clear and consistent, his entire discussion of the matter of tacit and express consent is confusing. Part of the problem derives from Locke's use of a confusing contrast; the rest of the problem derives from the superficial semantic similarities among the following phrases: "putting oneself under a government" (T2: 117, 118), "being a subject of a government (or country)" (T2: 118, 119), "being subject to a government" (T2: 120, 121), "being subject to the laws of a government" (T2: 119), "submitting to the laws of a government (or country)" (T2: 122), and "submitting to a government" (T2: 119, 120, 121, 122).

The misleading contrast occurs in the section in which Locke introduces the tacit/express distinction (I have numbered the parts for ease of reference):

> [1] There is a common distinction of an express and a tacit consent, which will concern our present Case. [2] No body doubts but an *express Consent*, of any Man, entering into any Society, makes him a perfect Member of that Society, a Subject of that Government. [3] The difficulty is, what ought to be look'd upon as a *tacit Consent*, and how far it binds, *i.e.* how far any one shall be looked on to have consented, and thereby submitted to any Government, where he has made no Expressions of it at all. [4] And to this I say, that every Man, that hath any Possession, or Enjoyment, of any part of the Dominions of any Government, doth thereby give his *tacit Consent*, and is as far forth obliged to Obedience to the Laws of that Government, during such Enjoyment, as any one under it; whether this his Possession be of Land, to him and his Heirs for ever, or a Lodging only for a Week; or whether it be barely travelling freely on the Highway; and in Effect, it reaches as far as the very being of any one within the Territories of that Government. (T2: 119)

In (2), Locke makes clear that no one doubts that express consent of a certain sort is sufficient for membership in a (political) society. In (3), Locke claims that there is a difficulty regarding how far tacit consent binds, and thereby suggests or conveys that it is a matter of debate both what is sufficient for tacit consent and whether tacit consent of a similar sort can be sufficient for societal membership. In direct response to this difficulty, Locke then avers in (4) that possession or enjoyment of any lands under government jurisdiction is sufficient for tacit consent, and that such tacit consent is sufficient for being obligated to obey the laws of that government, even when one is not a member of the relevant society (e.g., a temporary visitor or traveler). The problem is generated by two features of the text: (i) the contrast between express consent in (2) and tacit consent in (3), all in the context of a discussion of societal membership, and (ii) the fact that (4)'s discussion of tacit consent is described as a response to (3), even though (4) makes no reference to societal membership.

If one reads (3) as conveying that the question at hand is whether tacit consent is sufficient for societal membership, and one then reads (4) as providing a positive answer to the question in (3), then one will read Locke as conveying that it is possible to become a member of a society by tacit consent to abide by its laws. The problem with this reading is that Locke makes it clear in (4) that tacit consent, in the form of possession or enjoyment of land under a government's jurisdiction, is sufficient not for societal membership but rather for being under an obligation to follow the laws of the society. If this is so, then if (4) is to be read as a direct response to (3), then (3) must be read as raising the question of whether tacit consent is sufficient for being obligated to obey the law of a society (even if one is not a member of that society). But in that case Locke's contrast between (3) and (2) is unhelpful, because whereas (3) is concerned with whether *tacit* consent is sufficient for being *obligated to obey the law* of a society, (2) is concerned with whether *express* consent is sufficient for being *a member* of a society. Not only is there a contrast between express consent in (2) and tacit consent in (3), but there is also a contrast between what the two forms of consent might be thought to be sufficient *for*.

The various phrases Locke uses to discuss one's relation to government and to society appear to be identical in meaning. At first blush, it appears (a) that to put oneself under a society's government *is* to become a subject of that government, (b) that to be a subject of a government *is* to be subject to that government, (c) that to be subject to a government *is* to be subject to the laws of that government, (d) that to be subject to the laws of a government *is* to submit to the laws of that government, and finally (e) that to submit to the laws of a government *is* to submit to that government. If one accepts (a)–(e), then it is easy to argue that Locke takes tacit consent, in the form of possession or enjoyment of land under a government's jurisdiction, to be sufficient for societal membership. For Locke states that tacit consent, in the form of enjoyment of land under a government's jurisdiction, is sufficient for "*submitting to the Government of the Commonwealth*" (T2: 120). But, according to (a)–(e), to submit to the government of a commonwealth *is* to put oneself under that government. And yet Locke also assumes that to put oneself under a society's government *is* to become a member of that society: "and then he is a Free-man, at liberty what Government he will put himself under; what Body Politick he will unite himself to" (T2: 118).

As we have seen, however, Locke explicitly makes *express* consent a necessary condition for societal membership. There must therefore be something wrong with the argument that relies on (a)–(e). I suggest that the problem lies with either (c) or (d): the text does not determine which. Either Locke distinguishes between *subjection* to government/laws (sufficient for membership) and *submission* to government/laws (not sufficient for membership), or Locke distinguishes between submission/subjection *to government* (sufficient for membership) and submission/subjection *to the laws of a government* (not sufficient for membership).

It might at first seem odd for Locke to commit to the view that tacit consent could never on its own be sufficient for societal membership. After all, nowadays few if any persons become members of a society (citizens of a country) by taking an oath or signing a deed. How, then, would they become citizens if not by tacitly consenting to become members? The answer is that our membership conventions differ from Locke's. *We* take some sort of oath to be necessary for *naturalization*, but not for citizenship more generally: birth within the confines of the relevant society's territory is now taken to be sufficient for membership. But this is something Locke emphatically denies: "*a Child is born a Subject of no Country or Government*" (T2: 118). For Locke, a child "is under his Fathers Tuition and Authority, till he come to Age of Discretion [i.e., the age of reason]; and then he is a Free-man, at liberty what Government he will put himself under; what Body Politick he will unite himself to" (T2: 118). Because *we* take birth in a particular location to be sufficient for membership, it is no surprise that we do not treat membership as dependent on an oath or a signature at the "age of discretion." For Locke, the reverse is true.

Tacit consent, in the form of enjoyment or possession of anything lying within the territorial jurisdiction of a government, is sufficient not for societal membership but rather for obligation to obey the government's laws. If I purchase a villa in Tuscany and spend my summer holidays there (would that I could!), I do not thereby become an Italian citizen, obligated to defend Italy against all enemies, foreign and domestic. If I give a talk at Charles University in Prague, staying at a local hotel and paying local taxes, I do not thereby become a member of the Czech Republic. But, as Locke sees it, my being voluntarily on Italian or Czech territory counts as an agreement to abide by local laws and regulations, including rather stricter laws against jaywalking than I may be used to or laws mandating possession of a passport or identity card on one's person at all times. Were mere property possession or enjoyment within the jurisdiction of a society's government sufficient for membership in that society, no one who wished to remain a member of her own society would ever visit, rent, or purchase part of the territory controlled by the government of a different society. In Locke's eyes, such a result would be manifestly absurd.

12.2.3 The powers of a legitimate government

When a number of rational individuals in the state of nature join together to form a society for the preservation of their property (i.e., their lives, liberties, and estates), the express consent that is both necessary and sufficient for their membership in the society results in the transfer or alienation of rights from these individuals to their legislative. A government to which the members of a society have not transferred certain rights does not *have* those rights, and hence does not possess the authority to rule, to pass and enforce binding legislation.

The rights transferred from individuals to their society's government are two: the right "to do whatever [one] thinks fit for the preservation of [oneself] and others within the permission of the *Law of Nature*," and the right "*to punish the Crimes* committed against that Law" (T2: 128). As a result of the express consent of its members, the government of a society acquires the right to preserve the lives of those members by whatever means *it* thinks fit within the bounds of natural law, and hence none of the members of society is permitted to interfere with the government's decisions or with their implementation. Given that the preservation of life requires the preservation of what is needed to maintain life, and given that liberty and possessions are needed to maintain life, it follows that a government that acquires the right to protect the lives of its society's members *ipso facto* acquires the right to protect their liberties and estates as well. Given that in the state of nature *every* rational person has the right to punish *anyone* who violates natural law in *any* way, it follows from the principle of alienation by express consent that a society's government acquires *this very right*. And given that the right to enforce the laws passed by the legislative and the right to punish offenses against the law of nature would be meaningless without being backed by the threat of force, and given that this force rests on the willingness of society's members to serve as enforcers, the consent that transfers rights from a citizen to his government also "engages his natural force . . . to assist the Executive Power of the Society, as the Law thereof shall require" (T2: 130).

How far a government may go in exercising the rights transferred to it by its society's members is wholly determined by the society's end or purpose, which is to protect the members' property in the general sense by means that remedy the defects of the state of nature. The main defects of the state of nature, as we have seen, are ignorance of natural law, partiality and lack of concern for others in the resolution of disputes according to natural law, and wrongful excesses or deficiencies in the enforcement of natural law. The remedy for these ills requires that the legislative "govern by establish'd *standing Laws*, promulgated and known to the People, and not by Extemporary Decrees," that there be "*indifferent* and upright *Judges*, who are to decide Controversies by those Laws," and that the executive power be used "*only in the Execution of such Laws*, or abroad to prevent or redress Foreign Injuries, and secure the Community from Inroads and Invasion" (T2: 131). It follows that no legitimate government is permitted to tax any of its society's members without their consent – that is, without the consent of the majority; though, as Locke recognizes, the maintenance of any government requires taxation (see T2: 140).

Interestingly, Locke allows for many different forms of legitimate government, depending on the consent of the majority of a society's members:

democracy (in which the legislative is placed in the hands of elected officials), oligarchy (in which the legislative is placed in the hands of "a few select Men, and their Heirs or Successors"), or monarchy (in which the legislative is placed in the hands of "one Man"), whether hereditary or elective (T2: 132). Locke provides no demonstratively knowable moral principle favoring democracy over oligarchy or monarchy.

At the same time, Locke *does* think that *practical* reasons favor certain constraints on the proper structure of legitimate government. One of these constraints concerns the size of the legislative. Locke worries that if the legislative body consists of one person, then, at least when the same body possesses both legislative and executive power, there "may be too great a temptation to humane frailty apt to grasp at Power." If one person is given the job of making law and enforcing law, then he "may exempt [himself] from Obedience to the Laws [he makes], and suit the Law, both in its making and execution, to [his] own private advantage, and thereby come to have a distinct interest from the rest of the Community, contrary to the end of Society and Government" (T2: 143). In a context in which the same person makes and enforces the law, human frailty combined with a strong desire for power is a recipe for turning legitimate government into illegitimate government, one that no longer aims at the preservation of the lives, liberties, and estates of *all* members of society. Locke concludes, on empirical grounds, that it would be better for the legislative to be a plural body, rather than a single person: "Therefore in well order'd Commonwealths . . . the *Legislative* Power is put into the hands of divers Persons" (T2: 143).

Another practical constraint Locke mentions is the separation of legislative power from executive power. Here Locke *could* help himself to the same empirical reasons favoring the pluralization of the legislative: surely when the legislative power is placed in one body and the executive power is placed in another, it is more difficult for the second body to exempt itself from obedience to the rules established by the first. But this is not the reason Locke provides for separating the two powers. Instead, he points out that whereas "[i]t is not necessary, no nor so much as convenient, that the *Legislative* should be *always in being*," it is "absolutely necessary that the *Executive Power* should, because there is not always need for new Laws to be made, but always need of Execution of the Laws that are made" (T2: 153; see also T2: 144). Notice, though, that the fact that the legislative need not always be in session does not entail that it would be *undesirable* for it never to adjourn or recess. Locke's real practical reason against a perpetually active legislative is that it would be *inconvenient*. Although he does not explain what this inconvenience amounts to, we can speculate. If a plural legislative never adjourned, representatives would need to spend all their time near the seat of government, and would have little or no time to spend with their constituents. Under these circumstances, they would be removed from the people, whose interests they might well stop representing or protecting, contrary to the purpose of government.

Finally, Locke finds strong empirical reasons to support placing the power to execute the law and the power to make war and peace (as well as leagues and alliances) with other societies (i.e., the "federative" power) in the same body. For if one body were given the power to enforce domestic rules and another body were given the power to enforce international rules, then "the Force of the Publick would be under different Commands: which would be apt sometime or other to cause disorder and ruine" (T2: 148). Notice that all three of these recommendations have been taken up by successful democracies and republics since the time of Locke, testifying to his eminent good sense.

Locke emphasizes that, in all legitimate governments, the legislative is supreme, in the sense that all other powers are subordinate to the legislative (T2: 149). At the same time, Locke causes potentially serious, and probably in the end unnecessary, problems for himself with respect to the relation between the subordination of powers and the issue of legislative convocation. Locke recognizes that the legislative will need to meet in order to conduct the business of passing laws. In a well-ordered society, as Locke has already argued, the legislative is a plural body. This necessarily poses issues of convenience. As Locke sees it, "[c]onstant *frequent meetings of the Legislative,* and long Continuations of their Assemblies, without necessary occasion, could not but be burthensome to the People" (T2: 156). The most obvious practical remedy for this inconvenience is an "Original Constitution" requiring the legislative's "*assembling* and *acting* at certain intervals" (T2: 154). But Locke believes that it will not be possible for the framers of an original constitution to predict exactly when it would be most opportune for the legislative to meet, and thus concludes that, for practical purposes, the best original constitution of government is one in which the power of convoking the legislative (deciding when it will convene and for how long) "naturally [falls] into the hands of the Executive" (T2: 156). The problem this poses is that the executive, given that it has the use of force at its disposal as a necessary means of enforcing the laws passed by the legislative, might very well use that force "to hinder the *meeting and acting of the Legislative*" (T2: 155). In such a situation, the legislative would find itself unacceptably subject to the whims of the executive with respect to the time and place of its convocation (as in the case of the relation between Charles II and Parliament).

Locke has no response to this difficulty except to trust the executive to exercise its power of convocation wisely, in the interests of the people. And, as he argues, a similar response is called for with respect to other practical problems, such as how fair and equal representation (in the case of indirect democracy) is to be guaranteed. The worry is that districts with a single representative to the legislative may gain or lose population over time. If a district gains population, then it will be *underrepresented* in the legislative relative to the initial allotment of representatives to districts; and if a district loses population, then it will be *overrepresented* in the legislative relative to the initial allotment of representatives to districts. An obvious way to solve this problem is to fix a periodic census and reapportionment in the original constitution. But Locke's solution, as in the case of legislative convocation, is to leave this matter to the discretion of the executive, trusting that it will exercise power wisely for the sake of the overall good of the people (T2: 158).

In general, in Locke's well-ordered society, the executive should be left with a host of powers that go beyond mere law enforcement or the right to wage war and make peace and alliances, all of which fall under the general rubric of "prerogative." Prerogative, as Locke defines it, is the "Power to act according to discretion, for the publick good, without the prescription of the Law, and sometimes against it" (T2: 160). That the executive should have prerogative is required not only by the inconveniences that attach to regular convocation of the legislative or regular reapportionment, but also by the fact that "many accidents may happen, wherein a strict and rigid observation of the Laws [passed by the legislative] may do harm" (T2: 159). Locke's paradigm of this is a law penalizing the destruction of an innocent person's property in a situation in which pulling down someone's house may be needed to stop a fire from spreading (T2: 159). In such a case, the one who pulls down the innocent person's house would be guilty under the law, but "deserve[s] reward and pardon" (T2: 159). Mechanical application of the law would require punishment, but punishment would be unjust. Prerogative, in this case in the form of a power to pardon offenders lodged in the executive, is Locke's solution to this difficulty, as it is his solution to the problems of convocation and reapportionment.

Locke acknowledges that endowing the executive with prerogative might be thought to lay "a perpetual foundation for Disorder" (T2: 168). For if the executive is permitted to apply the law to some but not to others as she sees fit, depending on what she takes to be in the best interests of the people and in accord with natural law, then she essentially has the power to decide whether to enforce the law in any particular case. This power, then, appears to put the executive above the law. Indeed, armed with prerogative, the executive could exempt herself from the laws passed by the legislative, pleading that the welfare of the people as a whole requires it. As a result, the people might feel hard done by and rise up against the executive. But Locke does not treat this concern with the seriousness it deserves. Instead, he assumes that the people will not bother to resist the executive with violence "till the Inconvenience [caused by the assertion of prerogative] is so great, that the Majority feel it, and are weary of it, and find a necessity to have it amended" (T2: 168).

Locke may be right about this, but this kind of response should not give his supporters much solace. For the existence of executive prerogative is a very serious structural weakness of any government that is supposed to work for the benefit of every one of a society's members. If it is left to the executive to make exceptions to the implementation of laws whenever she believes that the law's application would be unjust or unfair, then, in practice, given the frailties of human nature and the desire for power (problems with which Locke is quite familiar), and given the understandable reluctance of the people to rise up against the executive except under the most draconian circumstances, the rule of law will effectively be transformed into the rule of the executive, and the executive will achieve supremacy over the legislative. If we are searching for mechanisms that will prevent this sort of result, then we will want to replace Locke's executive prerogative with a different constitutional arrangement.

12.3 Varieties of Illegitimate Rule

It follows directly from Locke's consent-based theory of governmental legitimacy that any government that does not rule with the consent of the people is illegitimate. Locke considers three main ways in which a government can become illegitimate: unjust conquest, usurpation, and tyranny. In the case of unjust conquest, a foreign invader in an unjust war dissolves the existing government and replaces it with another in the absence of popular consent and in contravention of properly enacted legislation (T2: 175). In the case of usurpation, the form of government does not change, but someone who has not been authorized (by the people in accordance with the legislative's properly enacted laws) to serve a particular governmental function (legislative or executive/federative) replaces the authorized person or group through the use of force or coercion (T2: 197–198). And in the case of tyranny, the form of government does not change and no one who is authorized to perform a governmental function is replaced, but either the legislative or the executive (or both) exercises power *"beyond Right . . . for [its] own private separate Advantage"* – that is, beyond what the people and their properly enacted laws permit and not for the good of the members of society as a whole (T2: 199).

Conquest, usurpation, and tyranny result in the dissolution of legitimate government. As Locke sees it, "Conquerours Swords often . . . mangle Societies to pieces." In such cases, the dissolution of society (as a group of people who have banded together for their mutual protection and advantage) automatically results in the dissolution of government as well: "Whenever the *Society is dissolved*, 'tis certain the Government of that Society cannot remain" (T2: 211). But Locke insists that the converse of this proposition is false: the dissolution of government does not entail the dissolution of society. This happens, as Locke puts it, when government is dissolved *"from within"* (T2: 212), but also when conquest does not involve all-out war or significant social disruption.

Governmental dissolution while society remains intact can occur in two ways: first, "[w]hen the *Legislative is altered"* – that is, "broken, or *dissolved,"* as happens in classic cases of usurpation and in some cases of conquest (T2: 212); and, second, "when the Legislative, or the [Executive], either of them act contrary to their Trust," as happens in classic cases of tyranny (T2: 221). Alteration of the legislative can itself happen in five ways: (i) when "a single Person or Prince [i.e., the executive] sets up his own Arbitrary Will in place of the Laws . . . declared by the Legislative" (T2: 214); (ii) when "the Prince hinders the Legislative from assembling in its due time, or from acting freely, pursuant to those ends, for which it was Constituted" (T2: 215); (iii) when "by the Arbitrary Power of the Prince, the Electors, or ways of Election are altered, without the Consent, and contrary to the common Interest of the People" (T2: 216); (iv) when the people are delivered "into the subjection of a Foreign Power, either by the Prince, or by the Legislative" (T2: 217); or (v) when the executive "neglects and abandons [his] charge, so that the Laws already made can no longer be put into execution, [thereby reducing] all to Anarchy" (T2: 219). The members of a plural legislative act contrary to their trust when "they endeavour to invade" the properties (i.e., the lives, liberties, and estates) of the members of society (T2: 221). The executive can act contrary to his trust in one of three ways: (i) when he tyrannically "goes about to set up his own Arbitrary Will, as the Law of the Society," (ii) when he corrupts the people's representatives to the legislative, or (iii) when he corrupts or threatens the electors of the legislative (T2: 222).

In all of these cases, when government is dissolved but society remains intact, Locke argues that the members of society have the right to reconstitute their government as they see fit (T2: 220). But the dissolution of government, as Locke describes it, often leaves persons with force of arms in positions of pretended authority, mistakenly claiming the right to make or enforce legislation. Locke is well aware that his prescription in the case of governmental dissolution might therefore be considered a recipe for rebellion and disorder (T2: 203, 224). In response, Locke makes a number of reasonable points. In some cases, he says, the illegal acts of persons who wrongfully claim authority affect a minority; in other cases, a majority. In the first case, minority resistance will not conduce to anarchy (T2: 208). And in the second case, if the abuses are sufficiently egregious, resistance is inevitable (T2: 209; see also T2: 224). But generally, Locke claims, even a majority of the people will endure a great deal of abuse before being driven to take up arms against those who wrongfully claim the power to govern. Empirical observation suggests that "[p]eople are not so easily got out of their old Forms," that there is "slowness and aversion in the People to quit their old Constitutions" (T2: 223). Revolution is likely only under extreme circumstances, such as when "a long train of Abuses, Prevarications, and Artifices, all tending the same way, make the [invidious] design [of their rulers] visible to the People," in which case it is desirable as a necessary, if unfortunate, remedy in any event (T2: 225).

Though these are reasonable rejoinders to the charge that his theory constitutes a recipe for perpetual disorder, Locke surely underestimates the extent to which it is possible for large numbers of generally unhappy, resentful, or prejudiced people to be whipped into a frenzy by false or exaggerated reports of governmental abuse. Sectarian or genocidal riots, sometimes powerful enough to successfully resist or overturn governments, are not unheard of. Locke may be thinking that the poor or downtrodden are too weak to form effective collective resistance to government, that any effective resistance must be led by people with estates, people with means and with a great deal to lose if resistance is unsuccessful. If so, then he is mistaken. At the same time, it is very reasonable for him to reply that, even if more resistance is likely if his theory is widely accepted than if the divine right of kings is taken for granted, that is a price that must be paid unless someone can come up with a better theory of governmental legitimacy that is less conducive to anarchy.

12.4 Toleration

In the seventeenth century, there was a serious debate, both within and outside the Anglican Church, about whether civil government is permitted (even obligated) to force non-conformists (in the case of England, non-Anglicans), on pain of punishment, to profess particular articles of faith or engage in particular forms of divine worship. Conservative Anglicans argued that Anglicanism was the only true form (among many false forms) of Christianity, and that non-conformists (including Quakers, Baptists, Presbyterians, Anabaptists, and Arminians among Protestant Christians, as well as Catholics, Jews, Muslims, pagans, and atheists) should be forced to embrace Anglicanism in order that their souls be saved from everlasting death or eternal damnation. Liberal Anglicans, of whom Locke was one, argued instead for a principle of toleration, according to which punishment (whether in the form of unilateral executive action or in the form of laws passed by the legislative and enforced by the executive) of non-conformism is morally impermissible.

Locke's considered and mature views on toleration are set out in *A Letter Concerning Toleration*. The letter caused a stir in Anglican circles, and Locke (under an assumed name) engaged in an extended and acrimonious exchange of public letters in defense of his original arguments on the subject with Jonas Proast, as we saw in Chapter 1. The substance of Locke's main arguments is contained in his original letter, with occasional helpful explications to be found in the second and subsequent letters.

Locke is often remembered for one particular argument in favor of toleration, but in fact he offers three (and insists on this at the beginning of his *Second Letter*). The conclusion of each of these arguments is that "the whole jurisdiction of the magistrate [cannot] be extended to the salvation of souls" (W6: 10). The first argument is that no civil magistrate, neither the executive nor the legislative, in a political society has any *authority* to punish non-conformists for their failure to profess or worship according to the established religion. Locke considers two ways in which a civil magistrate might acquire such authority: (i) from God, or (ii) "by the consent of the people." Making quick work of the first option, Locke insists that "it appears not that God has ever given any such authority to one man over another, as to compel any one to his religion" (W6: 10). Locke's evidence for this is that the New Testament, acknowledged by Anglicans to be the Word of God, speaks of bringing the good news of Christianity to non-believers, but never speaks of imposing Christianity on non-believers through force or coercion. As for popular consent, Locke argues (in keeping with the argument of the *Second Treatise*) that magistrates possess whatever authority they have as a delegated right transferred to them by the members of the relevant political society. But the purpose of a political society is to serve as a remedy for the inconveniencies of the state of nature through government by standing civil laws designed to protect the property (i.e., life, liberty, and possessions) of citizens, laws that are applied by impartial judges and enforced by an executive for the public good within the bounds of natural law. As such, the function of civil society (and hence, the function of government) does not extend to the protection or furtherance of its citizens' *otherworldly* interests: "The part of the magistrate is only to take care that the commonwealth receive no prejudice, and that there be no injury done to any man, either in life or estate" (W6: 34).

Locke assumes here that the state of nature is one in which each rational being has the right to pursue his own worldly or otherworldly interests as he sees fit without violating natural law (i.e., without threatening the life, liberty, or possessions of other persons). Moreover, religious beliefs by themselves do not threaten the lives, liberties, or possessions of others: "[N]o man or society of men can, by their opinions in religion or ways of worship, do any man who differed from them any injury, which he could not avoid or redress if he desired it, without the help of force" (W6: 212). According to natural law, then, persons have the natural right to profess whatever they wish and worship however they please, as long as this does not violate the rights of others. Given that no inconvenience attaches to each person being left at liberty to practice his own religion as he pleases (within the bounds of natural law), no person in the state of nature has the right to punish others for non-conformism. And no citizen of a new society can transfer to its government a right he does not have. Consequently, the government of any society cannot acquire the right to punish non-conformism by delegation from its citizens. Furthermore, given that every person in the state of nature would want to be (and has the right to be) protected from coercion by others in matters of religious belief and practice, the very ends of political society and government dictate that citizens be so protected: "For force from a stronger hand, to bring a man to a religion which another thinks the true, being an injury which in the state of nature every one would avoid; protection from such injury is one of the ends of a commonwealth" (W6: 212). So, far from having the right to force dissenters to conform, government in a political society is morally enjoined from punishing non-conformists.

Locke's second argument for toleration is the best known of the three, though there is reason to worry that it might not be as compelling as the other two. Locke represents his opponents as claiming that the punishment of non-conformists is designed to serve the purpose of saving their souls. But as Locke emphasizes, no one's soul will be saved except by actually *believing* what is needed for salvation: "[T]rue and saving religion consists in the inward persuasion of the mind, without which nothing can be acceptable to God." So if the magistrate is to succeed in saving the souls of non-conformists, he must force them to believe something that they do not currently believe. And if he is to do this, then he must use the only means at his disposal, which is the threat of punishment, given that "his power consists only in outward force." Unfortunately, coercing others to believe on pain of punishment is not possible: "[S]uch is the nature of the understanding, that it cannot be compelled to the belief of any thing by outward force" (W6: 11). Locke concludes that "penalties in this case are absolutely impertinent" (W6: 12). By this, he means that it is not only impossible but impermissible for the magistrate to punish non-conformists for the purpose of saving their souls. Most likely, Locke is assuming something approaching what is sometimes known as the Ought-Implies-Can principle, more often associated with Kant. According to this principle, if X ought to do A, then X can do A; or, contrapositively, if X cannot do A, then X ought not to do A. So, if the magistrate literally cannot change the minds of non-conformists under threat of punishment, then this is something he should not do (and thus, for Locke, something he has no right to do).

The reason why this argument is not as compelling as Locke might have hoped is that it underestimates the extent to which torture and brainwashing (or even mere threats of such torture) can result in doxastic change. Persons who are punished or who are threatened with punishment are highly motivated to avoid it. This motivation can result in biased forms of evidence gathering. Because I want very badly to believe something that will enable me to avoid punishment for non-conformism, I will be motivated to look for and pay close attention to evidence favoring Anglicanism and I will be motivated not to seek out or pay close attention to evidence against Anglicanism. As a result of paying attention to the evidence that I have gathered by these means, I will very likely find myself agreeing (without having been directly forced to agree) with Anglicanism.

Locke's third argument for toleration is that even if magistrates had the authority to, and effectively could, compel non-conformists to change their religious views and practices, it would not conduce to the saving of human souls for the punishment of non-conformists to be practiced in all societies. The reason, which Locke enjoyed repeating in his public exchange of letters with Proast, is that there can be only one true religion (and thus only one true way to salvation), and yet there are almost as many religious sects as there are societies and magistrates. So if it were generally acceptable for magistrates to punish non-conformism, then "one country alone would be in the right, and all the rest of the world put under an obligation of following their princes in the ways that lead to destruction." The result is that most human souls would *not* be saved, contrary to the purpose of any rule permitting the punishment of non-conformists; and, what might be even more absurd, "men would owe their eternal happiness or misery to the places of their nativity" (W6: 12).

In response to this argument, Proast complains that the rule he favors is one according to which only those magistrates who accept the *true* religion are permitted to force non-conformists to adopt his favored path to salvation (see W6: 142). Locke's reply is that the path to salvation is not something that can be *known*; rather, it is something that one has no option but to believe (at most with *assurance*) on grounds of revelation. But "if therefore it be the magistrate's duty to use force to bring men to the true religion, it can be only to that religion which he believes to be true" (W6: 144). And in that case, the only practicable rule would have to be one according to which non-conformists are punished by the magistrate for not accepting what the magistrate believes to be the true path to salvation. And this brings us right back to Locke's point that in matters of religion one, at most, of the many magistrates in power believes what is actually true, and all the rest are misguided. Thus a rule permitting *all* magistrates to punish those they *believe*, in the absence of conversion to the true religion, to be bound for eternal damnation would actually result in the perdition of the vast majority of human beings.

Locke argues explicitly that the principle of toleration applies not just to Protestant non-conformists (e.g., "Presbyterians, independents, Anabaptists, Arminians, quakers, and others"), but also to "pagans," "Mahometans," and Jews" (W6: 52). Given that permitting adherents of these various sects or religions would not endanger the lives, liberties, or estates of any persons in political society, none "ought to be excluded from the civil rights of the commonwealth, because of his religion" (W6: 52). (This was contrary to the views of Anglicans such as Proast, who did not believe that non-Christians should be allowed to be citizens and worried that even permitting non-Christians to live among Christians might lead the latter to abandon their faith.) But even as Locke defends the religious freedoms of pagans, Muslims, and Jews, he also insists that the principle of toleration does not extend to Catholics or to atheists. His reasons are different in each case. Catholics pledge to follow the dictates of the Pope (rather than follow the dictates of their own consciences). As such, they "deliver themselves to the protection and service of another prince" (W6: 46). But no one who pledges allegiance to a foreign government or society can also consistently promise to defend and uphold the laws of the society in whose territory he resides. Catholics, therefore, cannot be trusted to abide by the laws of any society other than the Catholic Church itself. Especially in time of war, Catholics are therefore potentially dangerous to any non-Catholic commonwealth, for if they were tolerated "the magistrate would give away to the settling of a foreign jurisdiction in his own country, and suffer his own people to be listed, as it were, for soldiers against his own government" (W6: 46). Atheists, on the other hand, cannot be trusted to uphold the civil laws or the laws of nature, because "[p]romises, covenants, and oaths, which are the bonds of human society, can have no hold upon" someone who denies "the being of God" (W6: 47). Taking God to be the ground of obligation, and the desire for eternal happiness in heaven to be the most important motivation for ethical conduct, Locke worries that atheists will break both civil and natural law whenever they find it in their own interest to do so. The mix of tolerance and intolerance towards religion that Locke's views represent may strike us at first as unprincipled and theoretically unstable, but in fact Locke's position makes perfect sense in the light of his own political theory and his account of moral obligation and moral motivation. In order to justify religious toleration across the board (excepting practices such as human sacrifice, practices that clearly violate the civil or natural rights of rational beings), appeal must be made to some alternative to Locke's own moral and political philosophy.

notes

1 It should be noted that this is not obvious. Imagine an island with 10 inhabitants, nine of whom get together to form a society, leaving Sally out. Although we may suppose that there is enough and as good left for Sally, it is clear that, as a result of their collective efforts, it will be possible for the nine to increase the wealth and power their society possesses in a way that will be impossible for Sally to do on her own. As a result, the society of nine will be able to use their collective clout in any trading agreements with Sally, leaving her at an increasing disadvantage. Although Locke's principles guarantee that Sally will survive, and the natural law duty of charity possessed by the nine entails that it would never be right for them to let Sally starve, there is nothing in Locke's moral or political theory (except perhaps an appeal to some general principle of fairness to which Locke never explicitly appeals in his discussion of the beginning of political societies) to prevent what some might see as morally impermissible exploitation.

It might be argued that the freedom to join does not entail the freedom to exclude. Perhaps it is Locke's view that all who want to join an already existing political society should be allowed to do so. But this seems like a restriction on the freedom of association in the state of nature that is nowhere required by the fundamental law of nature.

2 Article 107 of the *Fundamental Constitutions of Carolina*, which Locke was involved in drafting and editing relatively early in his life (1669), states that no adult shall "have any estate or possession in Carolina, or protection or benefit of the law there, who hath not, before a precinct register, subscribed these Fundamental Constitutions in this form: 'I A.B. do promise to bear faith and true allegiance to our sovereign lord King Charles the Second, his heirs and successors; and will be true and faithful to the palatine and lords proprietors of Carolina; and with my utmost power will defend them, and maintain the government according to this establishment in these Fundamental Constitutions'" (W9: 197).

further reading

Ashcraft, Richard, *Revolutionary Politics and Locke's* Two Treatises of Government. Princeton, NJ: Princeton University Press, 1986.

Ashcraft, Richard, "Locke's Political Philosophy," in *The Cambridge Companion to Locke*, edited by Vere Chappell. Cambridge: Cambridge University Press, 1994, pp. 226–251.

Dunn, John, *The Political Thought of John Locke*. Cambridge: Cambridge University Press, 1969.

Grant, Ruth W., *John Locke's Liberalism*. Chicago: University of Chicago Press, 1987, chapters 2–4.

Macpherson, C.B., *The Political Theory of Possessive Individualism: Hobbes to Locke*. Oxford: Clarendon Press, 1962.

Nozick, Robert, *Anarchy, State, and Utopia*. New York: Basic Books, 1974.

Simmons, A. John, *On the Edge of Anarchy: Locke, Consent, and the Limits of Society*. Princeton, NJ: Princeton University Press, 1993.

Tuckness, Alex, "Locke's Political Philosophy," in *The Stanford Encyclopedia of Philosophy* (Winter 2012 Edition), edited by Edward N. Zalta, http://plato.stanford.edu/archives/win2012/entries/locke-political/

index

Locke, First Edition. Samuel C. Rickless.
© 2014 Samuel C. Rickless. Published 2014 by John Wiley & Sons, Ltd.